The Cambridge Companion to Baudelaire

Charles Baudelaire's place among the great poets of the Western world is undisputed, and his influence on the development of poetry since his lifetime has been enormous. In this Companion, essays by outstanding scholars illuminate Baudelaire's writing both for the lay reader and for specialists. In addition to a survey of his life and a study of his social context, the volume includes essays on his verse and prose, analysing the extraordinary power and effectiveness of his language and style, his exploration of intoxicants like wine and opium, and his art and literary criticism. The volume also discusses the difficulties, successes and failures of translating his poetry and his continuing power to move his readers. Featuring a guide to further reading and a chronology, this Companion provides students and scholars of Baudelaire and of nineteenth-century French and European literature with a comprehensive and stimulating overview of this extraordinary poet.

ROSEMARY LLOYD is Rudy Professor of French and Professor of Gender Studies at Indiana University. She is the author of *Baudelaire's World* and *Mallarmé: The Poet and his Circle*.

THE CAMBRIDGE
COMPANION TO
BAUDELAIRE

EDITED BY

ROSEMARY LLOYD

Indiana University

CAMBRIDGE
UNIVERSITY PRESS

CAMBRIDGE UNIVERSITY PRESS
Cambridge, New York, Melbourne, Madrid, Cape Town, Singapore, São Paulo

Cambridge University Press
The Edinburgh Building, Cambridge CB2 2RU, UK

Published in the United States of America by Cambridge University Press, New York

www.cambridge.org
Information on this title: www.cambridge.org/9780521537827

First published 2005

Printed in the United Kingdom at the University Press, Cambridge

A catalogue record for this book is available from the British Library

Library of Congress Cataloguing in Publication data
The Cambridge companion to Baudelaire / edited by Rosemary Lloyd. – 1st ed.
p. cm.
Includes bibliographical references and index.
ISBN 0 521 83094 x (hardback) – ISBN 0 521 53782 7 (pbk.)
1. Baudelaire, Charles, 1821–1867 – Criticism and interpretation – Handbooks, manuals, etc.
I. Lloyd, Rosemary. II. Title.
PQ2191.Z5C24 2005
841′.8 – dc22 2005012929

ISBN-13 978-0-521-83094-2 hardback
ISBN-10 0-521-83094-x hardback
ISBN-13 978-0-521-53782-7 paperback
ISBN-10 0-521-53782-7 paperback

In memoriam Claude Pichois

CONTENTS

Notes on contributors   *page* ix

Preface   xiii

Chronology   xv

Abbreviations, references and translations   xviii

1   Charles Baudelaire, a life in writing   1
JOHN E. JACKSON

2   Baudelaire's politics   14
DOLF OEHLER

3   Baudelaire's poetic journey in *Les Fleurs du Mal*   31
BARBARA WRIGHT

4   Baudelaire's versification: conservative or radical?   51
RACHEL KILLICK

5   The prose poems   69
SONYA STEPHENS

6   Baudelairean ethics   87
EDWARD K. KAPLAN

7   Baudelaire's Paris   101
ROSS CHAMBERS

8   Baudelaire and intoxicants   117
E. S. BURT

CONTENTS

9   Art and its representation   130
    J. A. HIDDLESTON

10 Music and theatre   145
    MARGARET MINER

11 Baudelaire's literary criticism   164
    ROSEMARY LLOYD

12 Baudelaire's place in literary and cultural history   175
    BERYL SCHLOSSMAN

13 A woman reading Baudelaire   186
    MARY ANN CAWS

14 Translating Baudelaire   193
    CLIVE SCOTT

15 The stroll and preparation for departure   206
    JUDITH VOLLMER

    Afterword   213
    CLAUDE PICHOIS

    Appendix: Titles of individual poems and prose poems
        referred to in the text   221
    Guide to further reading   225
    Index   228
    Index to Baudelaire's works   232

NOTES ON CONTRIBUTORS

E. S. BURT, author of a book on nineteenth-century poetry and the political space, together with diverse articles on poetry and autobiography, teaches at the University of California, Irvine. A new project on the Other in autobiography, which treats Rousseau, Baudelaire, De Quincey and Wilde, is nearing completion.

MARY ANN CAWS is Distinguished Professor of Comparative Literature, English and French at the Graduate School of the City University of New York. Her many areas of interest in twentieth-century avant-garde literature and art include Surrealism, poets René Char and André Breton, Virginia Woolf and the Bloomsbury group and artists Robert Motherwell and Joseph Cornell. Conceptually, one of her primary themes has been the relationship between image and text. Among many other projects, she is currently working on a study of extraordinary women writers and painters.

ROSS CHAMBERS, Professor Emeritus of the University of Michigan, has earned a distinguished reputation for his many publications on nineteenth-century French literature; in the area of critical theory, notably *Room for Maneuver* and *Loiterature*; and most recently for his exploration of AIDS diaries.

J. A. HIDDLESTON is Professor of French at Oxford University, Fellow of Exeter College since 1966 and has published widely on nineteenth- and twentieth-century French literature (mainly Baudelaire, Laforgue, Hugo, Nerval, Rimbaud, Supervielle and Malraux). Recent publications include *Baudelaire and the Art of Memory* and an edited collection of articles on Hugo, *Victor Hugo, romancier de l'abîme*.

JOHN E. JACKSON is Professor of French Literature at Bern University (Switzerland). He is the author of fifteen books on French and European Poetry, including *La Mort Baudelaire*, and *Baudelaire*, as well as an edition of *Les Fleurs du Mal*.

EDWARD K. KAPLAN is Kaiserman Professor in the Humanities and Chair of the Program in Religious Studies at Brandeis University, where he teaches courses in French and comparative literature, and religious and ethical experience. He has interpreted the entire collection of fifty prose poems in *Baudelaire's Prose Poems: The Esthetic, the Ethical, and the Religious in 'The Parisian Prowler'*. His translation of *Le Spleen de Paris*, entitled *The Parisian Prowler*, was awarded the Lewis Galantière Prize from the American Translators Association in 1991. Professor Kaplan has also published books on Jules Michelet and the Jewish philosopher and social activist Abraham Joshua Heschel, and articles on Gaston Bachelard, Nerval, Hugo, Marceline Desbordes-Valmore, Baudelaire, Edmond Jabès and Yves Bonnefoy. He is especially interested in the relationship between poetic imagination, ethics and religious insight.

RACHEL KILLICK is Professor of Quebec Studies and Nineteenth-Century French Studies at the University of Leeds. She has published widely on post-Romantic French poetry (Baudelaire, Verlaine, Mallarmé, Valéry) and also on nineteenth-century French fiction (Hugo, Flaubert, Mérimée, Maupassant). She is the French section editor of *Modern Language Review*. Her current research project focuses on Quebec playwright Michel Tremblay.

ROSEMARY LLOYD is Rudy Professor of French and Professor of Gender Studies at Indiana University. She is the author of several books, most recently *Mallarmé: The Poet and His Circle* and *Baudelaire's World*. Her latest book is *Shimmering in a Transformed Light: The Written Still Life*. She has been awarded fellowships from the Leverhulme Trust, the National Endowment for the Humanities and the Guggenheim Foundation.

MARGARET MINER is Associate Professor of French at the University of Illinois at Chicago. She specialises in the interrelationship of music, literature and society in nineteenth-century France. In addition to her monograph, *Resonant Gaps: Between Baudelaire and Wagner* and a variety of feminist readings of Baudelaire, she has published articles on Jules Janin and Paris, and on Mallarmé, Rimbaud and music. She also has a particular interest in the fantastic and is currently working on a book devoted to music, women and the fantastic in nineteenth-century France.

DOLF OEHLER teaches in the Comparative Literature department at the University of Bonn, Germany, where he specialises in questions of European identity, the relationships between French and German literature and culture and the interplay of history and literature. He is the author of numerous articles on nineteenth- and twentieth-century literature as well as two major studies of Baudelaire and the political context of his time: *Pariser Bilder* and *Le Spleen contre l'oubli, juin 1848: Baudelaire, Flaubert, Heine*.

CLAUDE PICHOIS was known, among many other achievements, as the editor of the Pléiade edition of Baudelaire's *Œuvres completés*, his *Correspondance*, an edition of letters written to the poet and a diplomatic edition of *Mon cœur mis à nu*. He also wrote biographies of Baudelaire, his editor, Auguste Poulet-Malassis, Nerval and Colette. Until his retirement, Claude Pichois directed the Baudelaire centre at Vanderbilt University.

CLIVE SCOTT is Professor of European Literature in the Faculty of Humanities at the University of East Anglia, and a Fellow of the British Academy. His recent publications include *The Poetics of French Verse: Studies in Reading*, *Translating Baudelaire* and *Channel Crossings: French and English Poetry in Dialogue 1550–2000*, for which he was awarded the R. H. Gapper Book Prize. His most recent book is *Translating Rimbaud's 'Illuminations'*.

BERYL SCHLOSSMAN is the author of several books of literary criticism – *Joyce's Catholic Comedy of Language*, *The Orient of Style: Modernist Allegories of Conversion* (a work that explores the impact of Baudelaire on Proust) and *Objects of Desire: The Madonnas of Modernism* – as well as *Angelus Novus*, a collection of poems published by *Editions Virgile*. She teaches literature, cinema and the arts in society at Carnegie Mellon University, Pittsburgh. Her poetry and short fiction are published in France as well as in the USA, and she has published some stories related to Baudelaire in the *Bulletin Baudelairien* and in *L'Exterritorialité de la littérature allemande*. She is currently working on a book about Baudelaire's poetics.

SONYA STEPHENS is Reader in French at the University of London. She has published extensively on Baudelaire's prose poems, including a study entitled *Baudelaire's Prose Poems. The Practice and Politics of Irony*. She also edited *A History of Women's Writing in France*. Her current research projects include an edited volume of essays on Baudelaire's discursive practice across the range of his works and a book investigating the *non finito* as a cultural phenomenon in nineteenth-century France, *The Art of the Unfinished*. She is editor of *XIX The Journal of the Society of Dix-Neuviémistes*.

JUDITH VOLLMER is the author of three full-length collections of poetry, including *Reactor*, *The Door Open to the Fire* and *Level Green*; and the limited edition collection *Black Butterfly*. She is the recipient of the Brittingham and Cleveland State poetry prizes, the Centre for Book Arts prize, finalist honours for the Paterson Prize and poetry fellowships from the National Endowment for the Arts and the Pennsylvania Council on the Arts. She has also received artist residencies from the American Academy in Rome and the Corporation of Yaddo. She is Professor of English and Director of the Writing Program at the University of Pittsburgh at Greensburg, and a recipient of the Chancellor's Distinguished Teaching Award of the University of Pittsburgh. With Ed Ochester, she co-edits the poetry journal 5 AM.

BARBARA WRIGHT is Professor of French Literature at Trinity College, Dublin, having taught previously at the Universities of Manchester and Exeter. She is a member of the Royal Irish Academy and of the Academia Europaea. She specialises in nineteenth-century French studies, with particular reference to the interconnection between literature and painting, and has published books and articles on the works of Baudelaire, Fromentin, Gustave Moreau and Edgar Quinet. Her recent publications include *Eugène Fromentin: A Life in Art and Letters* and an edition of Fromentin's *Correspondance*. She is currently preparing a new edition of Narcisse Berchère's *Le Désert de Suez: cinq mois dans l'Isthme.*

PREFACE

Charles Baudelaire's place among the great poets not just of France, but also of the world, is undisputed. He figures prominently in canons of European and world literature, and his influence on poets worldwide has been enormous. In addition, he is considered one of the greatest art critics, a writer whose ability to convey colour, shape and texture in language, and to infuse his analysis with passionate intensity, has had a profound effect on the development of art criticism. As a translator and critic, he played a crucial role in presenting to a French audience both the American poet and short-story writer, Edgar Allan Poe, and Thomas de Quincey, the English Romantic writer, whose study of the influence of opium on the mind reveals so much about the workings of the imagination. Baudelaire's thinking about the strengths and limitations of the short story, revealed in his introductions to Poe's work, and his evocation of the powerful nature of addiction, especially to substances seen as enhancing the artistic imagination, in his adaptation of De Quincey's *Confessions*, continue to command attention. While he was not the first French writer to recognise the innovative genius of Richard Wagner, his study of *Tannhäuser* is still held to be a masterpiece both of insight and of descriptive power, the power to transform one artistic experience (music) into the modalities of another (critical writing). His literary criticism, devoted primarily to his contemporaries, is rich in insights not merely into the ambitions, restrictions and possibilities of the age, but also more particularly into his own aesthetic convictions and practice. The instigator of two poetic revolutions, as Barbara Johnson has argued, Baudelaire not only vastly extended the range of subjects and emotions available for verse-poetic treatment, increased the poetic lexicon and, especially through his manipulation of such fixed forms as the sonnet, expanded the possibilities of verse, but he also established the genre of prose poetry as we know it today, transforming it from the vehicle for the picturesque that it had become in the hands of an Aloysius Bertrand, and moulding it into the ideal expression for urban modernity. His great verse poem 'Le Cygne' is often considered to be the work that instigated Modernism, forging the disparate bric-a-brac of apparently chaotic contemporary existence into a means of setting the individual within both a cultural past and a physical present. Indeed, his influence on international Modernism was so far-reaching that we cannot fully understand that vital movement unless we are familiar with Baudelaire. Rimbaud saw him as a god, albeit one with feet of clay; Mallarmé and T. S. Eliot recognised him for the great genius he was; and his impact on twentieth-century poetry is both well documented and inescapable. Inspired by art, he in turn inspired artists as diverse as Gauguin, Matisse, Picasso and Nolan. His poetry has been set to music by a range of composers, and continues to challenge translators as varied and gifted as Richard Wilbur, Robert Fitzgerald, Seamus Heaney, Ciaran Carson, Richard Howard and Norman Shapiro. Infamously portrayed by the contemporary critic Sainte-Beuve as occupying a kiosk on Russia's remote Kamschatka peninsula, his work has been subjected to a huge range of critical analyses including those of Walter Benjamin, T. S. Eliot, Georg Lukács, Jean-Paul Sartre, Georges Poulet, Jean-Pierre Richard, Jacques Derrida, Jacques Lacan and many more. Baudelaire's own cultural roots go well back into the past, drawing sustenance from the great writers of antiquity, especially Ovid and Virgil, from Dante, Rabelais and Montaigne, from thinkers such as Vauvenargues and Sade, and from artists such as Rembrandt, Leonardo da Vinci, Michelangelo and above all Delacroix. Thus, while his voice is unique and instantly recognisable, his work draws together many disparate strands of thought and of aesthetics.

One of the goals of this volume has been to take full advantage of the challenging variety of Baudelaire's work. In general, it does not adopt a text-by-text response, the different chapters being organised instead around themes and techniques, those of painting or the use of the sonnet, for example. Such an approach both highlights the great variety of Baudelaire's corpus, and allows for a pertinent and flexible analysis of his modernity, the interdisciplinary nature of his work and thought and the complexity of his approach to ethical questions.

Like others in the series, the present volume includes a chronology and a bibliography, as well as a list of translations of his work.

I am deeply grateful to all my contributors, whose enthusiasm for, and commitment to, this volume have made it a truly collaborative production. I would also like to thank both Rachel de Wachter, who oversaw its early stages and Linda Bree, whose assistance over the past year has been exemplary.

Rosemary Lloyd

CHRONOLOGY

1759   Birth at La Neuville-au-Pont of Joseph-François Baudelaire, father of Charles.

1793   Birth in London of Caroline Archenbault Defayis, poet's mother.

1819   Marriage of Joseph-François Baudelaire and Caroline Defayis.

1821   9 April: birth of Charles-Pierre Baudelaire.

1827   Death of Baudelaire's father.

1828   Caroline Baudelaire marries Lieutenant-Colonel Jacques Aupick.

1832   Baudelaire and his mother go to Lyon, where Aupick is stationed.

1836   Return to Paris. Baudelaire attends the collège Louis-le-Grand.

1837   Expulsion from the collège Louis-le-Grand.

1841   Baudelaire sets out on a sea voyage, meant to take him to Calcutta. Stops at Réunion and Mauritius, refusing to go any further. He returns to France, arriving 15 February 1842.

1842   Inherits 100,000 francs from his father's estate. Becomes involved with Jeanne Duval, with whom he will live, off and on, for the rest of his life.

1844   Baudelaire's extravagant spending leads his family to create a *conseil de famille* which appoints Narcisse Ancelle trustee of his fortune.

1845   Publication of his review of the Salon, and of a poem, 'To a Creole Lady' ['A une dame créole']. First translations of the works of Poe begin to appear in the French press. 30 June: Baudelaire attempts suicide by stabbing himself.

1846   Publication of his *Salon of 1846*.

1847   Publication of his short story, *La Fanfarlo*.

1848   February Revolution and uprisings of the July Days. Baudelaire collaborates on a newspaper, *La Salut public*, of which only two numbers appear. 15 July: publication of Baudelaire's first translation of Poe, the tale *Magnetic Revelation*.

1851   Publication of his first study of wine and hashish, which contains a prose version of verse poems on wine to appear in *Les Fleurs du Mal*. 2 December: *coup d'état* in which Louis-Napoléon declares himself emperor.

1852   March and April: publication in *La Revue de Paris* of Baudelaire's first study of Poe.

1855   June: *La Revue des deux mondes* publishes eighteen poems under the title *Les Fleurs du Mal*. June: publication of the first of Baudelaire's prose poems, 'Le Crépuscule' and 'Solitude'.

1856   March: publication of Baudelaire's translations of Poe called *Histoires extraordinaires*.

1857   January–February: trial of Flaubert's novel, *Madame Bovary*. 8 March: publication of Baudelaire's second volume of translations of Poe short stories. 27 April: Death of General Aupick. 25 June: publication of *Les Fleurs du Mal*. 7 July: *Les Fleurs du Mal* accused of being an outrage to public decency. 20 August: Baudelaire condemned to pay a fine of 300 francs and suppress six of the poems. (The sentence would be quashed in 1949.)

1858   13 May: publication of Baudelaire's translation of Poe's novel, *Arthur Gordon Pym*.

1859   First notes for *Mon Cœur mis à nu*.

1860   1 January: Baudelaire sells Poulet-Malassis and de Broise the second edition of *Les Fleurs du Mal*, his study of the artificial paradises and his articles of literary and art criticism. 13 January: suffers first attack of illness. May: publication of *Les Paradis artificiels*. 11 December: Baudelaire presents his candidacy for the Academy.

1861   February: second edition of *Les Fleurs du Mal*. 15 June – 15 August: *La Revue fantaisiste* publishes nine of the ten prose articles that make up the *Réflexions sur quelques-uns de mes contemporains*.

1863   13 January: Baudelaire gives Hetzel for the sum of 1,200 francs the exclusive rights to publish his *Petits Poèmes en prose* and *Les Fleurs du Mal* previously sold to Poulet-Malassis.

1864   24 April: Baudelaire arrives in Brussels. 2 May: lecture on Delacroix. 11 May: lecture on Gautier. 12, 23 May and 3 June: lectures on artificial stimulants. 13 June: Baudelaire reads from his works. 25 December: under the title 'Le Spleen de Paris' *La Revue de Paris* publishes six prose poems.

1865   16 March: publication of Baudelaire's translation of Poe, *Histoires grotesques et sérieuses (Tales, Grotesque And Serious)*.

1866   Around 15 March, Baudelaire visits Namur and falls on to the ground in the church. 22–3 March: his condition worsens.

30 March: paralysis of the right side. 31 March: *Le Parnasse contemporain* publishes *Nouvelles Fleurs du Mal*. 2 July: Baudelaire's mother brings him back to Paris.

1867   31 August: death of Baudelaire. 2 September: burial in the Montparnasse cemetery.

1868   December: Michel Lévy begins publishing Baudelaire's complete works.

ABBREVIATIONS, REFERENCES AND TRANSLATIONS

The following abbreviations are used in this volume to refer to works by Baudelaire:

OC   *Œuvres complètes*, 2 vols. Ed. Claude Pichois (Paris: Gallimard, Bibliothèque de la Pléiade, 1975–6).

C   *Correspondance*. 2 vols. Ed. Claude Pichois and Jean Ziegler (Paris: Gallimard, Bibliothèque de la Pléiade, 1973).

FM   *Les Fleurs du Mal*. Trans. James McGowan (Oxford: Oxford University Press, 1993).

PP   *Les Petits Poèmes en prose*. Trans. Rosemary Lloyd (Oxford: Oxford University Press, 1991).

References to these works will be given in the form (OC I 75), (OC II 140), (C I 122), etc. References to other bibliographical items will be provided in full in a note on first mention, and in abbreviated form thereafter.

    All quotations are accompanied by a translation into English. The translation usually precedes the original, but the order is from time to time reversed for the sake of clarity or precision. The translations used for *Les Fleurs du Mal* are those of James McGowan (Oxford: Oxford University Press, 1993); those for *Les Petits Poèmes en prose* those of Rosemary Lloyd (Oxford: Oxford University Press, 1991). Where these have been adapted acknowledgment is made in the notes. For other works, the translations are those of the authors unless otherwise specified. Titles are in French in the text: an appendix gives the English version of each title.

I

Charles Baudelaire, a life in writing

Paradox is a way of being, at times a painful one: no poet's life illustrates this point more than Baudelaire's. Born with the richest constitution, endowed with the highest possible talent for writing, lucid to the point of near infallibility, this poet was at the same time not only a master of self-delusion, but also the craftsman of his mostly miserable existence. Reading his correspondence is an ordeal, so clear is the self-destructive leaning driving him again and again to place himself in impossible (financial) situations, which, in turn, bear heavily on his literary work. Such is the obsessive regularity with which Baudelaire creates for himself circumstances which he then vainly craves to escape from, that one comes finally to ask oneself if the need to despair doesn't belong to the very essence of his creative drive.

Sartre's 1947 essay[1] on Baudelaire, accusing the poet of 'mauvaise foi' (bad faith), recognises the paradox, but utterly fails to explain it. If Baudelaire's literary existence is to be described in terms of 'choice', surely it must be an unconscious one. Rather, if one wishes to apply Sartrean categories to Baudelaire, the notion of 'objective neurosis', as developed in the monumental biography of Flaubert, would be appropriate: it implies a parallel between the class contradictions in which, following Marxist analysis, a bourgeois would find himself and the personal constellation to which he owes his identity.[2]

Charles-Pierre Baudelaire was born in Paris on 9 April 1821, the son of François Baudelaire, a former priest who had left the Church to work for the State, and of his wife Caroline Archenbaut Defayis, his junior by thirty-four years. The dominant fact of the poet's youth was his father's death in February 1827. It had at least a double consequence for his son: it lifted or lowered the barrier which any child must experience in his desire for independence and increased his possessiveness of his mother. As he wrote to her more than thirty years later:

In my childhood I went through a stage when I loved you passionately. Listen and read without fear. I've never told you anything about it. I remember an outing in a coach. You'd just come out of a clinic you'd been sent to, and to prove that you'd given some thought to your son, you showed me some pencil sketches you'd done for me. Can you believe what a tremendous memory I have? Later, the square of Saint-André-des-Arts and Neuilly. Long walks, constant acts of tenderness. I remember the quays which were so melancholy at evening. Oh, for me that was the good age of maternal tenderness. I beg your pardon for describing as 'a good age' one that for you was doubtless a bad one. But I lived constantly through you, you were mine alone.

[Il y a eu dans mon enfance une époque d'amour passionné pour toi; écoute et lis sans peur. Je ne t'en ai jamais tant dit. Je me souviens d'une promenade en fiacre; tu sortais d'une maison de santé où tu avais été reléguée, et tu me montras, pour me prouver que tu avais pensé à ton fils, des dessins à la plume que tu avais faits pour moi. Crois-tu que j'aie une mémoire terrible? Plus tard, la place Saint-André-des-Arts et Neuilly. De longues promenades, des tendresses perpétuelles! Je me souviens des quais, qui étaient si tristes le soir. Ah! Ç'a été pour moi le bon temps des tendresses maternelles. Je te demande d'appeler *bon temps* celui qui a été sans doute mauvais pour toi. Mais j'étais toujours vivant en toi; tu étais uniquement à moi. (C II 153)]

There can be no doubt about the intensity with which Charles relished that period which is recalled in the beautiful untitled poem number XCIC, as another letter confirms (C I 445). All the more grievous must have been for him the 'treason' he felt eighteen months later when his mother elected to remarry (she wed lieutenant-colonel Jacques Aupick, a career soldier who died a general in 1857). The effects of this Hamlet-like situation are far-reaching. Charles' eighteen months alone with his mother had probably intensified both his fantasy that she belonged exclusively to him and the feeling of guilt which must have inevitably accompanied this oedipal transgression. The rage with which he discovered the truth about her real inclinations,[3] and which he still felt in later years long after the break-up with his stepfather which was so incisive as to force him to meet his mother in such places as the rose Salon of the Louvre,[4] testifies to the blow her second wedding dealt to his self-image. We can reconstruct the importance of this reaction through at least two decisive episodes of his later life. Having gone through the classical education of a future holder of the Baccalauréat, first in Lyon and then at the collège Louis-le-Grand in Paris, Baudelaire embarked on the carefree life of contemporary *bohème*, mingling with fellow young poets, artists and prostitutes, thereby also contracting a venereal disease from which he never properly recovered. During his twentieth year, his stepfather convinced the family council (Charles, being still a minor at the time, was legally subject to this council of which Aupick was co-guardian) that travelling might help redress the young man's tendency to a dissipated life and bring him back on to the right path. Thus in June 1840 Charles boarded the *Paquebot-des-Mers-du Sud* bound for Calcutta but which he disembarked from at Saint-Denis de la Réunion. The seven-month trip left lasting memories. These can be perceived in the persistent exotic images which animate his poems, especially those written with his later mistress Jeanne Duval in mind:

> When, eyes closed, on a pleasant autumn night,
> I breathe the warm scent of your breast, I see
> Inviting shorelines spreading out for me
> Where steady sunlight dazzles in my sight.
>
> An idle isle, where friendly nature brings
> Singular trees, fruit that is savoury . . .
>
> (FM 49)

> [Quand les deux yeux fermés, en un soir chaud d'automne,
> Je respire l'odeur de ton sein chaleureux,
> Je vois se dérouler des rivages heureux
> Qu'éblouissent les feux d'un soleil monotone;
>
> Une île paresseuse où la nature donne
> Des arbres singuliers et des fruits savoureux . . .
>
> (OC I 25)]

In spite of his assertion that he had 'pocketed wisdom' ('avec la sagesse en poche') on his return on coming of age in April 1842 he claimed his paternal inheritance and within the next eighteen months managed to dissipate 44,500 of the 100,000 *francs-or* he had received. At his stepfather's suggestion, his mother initiated a legal procedure to halt her son's profligacy, ending in the imposition of a *conseil judiciaire* which prevented him from having direct access to the money he had inherited from his father, forcing him to go through the intermediary of a lawyer. From 21 September 1844 and for the rest of his life, Charles only received the returns of the invested remains of his inheritance, as overseen by Narcisse-Désiré Ancelle, a notary of Neuilly. Baudelaire's enduring fury at this imposition is very revealing. Not only did he persistently complain that the *conseil* marked the beginning of his financial downfall (although in truth it probably saved him from the worst), but the very reasoning he later used against its usefulness shows how self-deluding he remained. Baudelaire's main argument against the *conseil* was that, had he been left to dissipate his inheritance completely, he would then have had no other choice than to start an (economically) sound life (as if he could not have done that anyway). Clearly, his intolerance regarding the imposition of the *conseil judiciaire* stems from the fact that it repeated and renewed the frustration experienced by the fact of having a stepfather imposed upon him at the very time he believed to have his mother to himself. Baudelaire's reluctance to accept any other authority than that of his mother doubtless has its root in this stark contrast between the indulgence of an elderly father and the military discipline his stepfather attempted to enforce. (Albeit at a very different level, his reaction to the legal condemnation of six poems of *Les Fleurs du Mal* in 1857 will confirm this point, as we shall see.)

There is more yet. While reining in the child's oedipal fantasy, the mother's remarriage also unleashed more destructive tendencies. Aggression is a natural component of any child's ambivalent relation to his or her mother. The fact that this mother was perceived to have 'betrayed' the child's confidence can only have increased his malevolence. In the case of Baudelaire, this was to have a lasting effect on his relation to women. Even where the poetic stance seems at first to be one of idealisation, there is an undercurrent of obsessive destructiveness: no reader of his poems can escape the impression of what an acclaimed essay by Georges Blin rightly called his sadism.[5] The last stanza of 'A une Madone' is a perfect example. Having feigned to humiliate himself before the revered aloofness of the beloved, he concludes the poem as follows:

> At last, so you're my Mary perfectly,
> And mixing love with pagan cruelty,
> Full of a dark, remorseful joy, I'll take
> The seven deadly sins, and of them make
> Seven bright Daggers; with a juggler's lore
> Target your love within its deepest core,
> And plant them all within your panting Heart,
> Within your sobbing Heart, your streaming Heart!
>
> (FM 121)

> [Enfin, pour compléter ton rôle de Marie,[6]
> Et pour mêler l'amour avec la barbarie,
> Volupté noire! des sept Péchés capitaux,
> Bourreau plein de remords, je ferai sept Couteaux
> Bien affilés, et, comme un jongleur insensible,
> Prenant le plus profond de ton amour pour cible,
> Je les planterai tous dans ton Cœur pantelant,
> Dans ton Cœur sanglotant, dans ton Cœur ruisselant!
>
> (OC I 59)]

The very sadistic pleasure taken in the murder of this Madonna can be felt in the final triple present participle whose trisyllabic regularity rhythmically mimics a male orgasm. There is no doubt that Baudelaire's greatness as a poet is directly related to his capacity to blend such dark sides – usually so difficult to admit – with more conventional feelings. This in turn seems less the result of a 'choice' than of some form of permanent exasperation which dates from his early years. Whether in his relation to his mother or to Jeanne Duval, the mulatto actress he met in 1842 and who was to remain his mistress over the following twenty years, this exasperation seems to have played a major role. This, for instance, is what he writes about her to his mother on 27 March 1851:

> TO LIVE WITH A PERSON who shows no gratitude for your efforts, who impedes them through clumsiness or permanent meanness, who considers you as a mere servant, as her property, someone with whom it is impossible to exchange a word about politics or literature, a creature who is *unwilling to learn a single thing*, although you've offered to teach her yourself, a creature who HAS NO ADMIRATION FOR ME, and who is not even interested in one's studies, who would throw one's manuscripts in the fire if that brought in more money than publishing them, who drives away one's cat, the sole source of amusement in one's lodgings, and who brings in dogs, *because* the sight of dogs sickens me, who does not know or cannot understand *that by being tight-fisted, just for* ONE *month* I could, thanks to that brief respite, conclude a big book – is all this possible? Is it possible? My eyes are full of tears of fury and shame as I write this . . .

> [VIVRE AVEC UN ETRE qui ne vous sait aucun gré de vos efforts, qui les contrarie par une maladresse ou une méchanceté permanente, qui ne vous considère que comme son domestique et sa propriété, avec qui il est impossible d'échanger une parole politique ou littéraire, une créature qui ne *veut rien apprendre*, quoique vous lui ayez proposé de lui donner vous-même des leçons, une créature QUI NE M'ADMIRE PAS, et qui ne s'intéresse même pas à mes études, qui jetterait mes manuscrits au feu si cela lui rapportait plus d'argent que de les laisser publier, qui renvoie mon chat qui était ma seule distraction au logis, et qui introduit des chiens, *parce que* la vue des chiens me fait mal, qui ne sait pas, ou ne veut pas comprendre *qu'être très avare, pendant* UN *mois seulement*, me permettrait, grâce à ce repos momentané, de finir un gros livre, – enfin est-ce possible cela? Est-ce possible? J'ai des larmes de honte et de rage dans les yeux en t'écrivant ceci . . .   (C I 193)]

A year later however, commenting on a temporary separation from her, he adds:

> She caused me a lot of pain, didn't she? How many times – and to you quite recently, just a year ago – have I complained about it? But faced with a collapse of such proportions, with a melancholy as deep as hers, my eyes fill with tears, and to tell the truth my heart is full of reproaches. Twice, I've devoured her jewels and her furniture, I've made her incur debts on my behalf, sign IOUs,

I've beaten her, and finally, instead of showing her how a man of my stamp behaves, I've constantly given her the example of debauchery and instability. She suffers – and is silent. Isn't there a cause for remorse in that? Am I not as guilty in this regard as in all the other matters?

[Elle m'a bien fait souffrir, n'est-ce pas? – Combien de fois – et à toi récemment encore, – il y a un an, – combien ne me suis-je pas plaint! – Mais en face d'une pareille ruine, d'une mélancolie si profonde, je me sens les yeux pleins de larmes, – et pour tout dire, le cœur plein de reproches. – Je lui ai mangé deux fois ses bijoux et ses meubles, je lui ai fait faire des dettes pour moi, souscrire des billets, je l'ai assommée, et finalement, au lieu de lui montrer comment se conduit un homme comme moi, je lui ai toujours donné l'exemple de la débauche et de la vie errante. Elle souffre – et elle est muette. – N'y a-t-il pas là matière à remords? Et ne suis-je pas coupable de ce côté comme de tous les côtés?
(C I 213–14)]

The mere juxtaposition of these two letters is revealing. The major complaint in the first is that Jeanne Duval doesn't *admire* him. In the second, that he feels *remorse* towards her. It is a feature of Baudelaire's psyche that narcissism and guilt belong together. Narcissism, though, is an ambivalent notion which includes what Rousseau once rightly distinguished as *amour de soi* and *amour-propre*. In Baudelaire's work, it refers both to fragilised self-esteem and to the ability to *identify* with others: 'The poet benefits from an incomparable privilege which allows him to be, at will, himself and others. Like those wandering souls in search of a body, he enters, when he so desires, into the character of each individual. For him alone, everything is vacant' (PP 44). ['Le poète jouit de cet incomparable privilège, qu'il peut à sa guise être lui-même et autrui. Comme ces âmes errantes qui cherchent un corps, il entre, quand il veut, dans le personnage de chacun. Pour lui seul, tout est vacant' (OC I 291)]. There is something haughty in the way Baudelaire at times elevates himself or allegorical figures of himself to the level of a quasi demiurgic height, as for instance in the case of the poem 'L'Albatros' in which he equates the poet to 'le prince des nuées' (prince of the clouds) whose 'ailes de géant' (giant's wings) prevent him from walking on the ground. This haughtiness is often accompanied by a streak of cruelty which modulates the poet's *distance* from his objects, letting the objects of his attention appear without illusion. Nowhere is this more true than in the first part of 'Les Petites Vieilles':

> They creep, lashed by the merciless north wind,
> Quake from the riot of an omnibus,
> Clasp by their sides like relics of a saint
> Embroidered bags of flowery design;

They toddle, every bit like marionettes,
Or drag themselves like wounded animals,
Or dance against their will, poor little bells
That a remorseless demon rings!

(FM 181–3)

[Ils rampent, flagellés par les bises iniques,
Frémissant au fracas roulant des omnibus,
Et serrant sur leur flanc, ainsi que des reliques,
Un petit sac brodé de fleurs ou de rébus;

Ils trottent, tout pareils à des marionnettes;
Se traînent, comme font les animaux blessés,
Ou dansent, sans vouloir danser, pauvres sonnettes
Où se pend un Démon sans pitié!   (OC 1 89)]

At the same time, the very reflection on this distance tends to colour it with a tenderness which is the very reverse of cruelty:

So you trudge on, stoic, without complaint,
Through the chaotic city's teeming waste,
Saints, courtesans, mothers of bleeding hearts,
Whose names, in times past, everyone had known.

You glorious ones, you who were full of grace,
Not one remembers you! some rowdy drunk
Insults you on the street with crude remarks;
A taunting child cuts capers at your heels.

O you ashamed of living, shrunken shades,
Fearful, with backs bent, how you hug the walls;
And no one greets you, strange and fated souls!
Debris of man, ripe for eternity!   (FM 185–7)

[Telles vous cheminez, stoïques et sans plaintes,
A travers le chaos des vivantes cités,
Mères au cœur saignant, courtisanes ou saintes,
Dont autrefois les noms par tous étaient cités.

Vous qui fûtes la grâce ou qui fûtes la gloire,
Nul ne vous reconnaît! un ivrogne incivil
Vous insulte en passant d'un amour dérisoire;
Sur vos talons gambade un enfant lâche et vil.

Honteuses d'exister, ombres ratatinées,
Peureuses, le dos bas, vous côtoyez les murs;
Et nul ne vous salue, étranges destinées!
Débris d'humanité pour l'éternité mûrs!

(OC 1 91)]

In other cases, tenderness springs not from a reflection upon the poet's own position, but from the feeling of guilt his very superiority induces towards those he dominates, such as in the beautiful 'La Servante au grand cœur', where the remembrance of Mariette, his long-deceased nanny, ends in an attitude of pious devotion devoid of any negative tone. It is not difficult to understand that the deep ambivalence which marks Baudelaire's relation to the other, although based on narcissistic ground, is at the same time the condition of his unique understanding of this other.

Following the decree of the *conseil judiciaire* (1844), Baudelaire's day-to-day life became a financial quagmire. The mechanism of this situation, which can be followed in his correspondence, is a very simple one. Unable to match his needs to his revenue, Baudelaire kept borrowing money from publishers, magazine directors, friends or, more frequently, his mother. The borrowed amount corresponded to the sum he believed his current writing would secure him when published. What happened nine times out of ten was either that the projected publication was delayed, or brought in a lower than expected fee, or that in the meantime he had incurred new debts. This led to new borrowing meant both for his sustenance and to allow him to repay the previous loans. The need to provide for Jeanne obviously complicated the matter further (all the more so since we can surmise that she had little education in household economy), as did the fact that the art-lover in Baudelaire periodically found it very difficult to resist purchasing paintings or etchings offered to him by several art-dealers he happened to know. So dire were the financial straits he found himself in at times that he could write to Mme Aupick:

> moreover, I have grown so accustomed to physical suffering, I know so well how to adjust two shirts under a torn pair of trousers that the wind cuts through; I am so skilful at fitting straw or even paper soles into shoes gaping with holes, that it's really almost only moral suffering that causes me pain. – Yet, I have to confess that I have reached the point where I dare not make any more abrupt movements or even walk too much for fear of tearing myself even more.

> [d'ailleurs je suis tellement accoutumé aux souffrances physiques, je sais si bien ajuster deux chemises sous un pantalon et un habit déchirés que le vent traverse; je sais si adroitement adapter des semelles de paille ou même de papier dans des souliers troués, que je ne sens presque que les douleurs morales. – Cependant, il faut avouer, j'en suis venu au point que je n'ose plus faire de mouvements brusques ni même trop marcher de peur de me déchirer davantage. (C I 242)]

He had often to change lodgings because he had not paid the rent or to disappear from a place to which his creditors might track him down – Baudelaire had more than seventy addresses after leaving his parents' home. He often took refuge in cheap hotels, but this increased the cost of his day-to-day expenses. All this bore heavily on his creative activity, as he rightly pointed out to his mother in innumerable letters. Why then didn't he change his lifestyle? The question is all the more natural as – at least after 1857, the date of General Aupick's death – he very clearly saw a way out: to leave Paris and join his mother in Honfleur, a small Normandy seaport to which she had retired. Indeed, the few weeks he spent there testify to the incredible creativity he could foster while living a sedate life. Even if one takes into account the reasons he invokes to himself or to Mme Aupick – the need to be in Paris to secure talks and contracts with his potential publishers – there is little doubt that the reasons for continuing such a stressful existence are to be found not on any conscious level, but on an unconscious one. Both in money matters and in the careless way he treated his venereal disease, Baudelaire was probably punishing himself. It may seem far-fetched at first to surmise an oedipal origin to be at the basis of one's dealings with one's fortune or with one's health, but guilt seems the only plausible reason for such an irrational way of living. This feeling of guilt probably stems, as we have seen, from the disappearance of his father at a time when boys do harbour such death-wishes against their genitor. The fact that its effect on Charles remained so powerful all his life bears witness both to the intensity with which he experienced that episode and to the relation between his literary vein and his darker sides.

Published in June 1857, *Les Fleurs du Mal* was condemned in August for its 'délit d'outrage à la morale publique' (offence against public morals), and its author was fined 300 francs and ordered to suppress six poems from the collection. Although this condemnation is evidence of the narrow-mindedness of the cultural policy that dominated the Second Empire (the reign of Napoleon III from 1852 to 1871) – Flaubert's *Madame Bovary* had just escaped a similar condemnation earlier that year – there is yet reason to wonder both at the way it was prepared and at Baudelaire's reaction.

As we have seen, one of Baudelaire's fundamental intuitions concerns the destructiveness he experienced first in himself. This experience – of which sadism is only one of several extreme forms – explains at least in part why he so unremittingly adhered to the doctrine of original sin which he stubbornly opposed to all the ideologies of Progress that were flowering in his time: sin was the term which theologians used for the destructive streak he felt only too well in himself. Thus if sin – or, as he would have preferred to say, Evil – is the basic fact of human life, it follows that if one is to continue being a Christian, it can only be in the severe form of Augustinian or even Jansenist Catholicism (it is perhaps not by chance that the most understanding contemporary reaction to *Les Fleurs du Mal*, that of Jules Barbey d'Aurevilly, came precisely from a similarly orientated mind). At the same time, Christianity was the official religion of the society which Baudelaire abhorred. Hence, he could neither be a Christian nor not be one (inasmuch as he shared its central belief). Baudelaire's solution was Satanism. Satanism was for him the inevitable but logical way to maintain both his creed and hope for salvation. By imploring Satan – as he does for instance in 'Les Litanies de Satan' – he was trying to short-circuit the all too comfortable beliefs of all the *hypocrites lecteurs* he expected and at the same time to reaffirm the need for a redemption he felt that the traditional figure of Christ could not provide because it was too compromised by contemporary society. One can only guess if this theological radicalism had a political counterpart. The matter of his views in that respect is a complex one. True, he wrote to Narcisse Ancelle in March 1852 that Louis Napoléon's 2 December *coup d'état* had left him *physiquement dépolitiqué*. But on the other hand he was keen to name Joseph de Maistre as one of his two *maîtres à penser* and wrote with 'Assommons les pauvres!', a prose poem of *Le Spleen de Paris*, a meaningful political allegory. If not a revolutionary (at least not in the socialist sense of the word), Baudelaire was nevertheless a rebel who might well have thought that the harshness of social inequality could lead to a social insurgency.

In much the same way as his dandyism, Baudelaire's Satanism was a mask. This in turns helps explain some of the dominant traits of his personality: the more repulsive he tried to show himself, the more he was protecting a moral integrity which he felt normal behaviour only too often corrupted. Hence also his incredulity at the indictment of his book. Far from being immoral, *Les Fleurs du Mal*, in his mind, was on the contrary of the highest morality precisely because of its subversion of conventional – and thus hypocritical – morals. As he complained several years later to Ancelle, his long-time nemesis whom he had nevertheless come to respect:

> Must I tell you, you who failed to guess it just as much as the others, that in that *atrocious* book I placed all my *heart*, all my *tenderness*, all my *religion* (disguised), all my *hatred*? It is true that I will write the opposite, that I will swear on all the gods that this is a book of *pure art*, of *pretence*, of *hypocrisy*. And I'll lie like a puller of teeth.

> [Faut-il vous dire, à vous qui ne l'avez pas plus deviné que les autres, que dans ce livre *atroce*, j'ai mis tout mon *cœur*, toute ma *tendresse*, toute ma *religion* (travestie), toute ma *haine*? Il est vrai que j'écrirai le contraire, que je jurerai mes grands Dieux que c'est un livre *d'art pur*, de *singerie*, de *jonglerie*; et je mentirai comme un arracheur de dents.   (C II 610)]

With Baudelaire, travesty comes close to being a (religious) art. There were however also other reasons for his fury at the censorship of his poems. By making him suppress six of them, the law court was acting in the way a moralising parent would. Thus it was repeating in its way what the *conseil judiciaire* had done: setting him back in the position of someone under-age. Such a tutelage was unbearable. It was in his eyes the confusion of conventional and artistic morality, it was a way of preventing him from setting his own (very high) standards, thus reimposing on him the brutal reality of the law when his father's premature death had induced him to believe his works depended on his decisions alone. Baudelaire's life was wholly dedicated to writing: this is why there is so little to report about it. His days were his works. Neither his literary connections – with Gautier, Flaubert, Sainte-Beuve, Asselineau, Poulet-Malassis his publisher – nor his artistic friendships – with Delacroix, Daumier, Meryon, Constantin Guys, Nadar or Manet – seem to have meant more than occasional moments of mutual understanding. Even Poe, whom he never met, or Wagner, whom he did, the objects of his greatest admiration, seem to have been chiefly pretexts for his writing. If Baudelaire was the first of what Verlaine was later to call the *poètes maudits*, it was because he strove to coincide entirely with his literary creation at a time when society showed very little respect for poetry. The price he paid for this effort (the financial misery) was in his eyes a sufficient reason for wanting to be judged solely by his writing. His *sacrifice*, so to speak, was in itself a proof of an irreproachable stance. Being at odds with French justice thus represented a fatal blow. Not only did it cause him prejudice, but it also split his writings between those which he was allowed to publish in France and those that had to be relegated to Belgium, where Poulet-Malassis published the forbidden poems under the title *Les Epaves* (wreckage).

Belgium was, however, to seal the poet's fate in an unexpected way. Ever more in financial trouble and vainly looking for a French publisher willing to buy his complete works, he decided to travel to Brussels in April 1864. Having agreed to give some talks, he was also hoping to find a publisher generous enough to relieve his plight. Alas, the disappointment with France's neighbour was to be immense. His lectures met with very little success and brought him only negligible returns. The two publishers he was hoping to attract, though formally invited, did not even turn up and later refused to deal with him. Baudelaire's bitterness soon turned to fury. Somewhat paradoxically he decided to remain in Belgium – though he had practically no means of living there – and to write two scathingly fierce pamphlets against the country: *Amoenitates Belgicae* and *Pauvre Belgique*!, both published posthumously. In March 1866, while visiting the Saint-Loup church in Namur, he suffered a cerebral stroke which soon left him hemiplegic and unable to speak. A few months later, he was taken back to Paris, placed in Dr Duval's nursing home near L'Etoile, and lodged in a room decorated with a painting of Manet and a copy of a Goya. There, both Mrs Manet and Mrs Paul Meurice tried to comfort him somewhat by playing some Wagner on the piano for him. He died there on 31 August 1867 and was buried in the cimetière Montparnasse, where he lies next to his mother and his stepfather.

Baudelaire's life was a frequently unhappy one. Although he had mainly himself to blame for this unhappiness, what must be understood is that it gave him certain insights into the fate of his Parisian contemporaries shared by no other writer of his time, with the possible exception of Flaubert. The paradox here is that it is Baudelaire's very narcissism which led him to such insights. As can be seen in so many of his poems, his mode of relating to the figures he stages is mainly one of identification. Even where the language he uses seems to indicate otherwise – as for instance in the celebrated opening line of 'Le Cygne': 'Andromaque, je pense à vous' (Andromache, I think of you) – his understanding of the fate of Hector's widow is based on the fact that he shares her feeling of deprivation. These figures are mainly victims, social victims: drunkards, old ladies, ragmen, prostitutes, beggars, maids, street cleaners, even thieves – they all testify to the dominantly proletarian composition of the French metropolis:

> Aurora, trembling in her gown of rose and green,
> Made her way slowly on the still-deserted Seine.
> Old Paris rubbed his eyes, woke to the day again,
> And gathered up his toils, that honest working man.
>
> (FM 211)
>
> [L'aurore grelottante en robe rose et verte
> S'avançait lentement sur la Seine déserte,
> Et le sombre Paris, en se frottant les yeux,
> Empoignait ses outils, vieillard laborieux.
>
> (OC I 104)]

The paradox of this predominantly proletarian world, with which his poems tend to identify ever more strongly, is that at the same time Baudelaire thinks of himself as an aristocrat. Andromaque is a case in point: the former Trojan princess, whom he depicts after the Virgilian narrative of the *Aeneid* Book III, has become 'vile property' ['vil bétail'] under Pyrrhus's arrogant rule before being given away to one of Hector's enslaved brothers. If, as Sartre has suggested, it was a reflex of Baudelaire's and Flaubert's generation to identify with the nobility of the preceding aristocratic class (so as to sever mental links with the stifling materialism of the Second Empire's bourgeoisie), it remains to his credit to have represented this fictive aristocracy in the degraded state of a downcast proletariat, thus laying bare the insensitivity and cruelty of emerging industrial capitalism. 'Charity' would have been the word

Baudelaire himself would rather have used. It was without a doubt the enduring merit of this form of charity to have included and to go on including the growing number of deprived human beings who cross our paths every day.

NOTES

1. Jean-Paul Sartre, *Baudelaire* (Paris: Gallimard, collection «Les Essais», 1947, «idées», 1963).
2. Jean-Paul Sartre, *L'Idiot de la famille. Gustave Flaubert de 1821 à 1857* (Paris: Gallimard, 1972). See in particular the chapter 'La névrose objective', vol. III, pp. 7–443.
3. All the more since she miscarried just one month after the wedding.
4. 'Later, you know what an atrocious education your husband wanted to put me through. I'm forty years old and can think of school only with pain, just as I think about the fear my stepfather inspired in me.' ['Plus tard, tu sais quelle atroce éducation ton mari a voulu me faire; j'ai quarante ans et je ne pense pas aux collèges sans douleur, non plus qu'à la crainte que mon beau-père m'inspirait'] (C I 153).
5. Georges Blin, *Le Sadisme de Baudelaire* (Paris: Corti, 1948).
6. There is here a pun inasmuch as the Marie/Madonna role described in the text alludes to Marie Daubrun, the woman who served as a model for the poem.

2

DOLF OEHLER

Baudelaire's politics

In the fewer than five decades that Baudelaire's life lasted, four different forms of government succeeded each other in France. His early childhood coincided with the end of the Restoration, the last decade of the renewed control of the Bourbons after the abdication of Napoleon. When Paris's July Revolution of 1830 brought the *ancien régime* to an end, and Louis XV's grandson, Charles X, was forced to abandon the throne, Charles Baudelaire was just nine years old. The hybrid bourgeois monarchy of Louis-Philippe, who inherited the throne from the last of the Bourbons, ran from Baudelaire's tenth to his twenty-seventh year. In other words, the period of his intellectual and literary formation fell in the time in which the bourgeoisie, with its catch cry of 'the golden mean' ['le juste milieu'], and its crowned figurehead from the House of Orléans undertook in large measure to modernise France, to industrialise it and to do so above all for its own economic and political advantage. This was the time of limited franchise in which only those who were rich or who were in a position to become so were allowed to participate in politics and the decision-making process, a period in which the plutocrats took over command and the slogan of the anglophile premier Guizot, 'Make money', became the catch cry, if not even a sort of categorical imperative of the age. The victim of this policy was the broad mass of the population, who found its representatives among the thinkers and especially the spokesmen of the very diverse republican and radical left-wing opposition parties and movements. Most of these representatives were in organisations outside parliament, indeed often taking the form of secret societies. Despite numerous economic crises, uprisings, attempted assassinations, strikes, corruption cases, moral scandals and so forth, the system of the July Monarchy nevertheless seemed so well established that the revolution of February 1848 burst on the European public like a bolt from the blue. The expulsion of the unloved citizen king to England, the proclamation of the Republic, the revolutionary conflagration that the events in Paris unleashed across the continent: all this seemed to ring in a new epoch of universal emancipation, of general freedom and brotherhood. And yet already in the spring of 1848 a conservative counter-movement held sway and no later than June 1848 the bloody suppression of the insurrections of the workers at the national workshops in Paris led to a horrible disillusionment. And in December 1848 the election of Louis-Bonaparte as president marked the beginning of the end of the Second Republic, since it contained in embryonic form the idea both of the coup d'état and that of the founding of a second empire. Indeed, the coup d'état of 2 December 1851 put an end to what contemporary capitalists saw as the horrific episode of the Republic. The Second Empire was proclaimed a year later, in December 1852. Its collapse was something Baudelaire would not live to experience, unlike the generation-older Victor Hugo, the literary adversary of 'Napoléon le petit', and unlike his friends Théophile Gautier and Gustave Flaubert. He died almost exactly three years to the day before the defeat of the imperial army at Sedan, a defeat that decided the Franco-Prussian War and cost Napoleon III his crown.

It was these historical fractures and events no less than personal crises that contributed to the fact that during his lifetime Baudelaire's work, creative as well as critical, could not be perceived as a self-contained and coherent whole. It is part of Baudelaire's modernity that he reacted with extreme sensitivity to the political and social movements of his time and it is part of his sensitivity that he, like Flaubert, distanced himself from those clichés with which his contemporaries expressed their aspirations, viewpoints, political programmes, historical philosophy and so forth. And that remains the case even when he was sympathetic to these ideas. The early aesthetic manifesto, the *Salon de 1846*, already provides an impressive example of Baudelaire's equally original and refined ways of dealing with the art- and socio-political discourses of his time. In the introductory dedication to the bourgeois, he pretends to defend the modern bourgeois above all from the educated classes and the artists who despise them, but also from all who cannot be won over to bless the dominance of the *juste-milieu*, and to stand up for a union of modern art and the new ruling classes. Anyone, however, who has an ear for ironic implications and undertones will not fail to notice that the author of this dedication is merely seeking a new, up-to-date form of an address to the bourgeoisie to replace the hackneyed insults levelled at the 'capitalist', the 'grocer', the 'philistine', an address to the reader that invites the latter to enter into the reading as if into the entrance of the shop where the wares of art can be brought to the client.

Now, you need art.

Art is an infinitely precious commodity, a refreshing and warming drink that restores to the stomach and the mind the natural balance of the ideal.

You can imagine its use, O bourgeois – you who are legislators or shopkeepers – when the hour of six or seven tolls and bends your weary head toward the coals of the fire or the cushions of the armchair . . .

Bourgeois, you have – you who are king, legislator or dealer – set up collections, museums, galleries. Some of those that sixteen years ago were open only to bailiffs have widened their doors to the multitude.

You have formed associations and companies and taken out loans to achieve the idea of the future with all its varied forms, political, industrial and artistic. In no noble enterprise have you left the initiative to the protesting and suffering minority which is, moreover, the natural enemy of art.

Because allowing yourself to be overtaken in art, as in politics, is to commit suicide and a majority cannot commit suicide . . .

You are the natural friends of art because you are either rich or erudite.

[Or vous avez besoin d'art.

L'art est un bien infiniment précieux, un breuvage rafraîchissant et réchauffant, qui rétablit l'estomac et l'esprit dans l'équilibre naturel de l'idéal.

Vous en concevez l'utilité, ô bourgeois, – législateurs, ou commerçants, – quand la septième ou la huitième heure sonnée incline votre tête fatiguée vers les braises du foyer et les oreillards du fauteuil . . .

Bourgeois, vous avez – roi législateur ou négociant, – institué des collections, des musées, des galeries. Quelques-unes de celles qui n'étaient ouvertes, il y a seize ans qu'aux accapareurs, ont élargi leurs portes pour la multitude.

Vous vous êtes associés, vous avez formé des compagnies et fait des emprunts pour réaliser l'idée de l'avenir avec toutes ses formes diverses, formes politique, industrielle et artistique. Vous n'avez jamais en aucune noble entreprise laissé l'initiative à la minorité protestante et souffrante, qui est d'ailleurs l'ennemie naturelle de l'art.

Car se laisser devancer en art et en politique, c'est se suicider, et une majorité ne peut pas se suicider . . .

Vous êtes les amis naturels des arts, parce que vous êtes, les uns riches, les autres savants. (OC II 415–17)]

At the same time, however, this bourgeois reader is being satirically exposed, not least through the mimicry of his own rhetoric. Baudelaire's satire here is visually inspired by the political caricatures of Honoré Daumier, but it also has its literary correspondents in writers like the early socialist Charles Fourier, the poet Heinrich Heine, who offered his own critical commentary on the rise of the bourgeoisie in Louis-Philippe's Paris, and Balzac, the author of the *Comédie humaine*, whom Baudelaire specifically acknowledges in the closing chapter of his critical assessment of the 1846 fine art

Salon. This kind of simulated recognition of bourgeois reasoning, in which lies hidden a dissimulated satire of the bourgeoisie, finds an intensification in the same *Salon* in that notorious introductory passage of the last chapter but one, *Of Schools and Workers* [*Des Écoles et des ouvriers*], to which even that rather sophisticated communist, Aragon, or Sartre, who was certainly no narrow-minded fellow-traveller, took offence, without noticing that here too Baudelaire's irony is at work:

> Have you experienced, all of you whom a *flâneur*'s curiosity has often led into the heart of an uprising, the same delight as I in seeing a guardian of the public tranquillity – a guardian of the peace for a town or a municipality, the real army – beat up a republican? And like me, have you said in your heart: 'Beat on, beat him even harder, beat again, watchman, you who take after my own heart, for in this supreme beating, I adore you, and judge you to be the equal of Jupiter, the great bringer of justice. The man you beat is an enemy of roses and perfumes, a fanatic of tools; he is an enemy of Watteau, an enemy of Raphaël, a rabid enemy of luxuries, of fine arts and of high literature, a sworn iconoclast, a torturer of Venus and Apollo! He no longer wants to work as a humble and nameless worker, on public roses and perfumes. He wants to be free, the ignorant man, and he is incapable of establishing a workshop of new flowers or new perfumes. Religiously beat the anarchist's back for him!'

> [Avez-vous éprouvé, vous tous que la curiosité du flâneur a souvent fourrés dans une émeute, la même joie que moi à voir un gardien du sommeil public, – sergent de ville ou municipal, la véritable armée, – crosser un républicain? Et comme moi, vous avez dit dans votre cœur: 'Crosse, crosse un peu plus fort, crosse encore, municipal de mon cœur; car en ce crossement suprême, je t'adore, et te juge semblable à Jupiter, le grand justicier. L'homme que tu crosses est un ennemi des roses et des parfums, un fanatique des ustensiles; c'est un ennemi de Watteau, un ennemi de Raphaël, un ennemi acharné du luxe, des beaux-arts et des belles-lettres, iconoclaste juré, bourreau de Vénus et d'Apollon! Il ne veut plus travailler, humble et anonyme ouvrier, aux roses et aux parfums publics; il veut être libre, l'ignorant, et il est incapable de fonder un atelier de fleurs et de parfumeries nouvelles. Crosse religieusement les omoplates de l'anarchiste!'
>
> (OC II 490)]

That such texts were long read at a superficial level, like, moreover, the late prose poem 'Assommons les pauvres!', whose closeness to the argument of Swift's *Modest Proposal* was overlooked, should, however, tell us more about the readers than the text. It must be the case, therefore, that the text is so intricately conceived in function to the tone expected by a public locked into its own ideological patterns that the misunderstanding represents its best testimony. On the other hand, however, the context of the *Salon de 1846* guards against such a misunderstanding. In this mode, ironically disguised passages alternate with nakedly polemical passages in which Baudelaire makes no secret of his own position and in which, moreover, he provides the reader with what might be called directions for using his text. I am thinking of the astonishing eleventh chapter on Horace Vernet, in which what Baudelaire terms the 'indirect panning' ['l'éreintage par la ligne courbe'] is replaced by a direct attack on 'the French' and France, that is the France of Louis-Philippe, an attack grounded in the following astounding reason:

> Nevertheless it is not imprudent to be brutal and go straight to the heart of the matter, when at each sentence the *I* covers a *we*, an immense *we*, a silent and invisible *we*, – *we* an entire new generation, an enemy of war and national follies; a generation bursting with health, because it is young, and already shoving its way along, elbowing in and making a space for itself, – serious, mocking and menacing!

> [Cependant il n'est pas imprudent d'être brutal et d'aller droit au fait, quand à chaque phrase le *je* couvre un *nous*, *nous* immense, *nous* silencieux et invisible, – *nous*, toute une génération nouvelle, ennemie de la guerre et des sottises nationales; une génération pleine de santé, parce qu'elle est jeune, et qui pousse déjà à la queue, coudoie et fait ses trous, – sérieuse, railleuse et menaçante! (OC II 471)]

Isn't the art critic turning himself here into a tribunal, a spokesman for a youth that is urging change, and which, two years later, side by side with the 'People of Paris', will become a protagonist in the February revolution? In his volume of poetry that will in the period 1845 to 1847 bear the title *Limbo* [*Les Limbes*], with connections no less to Fourier than to Dante, and then become known under the even more provocative name of *The Lesbians* [*Les Lesbiennes*] (1848–52) before it gains its final, scandal-rich title of *Les Fleurs du Mal*, Baudelaire clings to the idea that he is speaking as a representative of modern youth, whose agitation and melancholy (OC I 792) he promises to represent. In April 1851, Baudelaire has just turned thirty, and for the first time presents a selection of his poems in a newspaper, claiming that the published volume is 'destined to trace the story of the spiritual agitation of modern youth' ['destiné à retracer l'histoire des agitations spirituelles de la jeunesse moderne']. This is to reveal, in poetic language, the intellectual, political and sentimental novel of education for the youth of 1848, a youth which from this point of view had begun to realise that in shaking off the yoke of the bourgeois monarchy, it had only replaced it with the knout of Badinguet-Bonaparte.[1] (From its very conception Baudelaire's volume of poetry offered several similarities with Flaubert's novel *L'Education sentimentale*, which also ran through several stages before it reached its final form.) Even if the earlier, ironic, often almost devil-may-care Baudelaire was already an advocate of the Romantic great school of melancholy (OC II 125) and highlights, especially in his assessment of the painting of Delacroix, the melancholy above all of his portraits of women, as characteristic of modernity – it is not by chance that the *Salon de 1846* defines suicide as the heroic passion par excellence of the bourgeois age – his own melancholy after 1850 increasingly gains deeper tones. The consciousness of the *irréparable*, the awareness of unalterable historical processes and especially too the individual's own unalterable historical processes must have played a role in this. Nevertheless, in Baudelaire's writing, melancholy is never expressed in terms of tearful self-pity as is the case for example with Alfred de Musset or Paul Verlaine. Melancholy in his case is always a way of actualising, one might almost say sublimating, longing, and not least a utopic longing for the entirely different that he sometimes simply calls 'the new'.

The melancholy of the poet Baudelaire is on the other hand a kind of defence, a turning away from a present experienced as loathsome and unbearable, a present that of course, and therein lies the sleight-of-hand of say the *Tableaux parisiens* or the prose poems, is not Romantically ignored or skimmed over (as Jean-Paul Sartre claims in his study of Baudelaire) but instead is grasped critically. Baudelaire's melancholy poetry opens almost with a blow a double space, one dreamlike, appropriate to the demands and aspirations of the poetic genius, in which the I can feel itself at home, and one in which it is confronted in the most painful way with a reality which is as trivial as it is inexorable, the most disgusting prose of modern life. In poems like 'Bénédiction' or 'L'Albatros' this technique of the double room still has an element of the Romantic, while in 'A une passante', 'Le Cygne', 'Rêve parisien' or prose poems like 'La Chambre double', 'Perte d'auréole' etc. the reader is confronted with a new kind of poetic perception of the social.

Baudelaire makes the Realist manner of seeing and of writing appear strange, by inserting fragments of lived reality in a supernatural text based on dreams or experiences and he modernises the practice of the Romantic reverie through the preciseness with which facts from the bourgeois world are summoned and deployed. Characteristic of this method of composition is the value that the analysis of the (bourgeois) reader and more particularly the reading public has in his poems. Baudelaire does not limit himself to addressing the reader, at the beginning of his collection of poems, in order to win the reader's favour, but draws an allegorically distanced and excessive picture of the reader that simultaneously presents a characteristic of the bourgeois soul, as he puts it in the *Salon de 1859*. The introductory poem of the *Fleurs du Mal* is a typical example of Baudelaire's completely new approach to the reader: an examination of the reader's conscience, a confession, self-analysis or self-accusation of a collective, a confession that the reader is tricked or forced to undertake against his will. The famous, scintillating closing line 'Hypocrite reader, – fellowman, – my twin!' (FM 7) ['Hypocrite lecteur, – mon semblable, – mon frère!' (OC 1 6)] – is seen on closer examination as anything but a spontaneous identification of the poet with his public. It is a satanic brotherly kiss that the poet bestows on those who have betrayed the world with regard to the ideals of the revolution and whom he, just like the great revolutionary thinkers of the time, ironically reminds of the catch cry of the 1848 revolution, brotherhood, whose prosaic expression was civil war, as Marx wrote after the suppression of the June uprisings.[2] Baudelaire faces the order-loving bourgeoisie who in June 1848 as in December 1851 opted for the strong man, as a moralist who has read his Machiavelli. By 1855–7 his interpretation of the bourgeois soul goes well beyond the diagnosis that he had set in the *Salon de 1846* in the context of what meaning could be attributed to the familiar black suit:

> . . . an immense cortege of undertakers, political undertakers, undertakers in love, bourgeois undertakers. We are all celebrating some burial. A uniform livery of desolation bears witness to our equality.
>
> [. . . une immense défilade de croque-morts, croque-morts politiques, croque-morts amoureux, croque-morts bourgeois. Nous célébrons tous quelque enterrement. Une livrée uniforme de désolation témoigne de l'égalité.
>
> (OC ii 494)]

For 'Au lecteur' sketches an inner view of the 'âme publique' as one of a soul ruled by a thousand base passions and sick unto death. The most destructive evil, however, that Baudelaire apprehends in the bourgeois soul is that which is really the most unspectacular, the one whose existence hypocrisy most denies: ennui.

> But there with all the jackals, panthers, hounds,
> The monkeys, scorpions, the vultures, snakes.
> Those howling, yelping, grunting, crawling brutes,
> The infamous menagerie of vice,
>
> One creature only is most foul and false!
> Though making no grand gestures, nor great cries,
> He willingly would devastate the earth
> And in one yawning swallow all the world;
>
> He is Ennui! – with tear-filled eye he dreams
> Of scaffolds, as he puffs his water-pipe.
> Reader, you know this dainty monster too;
> – Hypocrite reader, – fellowman, – my twin!
>
> (FM 7)

[Mais parmi les chacals, les panthères, les lices,
Les singes, les scorpions, les vautours, les serpents,
Les monstres glapissants, hurlants, grognants, rampants,
Dans la ménagerie infâme de nos vices,

Il en est un plus laid, plus méchant, plus immonde!
Quoiqu'il ne pousse ni grands gestes ni grands cris,
Il ferait volontiers de la terre un débris
Et dans un bâillement avalerait le monde;

C'est l'Ennui! – l'œil chargé d'un pleur involontaire,
Il rêve d'échafauds en fumant son houka.
Tu le connais, lecteur, ce monstre délicat,
– Hypocrite lecteur, – mon semblable, – mon frère!
(OC I 6)]

The reader whom Baudelaire has in his sights here, whom he seizes and
exposes, the one whose ennui is preparing to transform the earth into a
field of ruins, is the one whom contemporary caricature portrays as someone essentially satiated; *les repus, les ventrus, les satisfaits*, were already the
satirical insults directed at the bourgeoisie in the days of Louis-Philippe.

It is striking that the obverse of the flourishing bourgeois world in 'Au
lecteur' is simply evoked in the form of a metaphor and then only in order
to give an image of the poverty of the soul of those who do not (want to)
know anything about the phenomenon of poverty and of social inequality:

And like a pet we feed our tame remorse
As beggars take to nourishing their lice,
(FM 5)

[Et nous alimentons nos aimables remords,
Comme les mendiants nourrissent leur vermine,
(OC I 5)]

Baudelaire writes in the very first stanza (consequently a bad conscience is
for the bourgeois what the vermin are for the poor, who for their part can
hardly allow themselves the luxury of a conscience). And the fifth stanza
extends the ironic comparison between poor and rich in four erotic lines:

As a poor libertine will suck and kiss
The sad, tormented tit of some old whore,
We steal a furtive pleasure as we pass,
A shrivelled orange that we squeeze and press.
(FM 5)

[Ainsi qu'un débauché pauvre qui baise et mange
Le sein martyrisé d'une antique catin,
Nous volons au passage un plaisir clandestin
Que nous pressons bien fort comme une vieille orange.

(OC I 5)]

The opening of the *Fleurs du Mal* is constructed in such a way that the dialogue between the poet and his public inevitably degenerates into an unequal duel, and gives rise to the impression that the space of art and the space of bourgeois society are and have been from the beginning incapable of coming together, that the poet is an intruder in the bourgeois social space, inevitably out of place and of use only as a scapegoat, a *souffre-douleur*, the predestined victim of sadistic horrors ('Bénédiction', 'L'Albatros'), if he is not willing to accept the role of an apologist or court jester:

You must, to earn your meagre evening bread,
Like a bored altar boy swing censers, chant
Te Deums to the never present gods

Or, starving clown . . .   (FM27)

[Il te faut, pour gagner ton pain de chaque soir,
Comme un enfant de chœur, jouer de l'encensoir,
Chanter des *Te Deum* auxquels tu ne crois guère,

Ou, saltimbanque à jeun . . .   (OC I 15)]

Pointing out the alternatives so sarcastically means making it clear to the regime – every regime, whatever it may be – that one is not willing to accept it. Anyone who expresses so dramatically the poet's role as victim reveals himself as an accuser. Despite the Romantic schematisation of the antithesis between artist and philistine society one cannot fail to notice that Baudelaire does not allow it to remain as a mere Manichean dichotomy, but demonstrates already in these first poems, most of which were written early in his life, what he has learned from contemporary caricatures and from his reading of the early socialists.

The beginning of 'Bénédiction' or the conclusion of 'La Lune offensée' thus present a blasphemous variety of caricature that pierces the marriage customs of the bourgeoisie, making the reader think of Hogarth, Goya, Daumier and the Fourier of the *Nouveau monde amoureux*:

Since from all women you chose me to shame
To be disgusting to my grieving spouse,
And since I can't just drop into the flames
Like an old love-note, this misshapen mouse . . .

(FM 11)

[Puisque tu m'as choisie entre toutes les femmes
Pour être le dégoût de mon triste mari,
Et que je ne puis pas rejeter dans les flammes,
Comme un billet d'amour, ce monstre rabougri . . .
(OC I 7)]

Other poems such as 'J'aime le souvenir', the physiognomic counterpoint of 'Au lecteur', contrast the physical world of his own contemporaries with the ideal of classical antiquity and in so doing demonstrate, as the latest song of modern poetry –['ces inventions de nos muses tardives'] – the inevitability of caricature in the representation of modern life:

Today, the Poet, when he would conceive
These native grandeurs, where can now be seen
Women and men in all their nakedness,
Feels in his soul a chill of hopelessness
Before this terrible and bleak tableau.
Monstrosities that cry out to be clothed!
Bodies grotesque and only fit for masques!
Poor twisted trunks, scrawny or gone to flab,
Whose god, implacable Utility,
In brazen wraps, swaddles his progeny!
(FM 21)

[Le Poète aujourd'hui, quand il veut concevoir
Ces natives grandeurs, aux lieux où se font voir
La nudité de l'homme et celle de la femme,
Sent un froid ténébreux envelopper son âme
Devant ce noir tableau plein d'épouvantement.
Ô monstruosités pleurant leur vêtement!
Ô ridicules troncs! torses dignes des masques!
Ô pauvres corps tordus, maigres, ventrus ou flasques,
Que le dieu de l'Utile, implacable et serein,
Enfants, emmaillota dans ses langes d'airain!
(OC I 12)]

(In the introductory poem to the prose poems, 'L'Etranger', which corresponds to 'Au lecteur' in terms both of its function and its construction, the public submits the 'stranger' to a painful interrogation: this reveals that the passion of the person questioned lies beyond the expectations of those posing the question and that they can certainly have no sympathy for the stranger's dream life.)

Were there to exist a literary *Dictionnaire des idées reçues*, then under the heading 'Baudelaire' there would surely be, right at the top, a piquant anecdote from the February Days of 1848. Its hero, the young poet and dandy, flourishing a brand new rifle, would be shouting to his fellow revolutionaries: 'Let's go and shoot General Aupick!' This alleged utterance has remained in the memory of posterity as ample explanation of Baudelaire's revolutionary intoxication: the oedipal hatred that the son, perverted, disinherited, even incapacitated, by his faithless mother, felt towards his stepfather, who was moreover a career soldier. The pendant to this stereotype of reception history is an epistolary exchange between Baudelaire and his guardian Ancelle. The coup d'état of 2 December 1851, he claimed had 'physically depoliticized' him ['*physiquement dépolitiqué*' (C 1 188)]. Even Walter Benjamin, who was fundamentally to change our view of the political dimension of the *Fleurs du Mal*, was yet another victim of this cliché, according to which Baudelaire, after the coup d'état, subjugated himself like a monk.[3] As a result of such prejudices certain texts have been and still are underestimated, texts that are striking proof that the coup d'état and the Second Empire in no way silenced the lyric poet Baudelaire, even and above all not as regards politics. However, Baudelaire's political criticism is not directed as Hugo's is against the 'hero of the coup d'état',[4] the third Napoleon, just as Baudelaire in general does not take aim at statesmen and politicians.[5] His criticism, even during the empire, is directed at bourgeois society as a whole. It is bourgeois society that Baudelaire holds guilty of the suffering of the post-aristocratic period, and not least for the fact that art has gone to rack and ruin, that poets and artists like himself now belong to the *déclassés*.

As a bohemian condemned to the most precarious of existences – one thinks of the constant changes of address of a man who never lived in his own home – sympathy with those who had nothing at all, and identification with the oppressed and browbeaten, with the proletariat and the beggars, was brought home to Baudelaire in the most painful way.

The despair, the spleen, that is expressed in so many of his poems is not simply metaphysical, but also has a completely concrete political and social basis. And because he recognises this, reflects it and designates it with a rhetoric that is frequently 'satanic', and therefore not without wit, black humour, irony and deeper meaning, Baudelaire despite all his kinship and loyalty to the Romantics, nevertheless goes beyond Romanticism. He is therefore not anti-bourgeois in a Romantic way, the bourgeois being for him no mere philistine, and the rift that runs through society does not merely separate bourgeois and artist. Baudelaire recognises in the bourgeois that politico-economical animal that claims supreme mastery of the world and that will allow no other being near itself, because it is incapable of understanding or tolerating the other, the alien.

This modern vision of the modern bourgeois, a vision which is the poetic and moral counterpart of Daumier's art and of the world view of the contemporary left, was already present *in nuce* in the early, pre-revolution work of the 1840s. Turning to the bourgeois, whose phobia of others he castigated, the poet Baudelaire demonstrated that his dandyism has nothing to do with idle narcissism or melancholy introspection, but that he was concerned about others, about those left behind, the victims of laissez-faire liberalism. The maxim of the philosopher Levinas: 'Autrui me regarde' (meaning both Others concern me and Others watch me) is also, however paradoxical this might seem in regard to a poet who boasts of his uniqueness and his loneliness, the leading idea of Baudelaire's poetic perception and interest. This idea is, however, at the very least just as polemical as it is moralistic. For the perception of others is always also the recollection that most of them are overlooked and ignored by those to whom the poet must willy-nilly turn.

The gesture that Baudelaire praises in his essay about Hugo's *Les Misérables*, the gesture with which 'the poet seizes the attention of the public and bends it, like the recalcitrant head of a lazy schoolboy, towards the prodigious chasms of social suffering' ['le poète s'empare de l'attention publique et la courbe, comme la tête récalcitrante d'un écolier paresseux, vers les gouffres prodigieux de la misère sociale' (OC II 218)] is also his own. With this difference, that Baudelaire's teaching of the reader does not let matters rest at school-mastering a refractory public in democratic and philanthropic affairs. Just as important for Baudelaire as the insistent reference to those prodigious chasms of suffering is the recollection of the gulf between him and his public and between the latter and those to whom he, above all in the prose poems, refers globally as the poor, 'les Pauvres'.

If the Hugo of *Les Misérables* brings the bourgeois reader through gentle coercion and, what Baudelaire tactfully refrains from mentioning, virtuoso tear jerking, to take a lively interest in the fate of pariahs who in their heart of hearts are good people, Baudelaire exerts over the reader his authorial power, a power that is admittedly symbolic, staged within the narrow space of a poem, but which is nonetheless exceptionally brutal. Nevertheless, this has a purpose other than the socio-pedagogical. The public shall not be won over for, say, the good cause of the poor, no. To mistreat the public is for Baudelaire a way of always renouncing it anew. Texts like 'La Fausse Monnaie', 'Les Yeux des pauvres', but also earlier, more 'traditional' poems from the *Fleurs du Mal*, are tokens of incommunicability and alienation. These certainly bear the signature of the capitalist social order, but they are nevertheless primarily not an ontological necessity but something to lay at the charge of the ruling classes. The 'friend' who gives the beggar a larger false

coin and then in addition congratulates himself for suddenly giving someone more than they had expected represents a monstrous social hypocrisy
which cannot be cured because it knows nothing of itself, because it com-
mits evil with a clear conscience, through stupidity; 'the most irreparable of
vices consists in doing evil through stupidity' (PP 74) ['le plus irréparable
des vices est de faire le mal par bêtise' (OC 1 324)]. And this stupidity may
be, as Baudelaire puts it at one point, a carapace, off which reason ricochets
like suffering itself. (One can't help wondering if Derrida's famous decon-
struction of 'La Fausse Monnaie', which drowns the point of the text in
more than 200 pages of commentary, unwittingly cultivates a certain solidarity with this *bêtise* and delights the public with hermeneutic counterfeit
coin.)

Like the 'friend' of this prose poem, the beloved in 'Les Yeux des pauvres'
takes the place of the reader. Her 'impermeability', which the first-person
narrator urges us to take as typically 'feminine', is in truth above all that
of the haves who cannot bear the silent accusation in the gaze of the have-
nots as they look at their luxurious intimacy. This is in contrast to the poet
who is ashamed of his own comfort, of the fact that he can enjoy the new
Paris of Haussmann, sitting by a beautiful lady in a magnificent new café.
The sudden arrival of the poor family in front of that café and above all his
reading of the gaze of their infant eyes would in themselves be enough to
throw into question his good fortune in love. But above all it is that cruel
heartless reaction of the beloved to the eye language of the ragged gazers that
sparks off the quarrel and allows the man's love to be turned into hatred.
(She asks her companion to have the head waiter drive off the poor voyeurs,
whose presence she cannot stand.) Paradoxically, it falls to the poet-narrator
to become the vehicle for the feelings that the haves assume exist in the minds
of the have nots ('Oh! so you want to know why I hate you today' (PP 67)
['Ah! vous voulez savoir pourquoi je vous hais aujourd'hui' (OC 1 317)]).
The poem certainly does not reveal any show of political solidarity from
the bourgeois intellectual towards the proletariat, as it would be portrayed
in politically correct literature of the twentieth century, but rather depicts
the impossibility of silencing the social conscience in order to establish a
lasting relationship with those who are not burdened with any conscience
whatsoever.

Contrary to the still dominant conviction that after 1851 Baudelaire turned
away from the revolutionary tendencies of his youth, there remains the fact
that both the themes and the tenor of his publicly engaged phase which find
their clearest expression in the cycle *Révolte* and in many of the wine poems
in the *Fleurs du Mal*, 'Le Vin des chiffonniers', 'Le Vin de l'assassin', 'L'Ame
du vin', return in certain of the *Tableaux parisiens*, and in the central poems

in prose. This does not, of course, occur in the form of a straightforward Satanism which attempts to correct by means of a post-Byronic rhetoric the dilettantism of typical 1848 poetry – that, for example, of his then-celebrated friends Pierre Dupont and Louis Ménard – as Baudelaire had attempted to do during the Second Republic. It happens, rather, through a new, more experimental form of art, which Baudelaire himself once claimed, in almost startled terms, had gone beyond the bounds within which poetry had until then been contained.[6]

This transgression naturally carries with it the risk of overtaxing not just poetry but also the public, 'to whom one must never present delicate perfumes which merely exasperate it, but carefully chosen ordure' (PP 38) ['à qui il ne faut jamais présenter des parfums délicats qui l'exaspèrent, mais des ordures soigneusement choisies' (OC I 284)], to quote 'Le Chien et le flacon'.

In a similar way, take such 1848 lines from the revolt cycle in the *Fleurs du Mal*, such as the 'Litanies de Satan':

> [Satan] Whose mark, astute accomplice, will be found
> On Croesus' mean and unforgiving brow
>
> . . .
>
> Adoptive father of those ostracized
> By God, and banished from his Paradise
> (FM 271–3)

> [Toi qui poses ta marque, ô complice subtil,
> Sur le front du Crésus impitoyable et vil,
>
> . . .
>
> Père adoptif de ceux qu'en sa noire colère
> Du paradis terrestre a chassés Dieu le Père.
> (OC I 124)]

or these from 'Abel et Cain':

> Race of Abel, multiply –
> Even your gold proliferates;
>
> Race of Cain, O burning heart,
> Take guard against your appetites.
> (FM 267–9)

> [Race d'Abel, aime et pullule!
> Ton or fait aussi des petits.
>
> Race de Caïn, cœur qui brûle,
> Prends garde à ces grands appétits.
> (OC I 123)]

Or the famous closing stanza of 'Le Reniement de saint Pierre', about which Benjamin has said that Blanqui's[7] deed was the sister of Baudelaire's dream. These are lines, in other words, whose scarcely hidden message goes far beyond what a Pierre Dupont as spokesman of the people dared to promote in his songs. Such revolutionary lines are answered, both dialectically and aesthetically in the work of the later Baudelaire by incomparably complex texts, some of which seem almost hermetic, while others appear deceptively simple. These poems not only renew the rhetoric of Satanism ('Les Sept Vieillards', 'Danse macabre', 'Le Voyage' or such prose poems as 'Le Gâteau', 'Le Mauvais Vitrier', 'Assommons les pauvres!' for example), but bring new life to the lyric of the city in general.

Baudelaire develops in them a technique which first of all duped the imperial censorship, a technique that involves a hitherto unheard-of mixture of on the one hand the political and the erotic, and on the other hand contemporary history and subjective everyday experiences. As a result the sonnet 'A une passante' is first a city love poem, the narration of a unique and individual encounter that is also about the nature of modern love. However, like a palimpsest it also reveals a subtext in which the lyric I undertakes a retrospective self-critical analysis of another encounter on the streets of Paris: that of the *rendez-vous manqué* of the generation of 1848 with the goddess of freedom and the Republic respectively. In such a reading the beautiful passer-by would be an allegory recognisable not merely through her majesty and her statuesque leg but also through other attributes: the way in which she suddenly appears among the noisy crowds of the street, and the fleeting nature of her presence. And also in the enthusiasm and inhibitions that she causes in the one who becomes so unexpectedly aware of her:

> I shaking like an addict, from her eye,
> Black sky, spawner of hurricanes, drank in
> Sweetness that fascinates, pleasure that kills.
> (FM 189)

> [Moi, je buvais, crispé comme un extravagant,
> Dans son œil, ciel livide où germe l'ouragan,
> La douceur qui fascine et le plaisir qui tue.
> (OC I 92)]

The presence of the goddess of freedom, or of the Republic, or related allegories belongs to the pictorial code of the time. A famous passage from Richard Wagner's youthful text, *The Revolution*, specifically provides evidence for the practice of eroticising politics with the aid of allegory, to which Baudelaire's lightly satanic Petrarchising around 1860 lends an ironic distance that breathes new life into it and brings it up to date. 'Yes, we know that the old world is going to pieces,' wrote Wagner in 1849,

> a new one will arise out the ruins of the old, for the illustrious goddess of revolution comes swirling up from those ruins on the wings of the storm, her august head surrounded with bolts of lightning, her sword in her right hand and a torch in her left, her eyes so dark, so piercing, so cold and yet what warmth of the purest love, what an abundance of luck streams from them towards whoever dares gaze steadfastly into those dark eyes! She swirls up to us, the ever rejuvenated mother of humanity, exterminating and delighting, she travels over the Earth . . . and the hem of her dress strips away the remnants![8]

In a similar manner the last prose poems can be understood as bold artistic and philosophical experiments through which Baudelaire strove to question and raise the level not only of contemporary socio-critical poetry and fiction, but also that of social philosophy. The most sensational of these texts, 'Assommons les pauvres!' refutes with devastating arguments and biting irony as mere old wives' tales (OC I 358) the salvation doctrines proposed in 1848 both by the left and by the right and above all the mutualism of the anarchist Proudhon, whom Baudelaire had once revered.

To see in such texts merely satanic paradoxes is tantamount to bringing them down to the level of the educated bourgeois, the very ones whom they are intended to deal a crushing blow. Conversely, for many readers the pleasure of the text is spoiled when they are forced to realise that these stories express a new highly unsettling critique of liberal society and distance themselves from Proudhon but not, however, from Blanqui.

Of course it would also be false to see in Baudelaire a poetic confederate of Marxist doctrine, which in any case he can barely have known at all. For Baudelaire believed neither in the complete definitive emancipation of the oppressed classes nor in a happy end to history (herein he is and remains the disciple of de Maistre and E. A. Poe). The most concise formulation of his philosophy of history is to be found in a letter to his publisher Poulet-Malassis: 'whatever transformations may take place in the races of humanity, however rapid may be their destruction, the necessity for antagonism will remain . . . It is, if you will agree to accept this formula, eternal harmony through eternal struggle' ['quelles que soient les transformations des races humaines, quelque rapide que soit la destruction, le nécessité de l'antagonisme doit subsister . . . C'est, si vous consentez à accepter cette formule, l'harmonie éternelle par la lutte éternelle' (C II 86)].

(Translated by Rosemary Lloyd)

NOTES

1. Badinguet was a satirical nickname applied to Napoleon III.

2. See 'Die Junirevolution', which Marx published in *Neue Rheinische Zeitung*, 29 June 1848. For more on this see D. Oehler, *Le Spleen contre l'oubli, Juin 1848. Baudelaire, Flaubert, Heine, Herzen* (Paris: Payot, 1996), pp. 75–81.

3. See Walter Benjamin: *Charles Baudelaire: A Lyric Poet in the Era of High Capitalism*, trans. H. Zohn (London: NLB, 1973). Benjamin is content here merely to give as an example Paul Desjardin's article 'Charles Baudelaire', *La Revue Bleue* (1887), p. 19.

4. Karl Marx, *Der 18. Brumaire des Louis Bonaparte*, ed. J. Weydemeyer (Frankfurt am Main: Insel, 1965), p. 138 (Preface to the second edition of *18. Brumaire* from the year 1869).

5. This refers to his epistolary judgment of Hugo's political satire against Napoleon III: 'although I consider political invective a sign of stupidity, I would tend more to side with Hugo than the Bonaparte of the coup d'état' ['bien que je considère l'engueulement politique comme un signe de sottise, je serais plutôt avec Hugo qu'avec le Bonaparte du coup d'Etat' (C II 41, in a letter to E. Crépet, 11(?)/05/1860)].

6. A letter to Jean Morel, to whom Baudelaire sent a first draft of his poem 'The Seven Old Men' ['Les Sept Vieillards'] includes this statement: 'this is the first number of a new series that I want to attempt, and I truly fear that I have simply overstepped the limits set down for Poetry' ['c'est le premier numéro d'une nouvelle série que je veux tenter, et je crains bien d'avoir simplement réussi à dépasser les limites assignées à la Poésie' (C I 583, late May(?) 1859)].

7. Louis-Auguste Blanqui (1805–81), French political activist, strongly opposed to Napoleon III.

8. Richard Wagner, *Dichtungen und Schriften. Jubiläumsausgabe in zehn Bänden*, ed. Dieter Borchmeyer, vol. v: *Frühe Prosa und Revolutionstraktate* (Frankfurt am Main: Insel, 1983), p. 234.

3

BARBARA WRIGHT

Baudelaire's poetic journey in *Les Fleurs du Mal*

In truth, Baudelaire made more than one poetic journey in *Les Fleurs du Mal*.

There was, first of all, the journey of the book itself. Condemned as an affront to public morality after its first publication in 1857, partly for its poems on lesbian love, partly for perceived sadism, partly for its questioning of conventional morality, the second edition, in 1861, dropped the six banned poems (published since then under the title 'Pièces condamnées') and added a further thirty-five. Baudelaire himself wanted to bring out what he hoped would be a definitive version, but death intervened and the third edition, in 1868, was posthumous.

As between the 1857 and the 1861 editions, the controversy turns on whether to prioritise the purity of Baudelaire's initial vision of *Les Fleurs du Mal*, before the trial of 1857, as opposed to the reworked version, with its new poems and an entirely new section, 'Parisian Scenes' ['Tableaux parisiens']. To strengthen the case of the defendant in the law court, in July 1857, Baudelaire's friend, Barbey d'Aurevilly, wrote an article in which he highlighted the '*secret architecture*' ['*architecture secrète*'] of *Les Fleurs du Mal*, a book which he maintained was 'a poetic work *of the strongest unity*' ['une œuvre poétique *de la plus forte unité*' (OC I 798)]. There is no doubt that this claim was well founded. It is corroborated by Baudelaire's own observation to Alfred de Vigny that *Les Fleurs du Mal* was not 'a simple album' ['un pur album'], but had a beginning and an end: 'All the new poems were written to fit a curious frame I had chosen' ['Tous les poèmes nouveaux ont été faits pour être adaptés au cadre singulier que j'avais choisi' (C II 196)]. In other words, the work was conceived as an integral whole, with interconnecting strands. It is equally true that the book is made up of poems composed *throughout* Baudelaire's career as a writer, most of them dating – at least in their earliest form – from the period running up to 1847. Notwithstanding internal contradictions, Baudelaire gave added significance

to these individual poems by virtue of their positioning in the overall constellation of *Les Fleurs du Mal*. The problem then arises as to *which* 'secret
architecture' to adopt as the ground-plan: the pre-trial version (1857) or the
post-trial version (1861), bearing in mind that the humiliating publicity and
scandal of the events of 1857 must necessarily have influenced Baudelaire
in the recasting of his work. In *Les Fleurs du Mal*, there was more than
one configuration. Had Baudelaire lived longer and enjoyed better health,
there might well have been others. The 1861 edition is the most commonly
accepted and most complete version and is the one which will be followed
here.

Even within the poetic journey itself, there are several 'itineraries'. There
is, first of all, the traditional one, leading from birth, in 'Bénédiction',
to death, in 'Le Voyage', tracing the outline of human destiny. Humanity is shown as seeking for some infinite satisfaction in art and love
('Spleen and the Ideal' ['Spleen et idéal']), in the life of the city ('Parisian
Scenes' ['Tableaux parisiens']), in stimulants ('Wine' ['Le Vin']), in perversity ('Flowers of Evil' ['Fleurs du Mal']), in rebellion against the nature
of things ('Revolt' ['Révolte']) and finally, in death ('Death' ['La Mort']).
Within each of these sections – and often within the poems themselves –
a threefold pattern may be detected of aspiration towards the ideal, followed by disillusionment and finally, a structurally forged intermediate
position.

It would, however, be an injustice to the deep complexity of *Les Fleurs du
Mal* to cast it exclusively in these terms. To do so would be to run the risk
of having the 'road map' degenerate into a 'system'. Flaubert, Baudelaire's
great contemporary, whose novel *Madame Bovary* was also trundled through
the courts of justice in the same year as *Les Fleurs du Mal* (though with
a happier outcome), believed that it was vital to set out the terms of an
argument, but folly to try to conclude: *'Ineptitude consists in wanting to
reach conclusions'* [*'La bêtise consiste à vouloir conclure'*].[1] That reflects
Baudelaire's position as well and is one of the reasons for the 'modernity'
of his enterprise, revealing the truth as fragmentary and partial, rather than
all-encompassing and absolute.

In the hard-hitting, opening poem, 'Au lecteur', the insidious corruption,
cowardice, stupidity and self-seeking hypocrisy of the world are related to all
human beings, in both mind and body – a recurring dichotomy throughout
Les Fleurs du Mal. Dominant among these sapping elements is 'l'Ennui' –
closer in spirit to the bad faith and inauthenticity later castigated in the
twentieth century by Existentialism than to the melancholy of Romanticism.
The reader is invited to share the poet's experience, not through adulation
of a lofty figure, nor through compassion for a reject of society, but as an

alter ego: '– Hypocrite reader, – fellowman, – my twin!' (FM 7) ['– Hypocrite lecteur, – mon semblable, – mon frère!'] (OC I 6).

The journey in art

The first twenty-one poems in 'Spleen and the Ideal' relate to Baudelaire's search for the ideal in art.

'Bénédiction' presents the Romantic artist as a poet misunderstood by his contemporaries – including his own mother, who rues the day he was born – just as, in 'L'Albatros', he will be persecuted by those who are unaware of his genius. Dramatically, the poet appears 'in this bored world' (FM 11) ['en ce monde ennuyé' (OC I 7)]. The challenge will be to rise above the 'dim existence' (FM 17) ['l'existence brumeuse' (OC I 10)] of daily life, as suggested in 'Elévation', with its soaring flight of rapture. Baudelaire described a similar sensation on hearing Wagner's *Lohengrin*: 'ecstasy *compounded of joy and insight*' ['ecstase *faite de volupté et de connaissance*' (OC II 785)]. This combination of body and mind is central to the holistic perception of reality by Baudelaire. Nowhere does it receive fuller expression than in the celebrated sonnet, 'Correspondances'.

The basic idea behind the octave of 'Correspondances' is that the material world suggests some abstract meaning, as, for example, in the 'language of flowers' ['le langage des fleurs'], suggested by the last line of the lead-in poem, 'Elévation'. The idea was not a new one. It had been developed by the Swedish theologian, Swedenborg, and proved to be a rich vein in Western European literature, from Balzac and E. T. A. Hoffmann to Nerval and Yeats. Here, the trees, or columns of a temple, seem to be winking knowingly, as though they contain a hidden message which only the poet can translate. What is posited, however, is a vertical movement in one direction only – from Earth to Heaven – and should not be confused with the combination of different modes of perception, known as 'synaesthesia', underpinning the sestet. The physical sensations are here shown to be interrelated in such a way that a perfume can suggest the softness of touch of a child's skin, the sound of an oboe or the green of a pasture. These, moving from one sense impression to another, are examples of horizontal synaesthesia. Other perfumes – in the instance adduced by Baudelaire, less pure – are rich, sultry and heady. They can lead ('Correspondances', line 14) to the rapture of mind ['l'esprit'] and body ['les sens'] and may be characterised as vertical, as well as horizontal synaesthesia. 'Correspondances' marks a powerful union of the physical and the non-physical.

To attain an aesthetic ideal of such complexity represents a major challenge. Whereas in the Romanticism of Lamartine or Musset the Muse was all-powerful and the poet had to do her bidding, Baudelaire's Muse is sick, insincere and hypocritical ('La Muse malade'). To avoid cold and hunger, the poet is driven to prostitute his art ('La Muse vénale'). He visualises himself as a medieval monk, charged with illustrating received theology on the walls of his cloisters, but stalled by inertia ('Le Mauvais Moine'). Baudelaire is plagued by a sense of time running out and by the perpetual hovering of his eternal foe, 'l'Ennui'. In 'L'Ennemi', he uses the image of a garden, devastated by storm damage, to suggest the 'autumn' of his ideas, by which he means paucity of inspiration. Fear of his own inadequacy insidiously attacks him from within. In 'Le Guignon', he likens the poet's fate to that of Sisyphus, the figure in Greek mythology who was condemned to push a rock up a mountain, from which it perpetually rolled down.

Most of Baudelaire's poems were written during the 1840s, often characterised as a period of anti-climax, following on the spectacular poetic output of the two previous decades. However, as Graham Robb has shown, the poetic scene was not as negative as is often suggested and provided a vital crucible for the art of Baudelaire. Many of the iconoclastic themes surrounding the scandal of *Les Fleurs du Mal* were developed by Baudelaire's contemporaries. His originality was to present these in deadpan terms, flouting the academic hierarchy of subject-matter (much as Manet would do, in 1863, in his *Déjeuner sur l'herbe*), blending 'high' and 'low' literature, and using verse forms as divergent as the sonnet (revivified by Sainte-Beuve), the *chanson* and the romance. It is noteworthy that the brilliantly evocative word-pictures of eight role-models for the artist, in 'Les Phares', should range in time from Leonardo da Vinci to Delacroix and that, of these, there should be seven painters, one sculptor and no representative whatsoever from the world of literature.

Beauty, for Baudelaire, is always strange (OC II 578). Multi-faceted, it can be cold and white ('La Beauté'), titanic in its energy ('L'Idéal'), immense in its dimensions ('La Géante'), paradoxical in its combination of extreme opposites and tantalising, at all times, by its elusiveness. In 'Le Masque', a poem inspired by the work of the sculptor Ernest Christophe, through a discordant dialogue between two voices, the face of a classically lovely woman is revealed as a smiling mask, concealing a face of sorrow. Beauty, then, is based on a lie, a deception, an illusion. The reader is, as it were, taken on a three-dimensional walk *around* the sculpture and gradually comes to see that what seemed like one head is in fact two: the real one and the mask held up before it. For Baudelaire, Beauty is only completely perceptible when it reveals its *other* side, the obverse face of a sculpted figure, the absolute and the relative, life and death.

The voyage in love

There are three traditionally established love cycles in *Les Fleurs du Mal*, which include most, but not all, of the love poems of Baudelaire: the Jeanne Duval cycle (XXII–XXXIX), inspired by the physical love of an exotic woman; the Madame Sabatier cycle (XL–XLVIII), inspired by spiritual love; and the Marie Daubrun cycle (XLIX–LVII), inspired by the love that comes in later years, when the first fine, careless raptures of youth have been lost irreparably, but may be compensated for, in some degree, by the complexities and ambiguities of maturity. Though very different, one from the other, the underlying ground-plan of these love cycles traces a threefold movement from aspiration to disillusionment and finally to a median position, born – not of compromise – but of an anguished awareness of the extremes and a determination to salvage something from them.

The first two poems in the cycle inspired by the mulatto woman, Jeanne Duval, 'Parfum exotique' and 'La Chevelure', take us on a voyage, no doubt inspired by the one on which Baudelaire was sent, by his mother and step-father, in 1841–2 – not in any anecdotal sense, but in terms of setting sail for tropical seas, with the inherent suggestive symbolism of such a theme. These two poems, characterised by both fecundity and languor, in a typically Baudelairean oxymoron, share common features with all the subsequent 'voyage-poems': the sense that it is more joyful to travel hopefully than to arrive; the destination as a non-specific 'elsewhere'; the experience as a combination of all the senses, in mind and body. The voyage is both physical and metaphorical. It starts from the poet's powerfully evocative sense of smell, as he embraces his mistress. Mentally, he moves to distant lands and far-off ports, where the *imagined* scent of the green tamarind tree is as real as the *actual* scent of his mistress. In 'La Chevelure', by plunging his head into the 'forest of perfume' ['forêt aromatique'] of her thick wavy tresses, with their blue-black sheen and heavy scent, the poet engages in a voyage on *two* oceans – the black (hair) and the blue (sea), in which the metaphorical subsumes the real. However, whereas 'Parfum exotique' (a youthful poem) focuses on the present and is dreamily non-specific, 'La Chevelure' (written in the period 1858–9) is a masterful navigation, through memory, of inner and outer worlds, in which analogies from both are a source of constant mutual enrichment, culminating in a mix of perfumes – coconut, musk and tar – the smell of tar, associated with ships and ports, being an essential part of travel for Baudelaire.

These two poems provide an excellent example of the holistic approach of the poet, in that the shaping of the verse is inseparable from its content.

There is no abstract statement. Instead, in addition to powerfully suggestive images, the complex of olfactory sensations in the octave of 'Parfum
exotique' is transformed, in the sestet, into a pattern of spiritual nostalgia
through the increasing richness of the rhymes: 'climats'/'mâts' (*ma/ma*: two
rhyming elements); 'marine'/'narine' (*marin/narin*: four rhyming elements);
and 'tamariniers'/'mariniers' (*tamarinje/marinje*: seven rhyming elements).
Indeed, there is an effect of call and echo between the two poems, with the
repetition of the rhymes between 'climats' and 'mâts' ('Parfum exotique',
lines 9–10; 'La Chevelure', lines 12, 15). In 'La Chevelure', which, by involving kinetic sensations as well as those normally classified in terms of the
five senses, is three-dimensional by comparison with 'Parfum exotique', the
pitching and tossing of the ship, ploughing its way through the ocean foam,
is conveyed through the use of five-line stanzas and the switching between
binary alexandrines (that is, with one caesura coming in the middle of the
line) and ternary alexandrines (that is, with three combinations of measure),[2]
similar in their effects of syncopation to that produced by Rimsky-Korsakov
in *Scheherazade*.

After these 'highs', there comes the inevitable downturn. In the Jeanne
Duval cycle, the woman becomes frigid ('Je t'adore'), a blood-sucking vampire ('Tu mettrais l'univers'), insatiable in her sexual appetite ('*Sed non
satiata*'), indifferent to the suffering she causes ('Avec ses vêtements') and
serpent-like in her sinuous movements and her perversity ('Le Serpent qui
danse'). '*Sed non satiata*' is inspired by Juvenal's account of the wife of
Emperor Claudius, Messalina, who, abandoning the Imperial couch for the
brothel and exhausted by her attempts to assuage her erotic desires heterosex-
ually, tires of men, but not of women. The eyes of the poet's mistress become
like vent-shafts to Hell, enabling him to penetrate to her soul. Woman, here,
is the destructive *femme fatale*. In the Jeanne Duval cycle, war is united with
love in a downward spiral, reaching its nadir in '*Duellum*', a sonnet said to
have been inspired by a Goya print of two witches, locked in deadly combat,
on the edge of a leopard-inhabited ravine.

The shaping of these experiences in art was to be an abiding preoccupation
of Baudelaire's. 'Une charogne' is, in essence, a reflection on the indestruc-
tibility of matter. It takes an age-old theme, that of the loved one who will be
remembered after death by the poetry she has inspired. The poet, who, up
to this, had addressed Jeanne Duval in the familiar 'tu' form of the pronoun,
now uses the ironically deferential 'vous' and the formal past historic. All
seems to augur well, as the poet and his mistress take a casual stroll on a
fine summer's day. They round a corner, however, to find a stinking carcass
looming into view. The position of the decaying animal is likened to that of
a woman in physical passion. The poet's mistress, who had been so heartless

and unfeeling, is confronted by reality and almost faints. Baudelaire takes the traditional *memento mori* and revolutionises it by uncoupling it from all association with transcendence or redemption, showing how the putrid carrion will be recycled by Nature ('Une charogne', line 11). The oozing particles will multiply and, in time, metamorphose into the swirling grain, winnowed in a sieve: dust to dust, allowing, however, for the possibility of *re*-composition through memory and art.

Despite bitter quarrels and treachery, Baudelaire was to protect Jeanne Duval through long years of illness (she had already been paralysed for three years when Manet painted her in 1862). The poet begins the conclusion of this love cycle on a note of tender recollection. In 'Le Balcon', he invites his mistress to recall with him their intimate moments together on quiet nights, by the fireside or on the balcony. These are sensations relived in the present, as recollected from the past and projected into the future. In 'Le Parfum', Baudelaire joins with the protagonist of *Les Fleurs du Mal* in asking the reader to share in reflecting on the role of perfume as a catalyst for triggering memories. Here, however, unlike earlier poems, such as 'Parfum exotique' and 'La Chevelure', it is the memory of the past which is being lived in the present. The cycle ends with a defiant assertion on the part of the poet, as both he and his mistress draw closer to death: their love will live in his memory; as long as his name and reputation survive, his poetry, inspired by this 'damned being' ['Etre maudit'] ('Je te donne ces vers', line 9), will carry her memory forward to the future.

Whereas the emphasis, in the Jeanne Duval cycle, was on the physical, the spiritual is the main focus of the cycle inspired by Madame Sabatier (whom Baudelaire met in or around 1849, and who held a salon, frequented by the writers, painters and sculptors of the time, where she was known as 'La Présidente'). Here, the woman is placed on a pedestal and worshipped in quasi-religious terms. Her flesh is holy ('Que diras-tu ce soir', line 7) and her scent angelic. Her very presence lights up the way before her. She orders the poet to love abstract Beauty for her sake and proclaims herself to be a blend of Guardian Angel, Muse and Madonna. There are shades of Dante and Petrarch in 'Le Flambeau vivant', where the woman's eyes are like guiding beacons for the poet. They shine in broad daylight, like candles in a mortuary chapel. Their role is sacred and is suggestive of awakening and perhaps resurrection.

In the Madame Sabatier cycle, with its close links between love and liturgy, the poet has recourse to a concept known in the Catholic Church as 'reversibility', according to which the voluntary sufferings of the innocent serve to redeem the sins of the guilty. Baudelaire adapts this principle to contrast the state of sin and wretchedness of the poet and the perfection of the angelic woman ('Réversibilité'). How, he wonders, can she share in suffering or empathise with a heart crushed like a piece of crumpled paper? How will she react when, in time, she sees herself grown old and wrinkled? However, Madame Sabatier's frivolity, as well as the mechanically forced smile, which a woman in her position had to put on at times when she felt least like being sociable, cause the spell to break. Behind the 'radiant delight' ['radieuse gaieté'] ('Confession', line 16) of her external image, the woman cannot refrain from emitting a plaintive cry, like a fractious child, complaining of her lot. She has shown herself to be an imperfect angel.

'Harmonie du soir', in the Madame Sabatier cycle, is like 'Le Balcon', in the earlier cycle, in that it is a moment of peace and reconciliation. Here, however, night is not a memory: it is a gradual unfolding in the present, echoed in the prosody, where the second line of each stanza becomes the first of the following one. In both poems, there is a gentle refrain, but, in 'Harmonie du soir', there is no suggestion of physical love and the imagery is liturgical (the memory of his mistress shines as though from a holy monstrance).

The Madame Sabatier cycle concludes with 'Le Flacon', in which an empty bottle, lying in the cupboard of an abandoned house, contains the heady perfume of a past love. The memories thus emitted are not of the woman's physical qualities, as in the Jeanne Duval cycle, but are symbolised by the delicate wings of a butterfly bursting out from the chrysalis or Lazarus rising from the dead. Similarly, the poet concludes, when he is dead and forgotten, like an old perfume-bottle, his verse will intoxicate the memory of future generations with its evocation of the bitter-sweet recollections of his love for his mistress. 'Le Flacon' has clear parallels with 'Une charogne', but there are subtle differences too, especially in its greater self-referentiality.

Marie Daubrun was an actress whom Baudelaire knew in the late 1840s and with whom he had a short-lived affair in 1854–5 and again in 1859. She was famed for her green eyes and was nicknamed 'The Girl with the Golden Hair', after a play of that title in which she acted in 1847. This third cycle of love-poems reflects the autumnal mood of the poet at the approach of middle age. 'A landscape is a state of mind', Amiel famously remarked. In 'Ciel brouillé', Baudelaire propounds the converse: 'Sometimes you're like horizons set aglow / By suns in rainy seasons here below' ['Tu ressembles parfois à ces beaux horizons / Qu'allument les soleils des brumeuses saisons' ('Ciel brouillé', lines 9–10)].

'Le Beau Navire' reflects the slow, indolent cadence of his mistress's footsteps in the syncopation of the poem: the first quatrain is repeated in the fourth, the second in the seventh and the third in the last. Sweeping along in her wide skirt, she is like a ship going out to sea. The same combination of outer and inner worlds is also characteristic of 'L'Invitation au voyage'. Unlike the 'voyage-poems' of the Jeanne Duval cycle, this is no passionate escape to a far-flung exotic destination. The woman here is addressed as 'child' or 'sister' ('L'invitation au voyage', line 1). The invitation is 'to love and to die' ['Aimer et mourir'] ('L'Invitation au voyage', line 5), in a setting which is an extension of her personality. Partially inspired by Weber's *Invitation to the Waltz*, this poem was the perfect definition of a work of art for Gide[3] and was the source of Matisse's exotic panels, *Luxe, calme et volupté*.

Ecstasy, as ever, is followed by suffering. In 'L'Irréparable', the poet cries out, full of remorse, but also in anguish that what has been done can never be undone. He appeals to the actress, Marie Daubrun, to act like the good fairy at the end of a pantomime and strike down the forces of evil, but he waits in vain.

As in the other love cycles, there comes the mood of resigned acceptance – here, with 'Chanson d'automne'. The thud of logs on the cobbles reminds the poet of approaching winter. Stocking up wood for fires is a comforting thought and there is, indeed, a moment of peace and calm in this poem. However, the poet will not allow himself to be lulled into a false sense of security, since the thudding sounds of the logs appear to him like the driving of nails into a coffin.

The Marie Daubrun cycle ends, like the other two, with the thought that a lasting memory can be forged from so much beauty and suffering. Jealousy, however, led the poet to be particularly cruel in 'A une Madone', where he lovingly constructs an altar to his mistress, on which he then sadistically sacrifices her, in a final mood of passion and sacrilege.

The descent into despair

Baudelaire entitled the first and by far the largest section of *Les Fleurs du Mal* 'Spleen and the Ideal', but it was in the opposite order that he tracked the ideal in art and love, ending with the downward spiral into the slough of despond, or 'Spleen'. 'Spleen' is more intense than the world-weariness of 'melancholy', associated by Baudelaire with Lamartine and the first-generation Romantics. Their attitude of lofty despair was generally born of frustration at the gap between the ideal and the real, attributable to circumstances beyond their control. Baudelaire's sense of 'Spleen' is far closer to clinical depression, an anxiety psychosis all the more galling for having its origins in perceived personal inadequacies. He does not define its nature, but suggests its effects, in a series of compelling images. This journey into despair involves travel in a kind of no-man's-land, intermediate between life and death, in which objects are anthropomorphised and the poet is depersonalised in a series of lucid self-explorations.

At first sight, 'La Musique' appears like one of the 'voyage-poems': through music, the poet can travel in his mind's eye, as though he were on the high seas, his chest thrust forward like the prow of a ship and his lungs inflated like sails. However, the ship is going nowhere. It is becalmed on a sea, which turns into a mirror, in which the poet can contemplate his own despair. He listens, in 'La Cloche fêlée', not so much to bells, as to the memories which they bring. For him, this is a bitter-sweet experience: sweet, because of the hopes and dreams thus evolved; bitter, in that these sounds no longer relate to the present. The poet's soul is like a cracked bell. He can take no comfort in its religious connotations ('La Cloche fêlée', line 7). This is the price he must pay for confronting reality unflinchingly.

The journey into despair is best tracked in four poems, each entitled 'Spleen' (LXXV–LXXVIII). In the first of these, Baudelaire begins with an allegorical figure pouring water from an urn. This death-like figure is none other than 'Pluviôse', the name given in the French Revolutionary Calendar to the rainy period from 20 January to 18 February. This is seen as a destructive, anachronistic force, which has upset the order of things: the inhabitants of the city are in the cemetery; a scrawny cat prowls, not on the roof, but about the house; meanwhile the soul of an old poet wanders in the gutters. 'Pluviôse' and 'Spleen' combine to dismantle reality, to the sound of a large church bell, a hissing log in the fireplace and a wheezy clock. In this dank atmosphere, objects are given a threatening personality. The only dialogue is that between two emblematic figures from a dirty pack of playing-cards, the Knave of Hearts and the Queen of Spades, who grimly chat about their lost love affairs.

In the remaining 'Spleen' poems, the poet brings himself directly into the picture, saying that he has more memories than if he were a thousand years old. His brain is like a large chest of drawers, into which have been stuffed old letters, poems and locks of hair, wrapped in receipts. Having identified with these objects, which are so evocative of his despair, he then declares that he *is* a moonless graveyard or an elegant interior, decorated with faded roses and pale pastels. In his self-alienation, he ends by turning into granite: as a forgotten sphinx, he sings only at sunset.

The accumulation of so many memories is oppressive. The nadir is reached ('Spleen: Quand le ciel bas et lourd') when there is no more hope and only despair prevails. The sky closes in and weighs on the mind. Earth is transformed into a dank prison cell. Sheets of rain pouring down are like the bars of a vast gaol and the lugubrious thoughts of the poet weave spiders' webs in his mind. Suddenly, ominous bells peal. Long, silent funeral convoys process through his soul. All the hopes fostered in his youth have been dashed.

Now, however, having reached the pit of despair, the only base, according to Baudelaire, which can empower true revolt and determination, he resolves to salvage what he can from the rubble of his world through his writing. Self and Other battle it out, in an obsessive conflict ('Obsession'), in which three main sources of human hope (forests, sea and stars) show themselves to be deficient. The poet cannot escape from his own self-image. The familiar glances of 'Correspondances', instead of being supportive (line 4), haunt him at every turn ('Obsession', line 14). Unlike Ovid, he has exiled himself and has no regrets. He has used the 'alchemy of sorrow' ['Alchimie de la douleur'] to make a Hell of Heaven and seeks the 'unknown' ['l'obscur'] and the 'uncertain' ['l'incertain'] ('Horreur sympathique', line 6) – the 'undecidable' – which alone will allow him the range and flexibility for which he yearns.

The split personality of the poet is nowhere expressed more forcefully than in 'Héautontimorouménos'. Here, the poet is both victim and executioner. He is caught in the grip of Irony, which has the advantage of showing him, in every phenomenon, its equal and opposite reaction, but has the deadly effect of sapping the unity of his overall vision, encompassing all extremes. Self-irony, furthermore, can stultify and destroy. This is the burden which he has brought down on himself. Irony and self-awareness are instruments of the Devil, but ones which the poet will use when he looks into his heart as into a mirror. In contradistinction to having role-models shine out ('Les Phares'), he here pays tribute to 'an ironic beacon' ['un phare ironique'] ('L'Irrémédiable', line 37), which will lead him to the ultimate justification of his mission: self-awareness in evil (line 40).

Old Man Time makes his presence felt throughout. In 'L'Horloge', a twenty-four line poem – one for each hour of the day – the poet tries to distance himself from the situation and has the hand of the clock speak autonomously. It tells of the merciless passage of the hours and of wasted opportunities, but stresses that, when our time is up, there will be no room for consolation or regret.

A stroll in the city

The addition of the new section, 'Parisian Scenes', along with the expansion of the 'Spleen' element, in 'Spleen and the Ideal', and the deletion of the banned poems, constituted the principal material changes in the 1861 edition. This marked a major alteration in focus, grouping together earlier poems and newly written ones, in the context of the city and of Paris, in particular.

The idea of 'pictures of Paris' was not a new one. In literature, it dates back to Mercier's *Tableau de Paris* of 1781. In painting, the view of a town from a window was well established in seventeenth-century Dutch art and the Italian eighteenth-century *vedute*. Given this inter-disciplinary background and Baudelaire's self-avowed desire here to operate in the domain of both painting[4] ('landscape' ['paysage']) and writing (composing 'eclogues' ['églogues'], or pastoral poems ('Paysage', line 1)), it is hardly surprising that he should open this new section with a pictorial 'landscape'. But this is a 'landscape' with a difference. It is a 'cityscape', or what Baudelaire himself described as 'landscapes of stone, now swathed in the mist, now struck in full face by the sun' ['paysages de pierre caressés par la brume ou frappés par les soufflets du soleil' (OC II 692)]. It is, moreover, contextualised historically, in that it shows the poet, in his attic, battening down the hatches against street demonstrations outside. This is generally taken to be a reference to the deep disillusionment of those *quarante-huitards* who, between the heady days of February 1848 and the repressions of July 1848, saw their dreams of a utopian society cruelly shattered. Gautier, like Baudelaire, retreated to the ivory tower of art and became 'depoliticised' ['dépolitiqué' (C I 188)], by contrast with Hugo and the other exiles who left France after the establishment of the Second Empire. However, the fact that the first letter of 'Riot' ('L'Emeute', line 21) is capitalised shows Baudelaire's intention to allegorise this reference to revolt, in such a way as to encompass all uprisings.

Paysage also marks a radical departure from the roughly contemporaneous 'landscape-poem', 'Ciel brouillé', where the correlation between the poet's mistress and the skyscape was so close that they were mutually interdependent and 'horizons' rhymed with 'saisons' ('Ciel brouillé', lines 9, 10), space with time. In both poems, Baudelaire uses the images of the outer landscape to conjure up an inner one: the goal is the creation, not the reproduction, of the real. However, whereas 'Ciel brouillé' is predicated on the infinite horizons of the pre-1848 days, in 'Paysage', the poet closes the doors and shutters, and wills himself, in his imagination, to construct, on the screen of his memory, 'fictive horizons' ['horizons fictifs' (OC II 89)], conditioned by experience and disillusionment to be framed rather than limitless. Literary artifice will replace direct contact with nature: the poet, with what Proust will later call the 'voluntary memory', will evoke the spring ('Paysage', line 24) and, from his 'furious thoughts' ['pensers brûlants' (line 26)], will conjure up a warm atmosphere. The *fin-de-siècle* art of decadence beckons.

There are still further ramifications. Given Baudelaire's well-known hostility to photography, it might seem perverse to establish a parallel between the *camera obscura* and the construction of his fairy palaces in the black of night ('Paysage', line 16). In his *Salon of 1859*, Baudelaire objected that photographers think they have a ready-made poem, when they open a window. Although this was true of the vast majority of the early practitioners of this burgeoning art, there were some notable exceptions, including photographers like Gustave Le Gray, who foresaw the death of subject-matter, long before Barthes and Foucault, in the twentieth century, spoke of the death of the author. In a photograph taken around 1849,[5] Le Gray shows a pile of paving-stones, making up the foreground and the background of the work, with no sky, and not even a post or column to give a sense of scale or context. These paving-stones, in other words, are fragments. Ruins, one could say, with Benjamin, of the old Paris which was being destroyed, at the command of Baron Haussmann, to make way for the vistas of the modern City of Light. For Benjamin, Paris, as portrayed by Baudelaire in 'Le Cygne', has become 'as brittle and as transparent as glass'.[6] The poet wanders through the new Place du Carrousel, in front of the Louvre, conscious of the rabbit-warren of houses and streets that had to be demolished to make way for the new order of things. All that is left is 'jumbled bric-à-brac' ['bric-à-brac confus'] ('Le Cygne', line 12), something like Le Gray's pile of paving-stones.

Baudelaire feels an exile in his own city, reduced – as he sees it – to a vast building site. This sense of exile illuminates, retrospectively, the opening reference to Andromache, exiled after the fall of Troy, following the defeat in battle of her husband, Hector. As one of the spoils of war, she was handed over to her brother-in-law, Helenus, but, as Virgil relates, she continued to venerate the spirit of Hector in Epirus, by a river named after the Trojan river Simois. She, too, was trying to reconstruct something of her lost past. As the poet continues his stroll, aware of the great city's mustering of its labour forces at dawn and the thundering sound of its transportation, he notices a swan, which had escaped from a local menagerie. Wandering through rubble and paving-stones, the swan, too, is in exile and longs for the beautiful lake of its birth ('Le Cygne', line 22), the equivalent, for the swan, of Andromache's Simois. The second part of the poem shows how this becomes allegorical (line 31) of exile. To the figures of fragility already mentioned is added a scrawny and consumptive woman of colour, searching wildly for the absent coconuts of Africa (a nostalgic echo of the early 'voyage-poems' in search of exotic destinations).

'Le Cygne' shows how far Baudelaire has travelled from the early poem, also inspired by a temporarily earth-bound bird, 'L'Albatros'. There, in the last quatrain, the point is rather laboriously made that the poet is 'like' this prince of the clouds ('L'Albatros', line 13). In 'Le Cygne', the multi-levelled allegory is suggested in a host of different ways. Together, the albatross and the swan mark the distance covered by Baudelaire in the development of his poetic genius.

This stroll in the city is no ordinary stroll. It is a *flânerie*, a word which implies both wandering and dreaming. What is so special about this *flânerie* is its timing. Lukács observed that the French Revolutionary and Napoleonic Wars made history, for the first time, a *'mass experience'*.[7] The Industrial Revolution, which followed in their wake, brought the masses from the countryside to the big cities. Indeed, the population of Paris doubled between 1800 and 1850. The resulting social problems were addressed by all classes, it seemed, in terms ranging from liberal to utopian. However, February 1848 marked the point at which the bourgeoisie took fright and, by June of that year, anxiously sought to hold on to its gains. The Second Empire consolidated the position of the bourgeoisie, modernising Paris in such a way as to clear the newly formed proletariat out of the city centre and to widen the streets – in part, at least, to prevent the construction of barricades. The sense of alienation and dispossession are palpable in Baudelaire's city poems. He identifies with all the marginal figures of society – a red-haired beggar girl ('A une mendiante rousse') or a rag and bone man – not in any sentimental way, but seeing them as 'exiles' like himself. That he should have dedicated 'Le Cygne' to Hugo is both fitting and ironic: fitting, because of Hugo's own political exile in Guernsey, as also because of his deep sense of compassion, which would manifest itself most famously in *Les Misérables* (1862); ironic, because Baudelaire shared none of Hugo's faith in 'Progress'. Technology had introduced the concept of mass production and led to mass migration between nations and into cities. Many traditional values were denigrated as being anachronistic and the public was infused with the desire for commodities. In the words of Benjamin, the masses appeared 'as the asylum that shields an asocial person from his persecutors'.[8] The *flâneur* had something in common with a spy and Baudelaire was acutely aware of the privilege of being both himself and someone else (OC II 692), in the anonymity of the crowd. He watched, from a position of detachment, the flotsam and jetsam of society. In 'Le Cygne', there is a collision of worlds (Paris and the ghosts of other lost cities), a shock-experience – as Benjamin has it – which is one of the determining factors in modernity.

The other two poems dedicated to Hugo, 'Les Sept Vieillards' and 'Les Petites Vieilles', clearly exemplify this. The first of these is based, not on allegory, but on hallucination. In the 'great colossus' ['colosse puissant'] ('Les Sept Vieillards', line 4) of the city, the poet comes across seven identical old men, bitter and acrimonious in their poverty. Appalled and devastatingly aware of his own inadequacy, he staggers back to his room, his soul dancing like a boat adrift on a sea without end (an image often likened to that of Rimbaud's 'Bateau ivre'). Between the poet and the seven old men, there is no exchanged glance, no encounter. The old men are remembered as dislocated body parts. Their procession to an unknown place ('Les Sept Vieillards', line 32) brings nothing new, only more of the unthinkable same. In 'Les Petites Vieilles', the parallel between the old women and, not just Paris, but all 'old capitals' ['vieilles capitales'] ('Les Petites Vieilles', line 1), is hinted at in the first line and developed in the fourth section of the poem. They share faded beauty and the loss of all that gave meaning to their lives. Baudelaire portrays the shrunken old women, as they are shaken about in the rattling horse-drawn omnibus or as, hunched over, they walk close to the walls of the buildings that they pass. Yet, their eyes have not lost their sharpness and they can still quietly enjoy a public concert of military music. Proust astutely noted that Baudelaire had, in this poem, 'created an exterior painting of their form, without sympathising with them',[9] an artistic detachment which, however, allows the odd glimpse of restrained compassion.

In 'A une passante', one of the loveliest of all the poems in *Les Fleurs du Mal*, a tall, slim woman, in deep mourning, emerges like a flash of lightning from the crowd, raising the hem of her dress as she passes. She disappears into the night, almost as soon as she has been noticed, leaving the poet to reflect on the love that might have been. This poem contains all the main interlocking factors in modernity: the grasping of the sensuous present, in all its transience; the contingency inherent in modern city life; the increasing fragmentation of experience under the impact of shock. It is a dissonant sonnet, full of noise – not merely because of the deafening traffic on the street, but also by virtue of the enjambments cutting across the line structure and an extraordinarily powerful line ('A une passante', line 12) made up exclusively of adverbs: 'Far away! Too late! *Never* perhaps!' (translation altered) ['Ailleurs, bien loin d'ici! trop tard! *jamais* peut-être!']). The encounter, such as it is, is marked by the points of suspension, where the glance is recognised as having been returned by the woman as she vanishes into the night. This virtual love is perhaps the closest Baudelaire would ever get to the ideal.

The trip with stimulants, perversity and revolt

From the crowd of the city to wine-induced intoxication, the transition appears seamless. All the people depicted in the section 'Wine' are on the margins of society. The rag-picker, in particular, emerges as an extension of 'Parisian Scenes', in that he, 'as poets do' ['comme un poète'] ('Le Vin des chiffonniers', line 6), sorts through the refuse on the city streets: together, in the words of Benjamin, they 'derive their heroic subject from this very refuse'.[10] Mud can be transformed into gold. Just as, in the earlier section, the poet was aware of being both himself and someone else in a city crowd, here wine is shown as enabling the fusion of subject and object, of inner and outer worlds, giving hope and courage to oppressed workers ('L'Ame du vin'). It rapidly emerges that such hope is illusory. When the drunken rag-picker staggers home, imagining himself to be a prince or a warrior, wine is shown to be no gift from God, but an invention of man, oppressed by God ('Le Vin des chiffonniers'). Wine can inculcate fierce pride and can induce a sense of god-like ecstasy ('Le Vin du solitaire'). Under its influence, the alco-holic murderer defies God ('Le Vin de l'assassin') and lovers can envisage an ecstatic flight into heaven ('Le Vin des amants').

It is at this point that there is the clearest intersection between the idea of a journey and that of the architecture of *Les Fleurs du Mal*. In the 1857 edi-tion, 'Wine' was placed after 'Revolt', presumably to suggest escapism into drunken torpor, after the blasphemous outrages and prior to death. How-ever, in the period between the trial and the 1861 edition, Baudelaire worked on *The Artificial Paradises* ['*Les Paradis artificiels*'] (1860), the first part of which, 'The Poem of Hashish' ['Le Poème du Haschich'], has been shown to be parallel in sequence to the rearranged order of the 1861 edition.[11] The complexities of self-consciousness within remorse, characteristic of the 'Spleen' poems, followed by the ability to participate dispassionately in the lives of countless others, in 'Parisian Scenes', have their counterparts in the world of drugs, as do the subsequent tendencies towards self-deification and revolt. The journey has informed the architecture and *vice versa*. Stim-ulants are points on the slippery slope of the rake's progress, rather than a 'blinder', dulling consciousness just before death.

There are sexual aberrations of all kinds in the following section, 'Flowers of Evil' – a title almost identical with that of the volume as a whole, save for the omission of the definite article. Lust manifests itself, in forms both sadistic and masochistic, in a vain attempt to escape from 'Ennui' ('La Destruction', line 11). Baudelaire feels compassion for lesbians, whom he sees as 'seekers of the infinite' ['Chercheuses d'infini'] ('Femmes damnées', line 23), in a search parallel to his own. Indeed, one of the forerunners of the title for *Les Fleurs du Mal* was *Les Lesbiennes*. The allegorised sister-figures of Death and Debauchery make their gifts of terrible pleasures and ghastly delights ('Les Deux Bonnes Sœurs', line 11), which are both attractive and lethal. The poet ends by becoming a sacrificial offering to these sisters, giving of his own lifeblood ('La Fontaine de Sang'). The most powerful poem in this section is a 'voyage-poem', 'Un Voyage à Cythère'. Here, against an intertextual background, drawn from an identical title used by the eighteenth-century painter, Watteau, and Baudelaire's own contemporary, Nerval, the poet sets sail in a spirit of joyous adventure. Unlike the previous 'voyage-poems', this one has an actual geographical destination, the island of Cythera, famed for love in myth and legend. However, as the island looms into sight, it is sad and black – a complete let-down (line 7). Worse is to follow. As the travellers sail close to the shore of this rocky desert island, they see a hanged man on a gallows, being pecked and torn asunder by birds and beasts of prey. The poet recognises himself in this hanged man and sees that this suffering is his own. Nauseated by self-disgust, he prays for the strength and courage to go on.

Going on means not only facing up to the reality of the human condition, but moving from the hell of destruction to a sustained mode of opposition against organised religion. The three poems in the section 'Revolt', like those in the two preceding sections, date from a relatively early period in the career of Baudelaire. They are rooted in Romantic admiration for the Luciferian rebel, which, in turn, goes back to eighteenth-century black masses, Hell Fire Clubs and particular interpretations of Milton's Satan in *Paradise Lost*. They are also close to the view of Christ as man, rather than as the Son of God, a view which informed the portrayal of the anguish of Jesus in the Garden of Olives by Vigny and Nerval in poetry and by Chassériau in painting. According to the Gospel, Peter, on three occasions, denied Christ. In 'Le Reniement de saint Pierre', Baudelaire gives an original twist to the theme by seeing himself as somewhat like Peter, but standing firm in his denial of Christ, criticising him for failing to fulfil his promise here on earth and for meekly handing over to a God, shown, at the beginning of the poem, to be a despotic tyrant, laughing in anticipation at Christ's pain on Calvary. For the poet, this created a cleavage between two worlds ('Le Reniement de saint Pierre', line 30): the kingdom which is 'not of this world' (dreams) and the vale of tears in which we live our daily lives (actions). Baudelaire outdid his predecessors by foregrounding Peter's denial of Christ, not in cowardice (as the Gospel has it), but in the sense that humanity was duped and that the scales have now fallen from its eyes. Partly, no doubt, to deflect the attention of his censors in 1857, Baudelaire composed a note (OC I 1075–6), in which he sought to downplay the significance of this type of 'pastiche'. Furthermore, he wrote that, as an author, he had to be 'faithful to his painful programme' ['fidèle à son douloureux programme'] and 'to train his mind in all forms of sophisms as well as all forms of corruption' ['façonner son esprit à tous les sophismes et à toutes les corruptions'].

In the reversed litany of 'Les Litanies de Satan', Baudelaire pastiches the *Kyrie Eleison* to pay homage to the Prince of Exile ('Les Litanies de Satan', line 4) and comforter to the dispossessed (lines 10–11). Indeed, so many of the attributes of Christ are accorded by the poet to Satan that, in the end, the two merge. Some believe that such a passionate acknowledgment of failure and misery is itself a paradoxical proof of the existence of God. The poet ends by choosing – like Adam – the Tree of Knowledge. The quest will continue.

Death: the last journey

Baudelaire always intended concluding with the theme of death, though, with the addition of the last three poems, in the 1861 edition, he modified his approach very significantly. The section 'Death' adopts the now familiar pattern of ecstasy, followed by its opposite – terror – and then by a fusion of the two extremes. Lovers dream of a consummation sublimated in death ('La Mort des amants'). For the poor, death is a source of consolation and a hope of peace ('La Mort des pauvres'). For artists, long years of striving after perfect expression may perhaps find fulfilment in death ('La Mort des artistes'). In all these poems, there is a sense of life after death. 'La Fin de la journée' suggests a sense of peace, after all that is haphazard, garish and futile in life.

Everything changes, however, with 'Le Rêve d'un curieux'. In a highly dramatic dream sequence, the narrator, terrified and fascinated at the thought of what death may bring, waits expectantly, like a child, for the curtain to rise at what appears to be a theatre. It is only the fiction of spectacle that causes 'the chilling verity' ['la vérité froide'] ('Le Rêve d'un curieux', line 11) to be revealed. Projecting into the future, the narrator is surprised to find that his own death caused him no surprise. On the contrary, it proved to be an anti-climax. 'And what! That's all there is to tell?' ['Eh quoi! n'est-ce donc que cela?' (line 13)], he finds himself exclaiming. Metaphysically, this cancels out all sense of transcendence in death. It does not even exclude the possibility that death may just mean more waiting, as in life. The poem was dedicated to 'F. N.', Félix Tournachon, better known as Nadar, one of the greatest nineteenth-century photographers. Jérôme Thélot[12] has convincingly argued that the setting in the poem is that of a photographer's studio. One might go further and suggest that, as the narrator poses in front of the lens and as the photographer, his head beneath a curtain, triggers the camera's shutter, the subject-becoming-an-object undergoes a process similar to the micro-version of death described by Barthes in *Camera Lucida*. A moment in time that once existed has now been documented and is no more. Baudelaire had mixed feelings of horror and fascination, not only about death, but also about the new art form of photography, practised with such mastery by his friend Nadar.

'Le Voyage' is the final poem of the series and of the book. This 'voyage-poem' is a microcosm of all the others and indeed of the entire work. It fol-lows the familiar threefold pattern: expectation, born of the dreams of youth, as the child traces chimerical journeys on maps and prints by lamplight; dis-illusionment, following on an imagined meeting with those who have been to that 'undiscover'd country from whose bourn no traveller returns', only to find that, in a supposed life after death, there will be a continuation of the 'numbing spectacle of human flaw' ['Le spectacle ennuyeux de l'immortel péché' ('Le Voyage', line 88)]; finally, the courage to go on, something in the spirit of Beckett's parallel determination in the twentieth century – with no illusions, but with an ineradicable sense of hope in what the 'new' may offer. It is as though the whole reel of film is being re-run in fast forward. The gap between the real and the ideal is captured in the gentle lulling of the voyagers' dreams of the infinite, cradle-like, by the finite sea (line 8). Travel may be motivated by a desire for political exile, escape from an intolerable family situation or the toils of a woman.

Travel, for its own sake, is best. It opens the way to unexpected features of delight, such as shifting cloud patterns in the sky, which may escape our attention if our minds are cluttered with a pre-existing agenda. We frequently invest so much in the expectation of our dreams that reality inevitably falls short of anticipation. This is equally true of political systems, such as the Icarian settlements, born of utopian socialism, one of the would-be destinations of the travellers in 'Le Voyage': from the look-out of the three-master on which this imaginary journey is being made, hope rapidly changes to despair when, instead of reaching Eldorado, the ship hits a reef. These travellers are no different from a drunken sailor imagining new Americas or a tramp – similar to our earlier rag-picker – by candlelight in his hovel, imagining places of voluptuous pleasure like Hannibal's legendary Capua. All the earlier forms of escape are recalled: the search for delight or oblivion in drugs; the pride of humanity, drunk on genius (line 101) and rebelling against God. A time–space continuum is created, in which the eternal enemy, Time, is depicted as the fighter with a net, in the Roman gladiatorial contests, capturing all before him – from the Wandering Jew and the indefatigable Apostles to those who never leave home and spend their lives 'killing time'. The final leave-taking is obligatory and high risk. Once we have committed to the old captain, Death, our only hope is to plunge into the depths of the unknown – as Baudelaire himself put it, in his prose poem of that name, 'Anywhere out of the world' – Heaven or Hell, in search of something new.

Various strands come together here: Baudelaire's unswerving belief in original sin (which he shared with Joseph de Maistre, one of his favourite authors); his Manichean conviction of the parallel existence of good and evil, God and Satan coexisting simultaneously in his personality (OC I 682). Linked with these is the loss of belief in transcendence. The infinite horizon of 'Ciel brouillé' contrasted with the framed horizon of the artefact in 'Paysage'. In 'Le Voyage', Baudelaire goes a step further, showing a constantly receding horizon (lines 29–30), one which gives the lie to any hope of there being another world behind it. There is a self-reflexive strength in

'Le Voyage', with the art of writing emerging as a permanent value when all else appears to be lost.

One last point. Like two bookends, Baudelaire has placed tributes to his contemporaries: the prefatory one to Théophile Gautier; the dedication of 'Le Voyage' to Maxime Du Camp. Both are, of course, salutations to friends. However, like the dedications to Hugo and Nadar discussed earlier, they bear with them a deeper message. The sense of humility in the wording of the Preface to Gautier is over the top and barely conceals Baudelaire's view of the role of Gautier as a Parnassian John the Baptist to his Christ as modernist. The dedication to Du Camp (who travelled to the Middle East with Flaubert) likewise draws a line in the sand between Du Camp's understanding of technological progress in *Les Chants modernes* (1855) and Baudelaire's deep aversion to the anonymity and alienation inherent in mass markets and urbanisation. The poetic journey in *Les Fleurs du Mal* is both rooted in its period and universal in its terms of reference.

NOTES

1. Letter, dated 4 September 1850, by Gustave Flaubert to Louis Bouilhet, from Damascus, in *The Letters of Gustave Flaubert*, selected, ed. and trans. Francis Steegmuller (Cambridge, MA and London: Belknap Press of Harvard University Press), p. 127.
2. Note especially the ternary 'Fortes tresses, soyez la houle qui m'enlève!' ('La Chevelure', line 13), a feature utterly lost in translation.
3. André Gide, *Incidences* (Paris: Gallimard, 1924), p. 89.
4. Significantly, for the plural of 'ciel', Baudelaire here ('Paysage', line 8) uses the form adopted in the world of painting, 'ciels', rather than the regular plural, 'cieux'.
5. See Anne de Mondenard, 'Le Gray et ses élèves, une école de l'abandon du sujet', *La Revue du Musée d'Orsay* (Printemps 2003), pp. 63–73, fig. 1.
6. Walter Benjamin, 'The Paris of the Second Empire in Baudelaire', in *Charles Baudelaire: A Lyric Poet in the Era of High Capitalism*, trans. from the German by Harry Zohn (London: NLB, 1973), p. 82.
7. György Lukács, *The Historical Novel*, trans. Hannah and Stanley Mitchell (Harmondsworth: Penguin, 1969), p. 20.
8. Benjamin, 'The Paris of the Second Empire', p. 40.
9. Marcel Proust, *Contre Sainte-Beuve* (Paris: Gallimard, 1954), p. 211.
10. Benjamin, 'The Paris of the Second Empire', p. 79.
11. Alison Fairlie, 'Some Remarks on Baudelaire's *Poème du Haschich*', in *Imagination and Language*, ed. Malcolm Bowie (Cambridge: Cambridge University Press, 1981), pp. 129–49.
12. Jérôme Thélot, '"Le Rêve d'un curieux", ou la photographie comme Fleur du Mal', in *Lire 'Les Fleurs du Mal' de Baudelaire*, Université Paris 7 – Denis Diderot, *Cahiers textuels* 25, Revue de l'UFR 'Science des Textes et Documents' (2002), pp. 147–60.

4

RACHEL KILLICK

Baudelaire's versification: conservative or radical?

Rhetorical and prosodic systems are not arbitrarily invented tyrannies, but a collection of rules determined by the way we as spiritual beings are ourselves organised.

[Les rhétoriques et les prosodies ne sout pas des tyrannies inventeés arbitraire-ment, mais une collection de règles réclamées par l'organisation même de l'être spirituel.

(OC II 626–7)]

Writing to Paul Demeny, some ten years after the publication of *Les Fleurs du Mal*, the sixteen-year-old Rimbaud hailed Baudelaire as 'the first of the visionaries, the king of poets, *a true God*' but nevertheless impatiently attacked what he saw as the master's formal conservatism: 'But he lived in a milieu that was too concerned with "art"; and his much vaunted form is paltry: the unknown and its inventions demand forms that are new.'[1] In strik-ing contrast, Baudelaire's poetic contemporaries Banville and Gautier were undisturbed by the challenging nature of Baudelaire's content, but, in line with the thinking of mid nineteenth-century theoreticians of versification,[2] were worried by his habit of contesting the 'rules' of traditional French verse, notably those of the sonnet.[3]

Banville set out his views on versification in his *Petit Traité de poésie française* (1871). Baudelaire's, characteristically, must largely be deduced from his actual poetry. He declined with mingled fatigue and irritation to reveal 'the backstage mechanics . . . all the horrors of the sanctuary of art' ['le mécanisme des trucs . . . toutes les horreurs qui composent le sanctuaire de l'art' (OC I 185)] to an unschooled and indifferent public, but the broad lines of his 'philosophy of composition'[4] do nevertheless emerge, albeit in fragmentary fashion, in the preface drafts for *Les Fleurs du Mal*, in *Mon Coeur mis à nu* and *Fusées*, and in his critical writings. Here he praises the Romantic writers of the 1820s and 1830s for their imagination, whilst criticising them for the laxity of their expression, and congratulates their 1840s and 1850s successors of the 'art for art' school for making beauty, not morality or truth, the goal of art, whilst castigating them in their turn for making technique an end in itself. Baudelaire's ideal, in contrast to both groups, is a poetry where the form does not draw attention to itself either by its patent carelessness or by its self-advertising virtuosity.[5] Rather, the poet must be a guardian of the unicity of idea and form,[6] exploring the fundamental rhythms of the human psyche through the rhythms of language as refined through the poetic structures of line and stanza. Baudelaire's task as poet is to reveal 'how poetry is linked to music by a prosody whose roots reach more deeply into the human soul than indicated by any classical theory' ['comment la poésie touche à la musique par une prosodie dont les racines plongent plus avant dans l'âme humaine que ne l'indique aucune théorie classique' (OC I 183)].

Baudelaire's prosody of the soul involves a complex struggle between opposing tendencies: between 'two simultaneous postulations, one towards God, the other towards Satan' ['deux postulations simultaneés, l'une vers Dieu, l'autre vers Satan' (OC I 682)]; between the yearning for perfect 'order and beauty' ['ordre et beauté'] ('L'Invitation au voyage') and the desire for the bizarre, the unknown, the new;[7] between apathetic 'horror of life' ['l'horreur de la vie'] and euphoric ecstasy (OC I 703); between the urge to escape 'Any where [sic] out of the world' ['N'importe où hors du monde' (OC I 356)] and the longing for security; between 'vaporisation' and 'centralisation' of the self (OC I 676). All these variations on the twin structuring principles of freedom and constraint, have an evident affinity with the regularities and flexibilities of versification, especially as focused through the tight conventions of the French tradition. Baudelaire's awareness of the challenges and opportunities of the way in which form and theme come together is a crucial element in his poetry, motivating an imaginative reinvigoration of prosodic convention, informed from within by the contradictory urgencies of his own moral and spiritual dilemmas.

As the ship by its sails and rigging (OC I 663–4) or the picture by its paints and brushstrokes (OC II 626) the verse poem is driven by the dynamic interplay of theme, metre, sentence structure, rhythm, rhyme and phonetic pattern. Where English metre, reflecting the strongly marked stress patterns of English, relies principally on beat, French metre, drawing on the more evenly distributed stress patterns of the Romance languages, is primarily based on syllabic count. The dominant metre in *Les Fleurs du Mal* is the twelve-syllable alexandrine, the defining metre of French versification, with the eight-syllable line a distant runner-up and the ten-syllable line barely visible.[8] Alongside these lines with an even number of syllables, Baudelaire makes a very limited use of lines with an uneven number of syllables, mostly in alternation with the alexandrine.[9] The sixteenth-century emergence of the alexandrine as the leading French metre was a function of its length, twelve syllables being capacious enough to accommodate an entire phrase or even a whole sentence and also balanced enough, through its central division into two parts of six syllables each, and flexible enough, through varied syllabic division in each half, to underpin the longer or shorter elements of the sentence. These qualities made the alexandrine the natural choice of French seventeenth-century verse theatre, where its aptitude as a vehicle for declamation and argument was further confirmed and codified.

The first four alexandrines of 'Au lecteur', the opening poem of *Les Fleurs du Mal*, locate Baudelaire, and the collection as a whole, immediately and firmly within the classical tradition.

> La sottis/e, l'erreur, /le péché, / la lésine
> Occupent nos esprits/ et travaillent nos corps,
> Et nous alimentons /nos aimables remords,
> Comme les mendiants/nourrissent leur vermine.
>
> (OC I 5)[10]

Line 1 expands the symmetrical capabilities of the alexandrine by creating four equal groups of three syllables each. The 6/6 symmetry of line 2 underlines an antithesis (the contrast 'mind'/'body'), and also simultaneously highlights a synthesis (their common destruction). The 6/6 balance of line 3 again underpins the contrast of the physical and the spiritual ('Et nous alimentons/nos . . . remords') while additionally introducing oxymoron ('aimables remords') as a subordinate contrast in the second half of the line. Line 4, matching illustrative analogy to the assertion of line 3, concludes a textbook illustration, neatly framing subject ('Comme les mendiants') and predicate ('nourrissent leur vermine') in the two halves of the line. These familiar, unsurprising symmetries are supported not only by the expected end-marking of rhyme but also by reinforcing sound patterns at the beginning of the line:[11]

> La sottise, l'erreur, le péché, la lésine
>   iz   zi
> Occupent nos esprits et travaillent nos corps
> ok   o   o k

The quatrain is thus at one level a model of metrical orthodoxy. However, this is no conventional dedication cajoling the 'gentle reader' through the soothing patterns of a familiar versification. Instead, these same patterns, in flagrant contrast to the generic norm, are the engine for a merciless assault on the 'hypocritical' audience. Furthermore, the surprise of this dissonance between form and content is complemented by a specific phonetic surprise, an expressive exploitation of intensified phonetic pattern, based on 'm' (lines 3–4):

Et nous ali*m*entons nos ai*m*ables re*m*ords
Co*mm*e les *m*endiants nourrissent leur ver*m*ine.

This not only highlights the individual semantic components of the imagery of M/mal-nourishment (the first in a key metaphorical series of consumption and self-destruction in *Les Fleurs du Mal*) but also, more originally, reinvigorates the etymology of 're-mords' (literally 'biting again'), transforming the banality of its rhyme with 'corps'/'body' by providing an acoustic enactment of the twin processes of invasion and erosion.

Baudelaire's use of the ten-syllable and the eight-syllable line shows a similar sensitivity to the specific qualities and potential of individual metres. The ten-syllable line, superseded in prominence in the seventeenth century by the more ample cadences of the alexandrine, only occurs in *Les Fleurs du Mal* in the four sonnets of 'Un fantôme', where its slighter dimensions appropriately match the ghostly theme, and in 'La Mort des amants' where metrical lightness, combined with fragile 5 + 5 metrical symmetry, suggests evanescent passage to the harmonious world of the beyond.[12] The eight-syllable line, on the other hand, is intermittently selected by Baudelaire as a tighter, more succinct alternative to the alexandrine. An all-purpose metre in French versification from the Middle Ages onward, often associated in the nineteenth century with 'chanson' or with humorous verse, it also attracted particular attention in the 1850s in Gautier's *Emaux et camées* (*Enamels and Cameos*) where the poet's desire to create poetry as bright and hard as enamels and cameos found a parallel in the tightness of the line. Gautier's descriptive lead seems evident in the successive cameos of 'L'Irrémédiable' and in the crystalline images of 'Rêve parisien', Part 1, but Baudelaire, characteristically, looks less to the virtuoso challenge posed by the eight-syllable line as a vehicle for description than to the gnomic or suggestive effects of metrical concision. 'Les Hiboux' and 'La Pipe', in which Baudelaire intensifies conciseness by choosing the sonnet form, have an emblematic quality, which in turn becomes a theme of 'Le Squelette laboureur'. Elsewhere metrical brevity and the resultant rapid return of the rhyme effectively convey latency and potential. Thus the quality of magical expansion, inherent in the cat's discreet mewing and the delicate scent of its fur ('Le Chat', no. 51) is formally replicated by the eight-syllable line, which, though barely attaining the dimensions of a 'vers nombreux' (literally 'a multi-syllabled line') (line 11), is nevertheless able to capture the essence of 'the longest sentence' ['les plus longues phrases' 1.15]. Similarly, in 'Tout entière', the fascination of the poet's mistress and the way it elusively exceeds the sum of 'the many charming things of which her body is composed' ['toutes les belles choses . . . Qui composent son corps charmant'], is suggestively indicated by the glancing rapidities of rhythm and rhyme. In contrary fashion, the effect created can also be one of claustrophobic confrontation. 'Le Vampire' tightly binds the addict and the object of his obsession within the narrow confines of the eight-syllable line; '*Héautontimourouménos*' replays the 'vampiresque' paradigm with an explicit sado-masochistic focus; and 'L'Irrémédiable' cements its insistent reiteration of images of imprisonment with the most potent example of Baudelaire's exploitation of the compressive energy of the octosyllable, the celebrated formula: 'Evil aware of itself!' ['La conscience dans le Mal!'].

Orderly repetition is a key aspect of metrical structure. The alexandrine, combining the even 6/6 balance of its two halves with their subsidiary flexibilities, is the lynchpin for this in traditional French versification, but it carries within it the danger that it may come to seem too predictable. The Romantic poets of the 1820s and 1830s therefore attempted to vary the twelve-syllable line by dividing it into three groups of four syllables. Baudelaire uses this arrangement occasionally, for example in the third line of the stanza 8 of 'Un voyage à Cythère':

> De féroces oiseaux/perchés sur leur pâture
> Détruisaient avec rage/ un pendu déjà mur
> Chacun plantant/ comme un outil/ son bec impur
> Dans tous les coins saignants/de cette pourriture.
>
> (OC I 118)

The departure from the 6+6 rhythm is successful in drawing attention to the physical detail of the birds' attack on the body rotting on the gibbet, but as the Romantics had discovered earlier and as this example shows, the subversive effect of the variant arrangement is highly specific and crucially dependent on the very metrical pattern it seeks to disrupt.[13]

Metrical structure does not of course presuppose that each individual line is complete in itself as a sentence or a phrase and greater flexibilities are to be achieved by the interplay of metrical and syntactic structures across pairs of groups of lines, or more daringly across stanza divisions. Baudelaire, in common with poets generally, runs sentences over several lines and sometimes exploits such overruns in ways that draw particular attention to the device and thus serve to highlight particular aspects of theme. Thus, for example, in the opening lines of 'Le Flacon':

> Il est de forts parfums pour qui toute matière
> Est poreuse. On dirait qu'ils pénètrent le verre
>
> (OC I 47)

he highlights the pervasiveness of the perfume by the overrun which places 'matière' at the rhyme and 'poreuse' in a heavily stressed position in line 2. Alliteration on 'p' across both lines, emphasising the key words 'parfums, poreuse', 'pénètrent' and also, through its multiplicity, suggestively reproducing porousness phonetically ('pour' is an additional element here), further supports the effect. Continuation of sentences across two or more stanzas is also normal practice, provided sentence structure and stanza structure remain in parallel. In 'L'Amour du mensonge' Baudelaire uses repetition of subordinate clauses of time across stanzas 1 and 2 in this way ('Quand je te vois passer . . . Quand je contemple . . . ton front pâle' (OC I 98)) ['When I watch you go by . . . And when I contemple . . . Your pallid brow' (FM 201)] to prepare the expansiveness of presence and memory achieved in stanza 3 ('Je me dis, 'Qu'elle est belle! Et bizarrement fraîche! Le Souvenir massif . . . La couronne' (OC I 99)) ['I think, how lovely! And how oddly innocent! Massive remembrance . . . Crowns her' (FM 201)]. Stanzas 1–3 of 'Spleen (IV)' use precisely the same technique but this time the repetition of temporal clauses insistently reinforces the oppressive tension of 'ennui' that finally explodes into the frenzied outburst of stanza 4, where:

> Des cloches tout à coup sautent avec furie
> Et lancent vers le ciel un affreux hurlement.
>
> (OC I 75)

> [Bells all at once jump out with all their force,
> And hurl about a mad cacophony.
>
> (FM 151)]

Baudelaire also demonstrates, however, a wish to extend these limited flexibilities, sometimes by drawing more intensely on standard devices, sometimes by blatantly subverting them. Alternation of metre is one means he adopts to prolong or collapse anticipated patterns of rhythm, as in 'Le Poison', where twelve- and seven-syllable lines, further supported by a fifth rhyming line, provide a metrical echo of both expansive drug-induced 'high' (stanza 2) and dizzy faint (stanza 4). In contrast, distinctly unorthodox variations from standard procedures occasionally point to a more radical undermining of metrical expectation. Stanza 7 of 'Le Chat' is an outstanding example:

> De sa fourrure blonde et brune
> Sort un parfum si doux, qu'un soir
> J'en fus embaumé, pour l'avoir
> Caressée une fois, rien qu'une.
>
> (OC I 51)

> [From its soft fur, golden and brown,
> Goes out so sweet a scent, one night
> I might have been embalmed in it
> By giving just one little pet.
>   (FM 105) (Translation altered)]

Here the single sentence of which the stanza is – quite normally – composed, overruns the individual lines in ways which become increasingly strange and surprising. The detachment of 'un soir' at the end of line 2 and its separation from the rest of its clause in line 3 are striking but not in themselves unusual as a device for poetic emphasis. The chief aim here, though, is not to highlight an aspect of theme, but rather to prepare the daring overrun between the third and fourth lines – an audacious departure from standard metrical practice – that disrupts the normally unbreachable group of the past infinitive 'avoir caressé', setting the unstressed auxiliary 'avoir' at the stressed position of the rhyme. The disturbing effect is then further intensified by a second highly unorthodox rhyme placing the single unstressed syllable of the indefinite article 'une' as the final word of the stanza.

'Le Chat', however, is an exceptional example and these disruptive procedures are moreover limited to the four lines of stanza 7. However, Baudelaire uses the blurring of line and stanza divisions with increasing frequency in the poems added to the 1861 edition of *Les Fleurs du Mal*. In 'Les Sept Vieillards', for example, he deliberately mismatches sentence and stanza division to underline the theme of physical and mental dislocation. Thus the subordinate clauses of stanza 2 overlap into stanza 3, so that the subject and main verb 'I followed', controlling all of lines 5–12, do not appear until line 2 of the third stanza. The subsequent sentence ('Tout à coup un vieillard . . .') ['Then, an old man . . .'], contained for the most part in stanza 4, takes dislocation a stage further, encroaching on the first three syllables of stanza 5, where the long-awaited main verb 'M'apparut' ['Appeared quite suddenly to me'] finally surfaces. Stanzas 6 and 7 bring disarticulation to a climax, as the presentation of the grotesquely disjointed old man awkwardly straddles the stanza division:

> Il n'était pas voûté, mais cassé, son échine
> Faisant avec sa jambe un parfait angle droit,
> Si bien que son bâton, parachevant sa mine,
> Lui donnait la tournure et le pas maladroit
>
> D'un quadrupède infirme
>   (OC I 88)

[You would not call him bent, but cut in two –
His spine made a right angle with his legs
So neatly that his cane, the final touch,
Gave him the figure and the clumsy step

Of some sick beast . . .

(FM 179)]

Similar incompatibilities of sentence and quatrain structure in 'Les Petites Vieilles' and 'Le Cygne', and of sentence and sonnet structure in 'La Fin de la journée' are used to distort and blur received metrical groupings to provide expressive reinforcement to the portrayal of disorientation and agitation.

Baudelaire's choice of stanzaic forms, like his choice of metre, is essentially conventional with three main focuses: the quatrain sequence; the sonnet; poems with refrains, notably poems of five-line stanzas. As analysis of 'Au lecteur' has suggested, the quatrain, generally speaking, offers a natural match of length and structure for Baudelaire's discursive sentences. The sequence of quatrains also has the advantage of being able to expand according to his needs, sustaining the patterns of progress, contrast or repetition that underpin his preoccupation with the themes of constriction and expansion.[14] The sonnet, on the other hand with its restricted length and its sharply delineated divisions into quatrains and tercets provides an excellent complement and contrast to the quatrain sequence. Baudelaire's extensive use of the sonnet in *Les Fleurs du Mal* has sometimes been presented as a major formal innovation in French nineteenth-century poetry. As a choice, though, it was conventional enough for the time. The sonnet had been a key vehicle for the sixteenth-century Pléiade poets and their interpretation of the Renaissance aesthetic of originality through imitation, but like lyric poetry in general it had gone into eclipse in the seventeenth and eighteenth centuries. It had returned to prominence following the publication of Sainte-Beuve's *Tableau historique et critique de la poésie française et du théâtre français au XVIe siècle* (1827–8), and in the 1830s and the 1840s, as Baudelaire began to write, was a popular, multi-purpose genre, combining, for the talented as for the untalented, a moderate formal challenge with a degree of thematic freedom. As Baudelaire put it in a letter to Armand Fraisse of 18 February 1860, 'the Sonnet suits everything, clowning, compliment, passion, reverie, philosophical meditation' ['tout va bien au Sonnet, la bouffonerie, la galanterie, la passion, la rêverie, la méditation philosophique' (C I 676)]. For Baudelaire, moreover, the sonnet as a 'fixed form' also embodied the 'eternal benefits of constraint' ['bénéfices éternels de la contrainte' (OC II 119)]. It thus had the particular attraction of offering a concise alternative to Romantic prolixity, whilst still leaving thematic integrity uncompromised by excessive formal display.

The divisions of the sonnet into quatrains and tercets and the ways in which parallels and contrasts are set up from stanza to stanza readily fit Baudelaire's dualistic view of human experience. In matters of love, the Renaissance sonnet had ritually exploited these structures to portray the power struggle of the male and the female: his humanity/her divinity, his ardour/her coldness, his sensitivity/her superficiality, the eternity of his verse/the mortality of her beauty. A number of sonnets in *Les Fleurs du Mal* closely replicate these models. 'Le Flambeau vivant', 'L'Aube spirituelle', 'Sisina', 'A une dame créole' pastiche the idealisation of the beloved, while 'Remords posthume', 'Le Revenant', 'Sépulture', on the other hand, imitate the equally traditional counter-model of the macabre post-mortem revenge of the disappointed lover. But more significantly and more frequently in *Les Fleurs du Mal* these well-worn tropes are rejuvenated by Baudelaire's obsessive preoccupation with the sinfulness of sex. The contrastive potential of the sonnet is thus consistently used to foreground woman's animal sensuality and spiritual sterility ('Le Chat' (no. 34), 'Avec ses vêtements ondoyants et nacrés'), her sexual dominance and his sexual subjugation ('Le Possédé', *'Sed non satiata'*), her thoughtless 'joie de vivre', his tortured 'conscience dans le mal' (*'Semper eadem'*, 'Causerie').

But love is only one of the ways through which access to the Ideal is attempted and Baudelaire, building on the early initiative of Sainte-Beuve in the *Vie, poésies et pensées de Joseph Delorme* (1829), decisively extends the thematic range of the sonnet to incorporate other experiences of aspiration and failure. He thus draws on the structural oppositions of the sonnet to reveal the contrast between the vitality and the commitment of earlier creators and the sterility and loss of focus of their modern counterparts ('L'Idéal', 'La Muse malade', 'La Muse vénale', 'Le Mauvais Moine'). He also expands this contrast to encompass the difficulties experienced by humanity in general when faced with the chasm between the finite and infinite ('La Beauté'), effort and attainment ('Le Guignon', 'La Cloche fêlée'), and the fragile, unrealised hopes of youth and the frustrated despair of an unfulfilled old age ('L'Ennemi').

If the contrasting themes Baudelaire explores in 'Spleen et idéal' readily match the sonnet's characteristic 'turn' from octave to sestet in line 9, his handling of 'la pointe', another frequent feature of the sonnet involving the decisive summation or reversal in the final line (or couplet) of a previously developed theme, argument or image, is more problematic and more subversive. 'La Musique' offers a virtuoso example of Baudelaire's upending of the traditional device. His choice of an alternation of twelve- and five-line syllables and the forward movement of rhyme across lines 1–12/13 mirror the surging of the sea which is the metaphor for the poet's elated response to the stimulation of music. But Baudelaire then uses the final couplet to bring this movement to a sudden halt:

> . . . D'autres fois, calme plat, grand miroir
> De mon désespoir

> . . . At other times, dead calm, the glass
> Of hopelessness   (OC I 68)

and exploits the imbalance of the 12/5 alternation in lines 13 and 14 and the almost immediate return of the rhyme to underline and also to simulate the monotonous 'flat calm' of despair. Less showily, he repeatedly modifies or undermines standard procedures of progression and climax. 'Bohémiens en voyage' and 'La Géante' imaginatively insist on formal 'irresolution', avoiding 'la pointe' and developing an open-ended cross-stanza accumulation of verbs and infinitives that mimics the ceaseless journeying of the 'tribe of prophets' ['tribu prophétique'] or the immensity of the 'mighty forms' ['magnifiques formes'] of 'the young giantess' ['jeune géante']. In contrast, the many images of death in 'La Mort des pauvres' culminate in a curiously ambiguous line 14, where the repetitive predictability of the syntax ('C'est . . ./ C'est . . .') seems to subvert as much as to support the final presentation of death as 'the porch looking out on mysterious skies' ['le portique ouvert sur des Cieux inconnus' (OC I 127)]. A more decisive undercutting of the sonnet's dynamic of progression and resolution can be seen in 'Brumes et pluies' where the formal climax of the couplet (lines 13–14) places the emphasis not on change, but on a continuing failure of the will and vaporisation of the self. 'Pluviôse, irrité contre la ville entière' ('Spleen (1)'), goes a stage further, offering a series of fragmented notations linked by the twin motifs of liquefaction and liquidation. The poet as subject has been eliminated; instead it is the overall structure of the sonnet that imposes its own confining shape, enacting the paradox of disintegration and claustrophobia which is the defining feature of 'spleen'.

In France convention had long had it that the quatrains of the sonnet should ideally use only two rhymes. Purists such as Gautier and Banville held strict views on this (and other) sonnet 'rules' and criticised Baudelaire for his persistent failure to comply. At the same time, a further complicating factor was their emphasis, in common with many other nineteenth-century poets, on the importance of 'rich' rhyme (that is, rhyme comprising three or more matching phonetic elements rather than the standard two). Baudelaire was in fact equally capable of both 'regular' quatrain rhyme and rich rhyme when it suited his purpose and throughout his career insisted on mastery of rhyme as an essential poetic tool. His criticism, in 1846, of Louis de Senneville's incompetent rhymes in his *Prométhée délivré*: 'His work shows no awareness of the intense colorations of rhyme as lanterns lighting up the route of the idea' ['il ignore les rimes puissamment colorées, ces lanternes qui éclairent la route de l'idée' (OC II 11)] shows sympathy with contemporary thinking on the importance of the phonetic quality of rhyme, whilst also, and more importantly, signalling Baudelaire's constant awareness of the primacy of theme. Ten years or so later, a preface draft for *Les Fleurs du Mal* confirms both the importance of the mastery of rhyme and its essential link to content: 'Any poet, who is unaware of the exact number of rhymes there are to each word, is incapable of expressing any idea whatsoever' ['Tout poète qui ne sait pas au juste combien chaque mot comporte de rimes est incapable d'exprimer une idée quelconque' (OC I 183)]. The challenge of consistently producing sonnet quatrains with only two sets of (preferably rich) rhymes, was not, then, something which Baudelaire, with his sceptical attitude towards formal virtuosity, felt bound to accept. He remained keen, however, to exploit the repetitiveness of sonnet *structure* to suggest, for example, the expansive mirroring relationship between the self and the cosmos on the one hand, and between the different senses on the other, as depicted in 'Correspondances', lines 1–4 and 5–8, or, conversely, the inescapable reflection of the self and its limitations in the spectacles of the natural world, as portrayed in 'Obsession', 'Alchimie de la douleur' and 'Horreur sympathique':

> Cieux déchirés comme des grèves,
> En vous se mire mon orgueil;
> Vos vastes nuages en deuil
>
> Sont les corbillards de mes rêves,
> Et vos lueurs sont le reflet
> De l'Enfer où mon cœur se plaît.
>
> (OC I 78)

> [Skies torn apart like wind-swept sands
> You are the mirrors of my pride;
> Your mourning clouds, so black and wide,
>
> Are hearses that my dreams command
> And you reflect in flashing light
> The Hell in which my heart delights.
>
> (FM 154)]

In a small but significant number of instances, however, Baudelaire seeks actively to intensify the repetitive principle inherent in sonnet structure by exaggerating the demands of 'regular' sonnet *rhyme*. '*Sed non satiata*' is a particularly striking example. The first rhyme 'nuits' [nɥi] has three matching phonetic elements and, in addition, exploits the density of homonym: 'nuits'/'night' and 'nuits'/'wine'. The second rhyme raises this resonant richness to a new level of intensity. Each of the rhyme words 'havane,' savane', 'pavane', 'caravane', already incorporates a mirroring of sound (the repetition of [a]). By bringing these words together as highly developed rhymes with two matching vowels and two matching consonants, [a-v-a-n], Baudelaire multiplies the reflective impact. The tercets provide a brief pause with two unremarkable rhymes, one of them ('âme'/'flamme') arguably the most over-used rhyme of all love poetry in French. These serve to set off the phonetic richness of the final rhyme ('li*bertine*'/Proser*pine*') and also its quality as a 'rare' rhyme involving, in this case, a proper name.[15] The effect is the re-creation, stylistically, as incantation, of the mesmeric fascination exercised by the insatiable mistress over her poet/lover.

Intensification of the rhyme-scheme is extended to an entire sonnet in 'Parfum exotique'. Strictly 'regular' use of two rhymes only in the quatrains is accompanied here by the richness of all the rhymes, producing a density of phonetic pattern that enacts that perfect unbroken harmony, characteristic of the 'other country' of the Ideal. The expanding of rhyming elements in the tercets takes the process further, mimicking the expanding amplitude of the convergence of the sensations of smell, sight and sound. Thus the single rhyming syllable of 'Cli*mats*/*mâts*' (lines 9–10 leads to the two rhyming syllables of '*m*/*narine*' (lines 11–12), and from '*m*/*narine*' to the many-syllabled repetition of '*tamariniers*/*marininers*' (lines 13–14). 'La Vie antérieure' similarly uses sonnet rhyme and associated phonetic effects within the line to support the mirroring and reflection that is one of its central motifs:

> Les houles, en roulant les images des cieux,
> Mêlaient d'une façon solennelle et mystique
> Les tout-puissants accords de leur riche musique
> Aux couleurs du couchant réflété par mes yeux.
>
> (OC I 18)

Baudelaire exploits the phonetic intensity of the 'rule' whereby the two quatrains share the same rhymes, and uses richness of rhyme ('portiques'/'basaltiques'/'mystique'/'musique' in the quatrains and 'calmes' and 'palmes' and 'splendeurs'/'odeurs' in the tercets) to boost further the theme of harmonious synthesis, metaphorically figured in the fusion of sea and sky and in the marriage of expansive structure ('vast and columned vaults', line 1 ['vastes portiques']) and voluptuous calm.

Conversely 'Brumes et pluies' provides the opposite reading of 'monotony', focusing on uniformity not as vibrant order but as a drift into formlessness.

> Ô fins d'automne, hivers, printemps trempés de boue
> Endormeuses saisons! je vous aime et vous loue
> D'envelopper ainsi mon cœur et mon cerveau
> D'un linceul vaporeux et d'un vague tombeau.
>
> (OC I 100)

Fourfold repetition of quatrain rhyme again is key, but now, instead of choosing rich rhymes, Baudelaire turns instead to imperfect ones, the first composed only of assonances ('boue'/'loue'/'joue'/'s'enroue'), the second only partially fulfilling the basic rhyme requirement of a matching vowel and a matching consonant element, since 'cerveau' and 'tombeau' in the first quatrain and 'renouveau'/'corbeau' in the second are linked only by assonance (eau [o]), though each has a fully rhyming counterpart ('cerveau'/'renouveau' and 'tombeau'/'corbeau') in the opposite quatrain. This formal suggestion of collapse is further promoted by an aberrant arrangement of the quatrain rhyme, that replaces the intertwining of enclosed (abba abba) or alternate (abab abab) rhyme with the monotony of couplets (aabb). Alongside these subversions of structural shape, dense internal phonetic patterning works towards an acoustic assertion of sameness, as repetition of nasal vowels, together with the repetition of other vowels and consonants, weakens the importance of the rhyme at the end of the line.

Baudelaire's imaginative reinterpretation of the 'rules' of 'regular' sonnet rhyme provides him with one way of enhancing the expressive sound of his verse to suggest, as appropriate, either the expansive intensity of the Ideal or the invasive amorphousness of Spleen. An alternative possibility, supporting each of these opposing tendencies, is offered by stanzaic forms based, like traditional forms of *chanson*, on refrain. One very specific realisation of this is 'L'Invitation au voyage', where the paradox of sensuous calm is formally re-created by the lulling alternation of five- and seven- syllable lines in the three stanzas and the delicate amplification and momentary stabilisation of this gentle rocking in the seven-syllable refrain 'Là, tout n'est qu'ordre et beauté / Luxe, calme et volupté' (OC I 53). Another similarly specific experiment is 'Harmonie du soir', where the second and fourth line of each stanza become the first and third line of the stanza following, reproducing for the ear the 'languid vertigo' ['langoureux vertige'] of the slow decline of evening into night.[16] However, though each is a highly successful poetic creation, their virtuoso aspect is also a crucial limitation. Where the sonnet permutations are legion (always leaving open an element of surprise), these are 'one-offs' dependent for their effect on their singularity. A more flexible model is provided by the five-line stanza where the opening line is repeated as the fifth line. Though more mannered and 'visible' than the sonnet, it offers a varied set of repetitive options depending on whether repetition is total or approximate, on the way it is incorporated into individual stanzas and how it is handled across the poem as a whole. In 'L'Irréparable', the constant repetition of first and last lines serves to highlight fatality and implacability, though the suggestively repetitive character of the refrain is to some extent diluted by the discursiveness of the series of questions, commands and assertions upon which the poem is constructed. In somewhat similar fashion in 'Réversibilité' (XLIV)], the quasi-liturgical supplication 'Ange, plein de . . .' is memorably inaugurated by subtly intertwined modulations of sounds and letters in line 1, cross-weaving nasalised [ã] and [g] in balanced phonetic repetition for the ear: '[ã] Ange . . . [g] gaiété . . . [ãg] angoisse' with balanced orthographic repetition for the eye: 'Ange . . . gaiété . . . angoisse'. But the repetitive effect is then ironically subverted by the sharp, thematic contrast between her insouciant well-being (lines 1, 5) and his mental and physical torment (lines 2–4), a pattern that will be insistently repeated in successive stanzas. In contrast, 'Le Balcon' and 'Moesta et Errabunda' intensively exploit the principle of repetition as 'magical incantation' ['sorcellerie évocatoire' (OC I 658)], evoking an all-encompassing experience of euphoric harmony as it might be recaptured through memory.

In 'Le Balcon', the repeated line extends and enacts the twin principles of expansive echo and globalising synthesis that underpin an intensive thematics of all-encompassing love. All of space becomes part of this love, as symbolised in the balcony, poised 'vertically' between earth and heaven, and 'horizontally' between domestic intimacy and the open infinities of the cosmos. All the senses come into play, creating an experience more intense than any one of them can convey. Love is both a physical and an emotional relationship, engaging body, breast and heart, and embracing the different qualities of mother, mistress, queen and sister within the single figure of the poet's adoration. And love reaches out across the days and the seasons, fusing the past with the present in the fullness of memory.

'Moesta et Errabunda' similarly uses the refrain as an incantatory device to recall and suggest the ample harmony of 'the green paradise of youthful loves' ['le vert paradis des amours enfantines' (OC I 64)], but the emphasis here, in contrast to 'Le Balcon', is on a 'land of lost content',[17] infinitely perfect but also infinitely remote, the insistent repetition of 'loin' ('faraway') in four of the six stanzas establishing a clear counterpoint of non-recovery of the past to the pattern of recall promoted by the repetition of the first and last line of each stanza. A final variation, both of theme and form, is provided by 'Le Goût du néant'. Consisting of only fifteen lines, it avoids an explicit refrain, and as an alternative device, 'displays' the fifth line of each of the three groups, as a typographically free-standing line. Each of these lines summarises the mood of its respective stanza: apathetic exhaustion in line 5, 'Give up, my heart, and sleep your stolid sleep' ['Résigne-toi, mon cœur; dors ton sommeil de brute']; loss of youthful vitality in line 10, 'The Spring, once wonderful, has lost its scent!' ['Le Printemps adorable a perdu son odeur']; detached expectation of obliteration in line 15, 'Avalanche, sweep me off within your slide!' ['Avalanche, veux-tu m'emporter dans ta chute?' (OC 1 76)]. At the same time, the five-line rhyme-scheme is hyperbolically intensified by limitation to two rhymes throughout. Symmetrically arranged in the pattern *abba-a/baab-b/abba-a*, the obsessive return of the rhyme, rendered still more monotonous by the richness throughout of the *b* rhyme -*deur*, renders acoustically the effacement of individual difference in the undifferentiated expanse of Time:

> Et le Temps m'engloutit minute par minute
> Comme la neige immense un corps pris de roideur.

The linking of the *a* rhyme -*ute* to the repetition of *ch* in lines 14–15, the final lines of the poem:

> Et je n'y *ch*er*ch*e pas l'abri d'une cahute
> Avalan*ch*e, veux-tu emporter dans ta *ch*ute?

contributes a final phonetic support to the image of 'white-out', the rhyming of 'c(a)hute' with 'chute' contributing a final orthographical suggestion of obliteration.

The poems making up *Les Fleurs du Mal* were written at a time of radical changes in attitudes to versification. The Romantics had initiated the undermining of the rhythmic predictability of the alexandrine but their questioning of the banalities of classical rhyme had paradoxically led to an increased emphasis on the potential of rich rhyme as an alternative indicator of formal structure. The scene was thus set for the large-scale debate amongst French nineteenth-century poets as to the role of versification in the definition of poetry and poetic language. Baudelaire stands at the centre of this debate, shaped by the cadences of traditional versification but responsive less to 'rules' than to the fundamental principles they embody, including, crucially, the need for freedom and surprise. His work thus points forward to the metrical experimentation of Verlaine and the Symbolists, culminating in their development of 'liberated verse' and 'free verse', and also in the prose poem, a genre where Baudelaire himself played a major role (see chapter 5). It also prompted further experimentation with rhyme, not only its diffusion within patterns of generalised 'musical' suggestion as explored by Verlaine, but also, in its most hyperbolically 'regular' manifestations, as a key element in Mallarmé's intensive interrogation of the metaphysics of form. Contrary, then, to the perception of Rimbaud, on the one hand, and those of Gautier and Banville on the other, Baudelaire is interested neither in the mechanical observance nor the unconsidered flouting of 'rules'. Rather, he harnesses the fundamental energies of versification as the driving force in the portrayal of what we might now define as a Modernist or even post-modern crisis of identity. Baudelaire's great achievement is not only to have encapsulated the crucial dilemma of attempted self-construction and persistent self-loss on the level of his images and themes but to have made the challenges and vicissitudes of versification an integral and organic part of his reflection on the human condition.

NOTES

1. In a letter of 15 May 1871, commonly known as 'The Letter of the Visionary', in which Rimbaud sets out his radical ideas about poetry. Arthur Rimbaud, *Oeuvres complètes*, ed. Antoine Adam (Bibliothèque de la Pléiade) (Paris: Gallimard, 1972), p. 251.

2. Notably Wilhelm Ténint, *Prosodie de l'école moderne* (Paris: Didier, 1844) and Louis Quicherat, *Traité de versification française* (Paris: Hachette, 1850).

3. Gautier's negative reaction to the number of 'libertine sonnets, that is non-orthodox sonnets, deliberately breaching the rule of two rhymes only in the quatrains' ['sonnets *libertins*, c'est-à-dire non orthodoxes et s'affranchissant volontiers de la règle de la quadruple rime'], submitted to him by Baudelaire at their first meeting in the 1840s, is recounted by Baudelaire in his 1859 article, 'Théophile Gautier' (OC II, 107–9), and by Gautier in the preface to the 1868 (posthumous) edition of *Les Fleurs du Mal* (Théophile Gautier, *Portraits et souvenirs littéraires* (Paris: Charpentier, 1885), pp. 233–6). Banville's views, as laid down in his *Petit Traité de poésie française* (*Œuvres* IX (Paris: Lemerre, 1885), pp. 198–208) are even more rigorous, presenting the rhyme scheme *abba abba ccd ede* as the only permissible arrangement for the 'regular' sonnet.

4. Edgar Allan Poe's essay, *The Philosophy of Composition* (1846) was translated by Baudelaire as *Méthode de composition* and published by him along with a short introduction and *Le Corbeau*, his translation of *The Raven*, under the collective title *Genèse d'un Poème* in the *Revue française* of 20 April 1859.

5. See Baudelaire's comment on the carelessness of Auguste Barbier's poetry: It is a painful thing to see such a gifted poet suppressing articles and possessive adjectives, when these monosyllables or dissyllables do not fit the line, and using a word in an opposite sense to the one it normally has because that word has the number of syllables he needs.

   [C'est une chose douloureuse de voir un poète aussi bien doué supprimer les articles et les adjectifs possessifs, quand ces monosyllabes ou ces dissyllabes le gênent, et employer un mot dans un sens contraire à l'usage parce que ce mot a le nombre de syllabes qui lui convient. (OC II 144)]

Conversely, on 'art for art' writing, he remarks: 'Immoderate preoccupation with form leads to monstrous, unimaginable aberrations. Swallowed up by a ferocious passion for the beautiful, the odd, the pretty, the picturesque . . . notions of the just and the true disappear.

[Le goût immodéré de la forme pousse à des désordres monstrueux et inconnus. Absorbées par la passion féroce du beau, du drôle, du joli, du pittoresque . . . les notions du juste et du vrai disparaissent. (OC II 48)]

6. 'Auguste Barbier': 'Idea and form are two beings in one' ['L'idée et la forme sont deux êtres en un' (OC II 143)].

7. 'The beautiful is always bizarre' ['Le beau est toujours bizarre'] (OC II 578)]. The last line of 'Le Voyage' concludes *Les Fleurs du Mal* with confirmation of the continuing desire 'To fathom the Unknown, and find the *new*' ['Au fond de l'Inconnu pour trouver du *nouveau*' (OC I 134)].

8. Of the 127 poems of the 1861 edition, 89 are in alexandrines, 19 in eight-syllable lines, and 2 ('Un fantôme' and 'La Mort des amants') in lines of ten syllables.

9. Subsequently Paul Verlaine in his 1873 collection *Romances sans paroles* would consistently use lines with an uneven number of syllables in pursuit of a musically suggestive poetry.

10. Final 'e', followed by a consonant as the first letter of the next word, as here with 'sottise', continues to be sounded in French poetry and counts as a syllable, even though it has disappeared from everyday pronunciation. This so-called 'atonic e' or 'mute e' provides an important element of flexibility in a verse system based on syllabic count.

11. For a detailed and very clear discussion of Baudelaire's complex and varied use of sound patterns, see Graham Chesters, *Some Functions of Sound-repetition in 'Les Fleurs du Mal'*, Occasional Papers in Modern Languages, 11 (Hull: University of Hull Publications, 1975) and Graham Chesters, *Baudelaire and the Poetics of Craft* (Cambridge: Cambridge University Press, 1988).

12. The ten-syllable line, as a line of some length, is divided like the alexandrine by a pause, but, unlike the alexandrine, the position of the pause may vary. The most usual syllabic patterns involve even numbers of syllables, 4/6 and 6/4, as can be observed in 'Un fantôme'.

13. The division into three groups of four syllables immediately precludes the shifting syllabic subgroups of the standard alexandrine and is less flexible therefore than the traditional 6+6 pattern.

14. Only eighteen poems of the 1861 edition of *Les Fleurs du Mal* are in couplets. This contrasts sharply with the extensive use of couplets by Baudelaire's great Romantic predecessor, Victor Hugo, and reflects Baudelaire's dislike for uncontrolled prolixity. Significantly, when Baudelaire does use couplets, they are often syntactically linked in four-line groups.

15. Conventionally, poets were encouraged to avoid 'banal' rhymes, that is, those using the same parts of speech, words with the same root or words that regularly occur together ('flamme'/'âme', ['fire'/'desire']). At the opposite extreme, 'rare' rhyme, as its name indicates, involves words that only occasionally appear as rhymes. Often these are proper names, but they can also be words not normally associated with poetic register, for example 'cloison' ['partition'] in 'Le Balcon' or 'couvercle' ['lid'] in 'Spleen (IV)'.

16. 'Harmonie du soir' has been frequently described as a 'pantoum'. Hugo had included a translation of a Malay 'pantoum' in *Les Orientales* (1829).
17. A. E. Houseman's phrase from *A Shropshire Lad* is used by Rosemary Lloyd in the title of her book, *The Land of Lost Content. Children and Childhood in Nineteenth-Century French Literature* (Oxford: Clarendon Press, 1992).

5

SONYA STEPHENS

The prose poems

'Who among us has not, in moments of ambition, dreamt of the miracle of a form of poetic prose' (PP 30) ['Quel est celui de nous qui n'a pas, dans ses jours d'ambition, rêvé le miracle d'une prose poétique' (OC I 275)], asks Baudelaire in his letter to Arsène Houssaye, before going on to gloss – within his question – just what he means by poetic prose:

> musical but without rhythm or rhyme, both supple and staccato enough to adapt itself to the lyrical movements of our souls, the undulating movements of our reveries, and the convulsive movement of our consciences?   (PP 30)

> [musicale sans rythme et sans rime, assez souple et assez heurtée pour s'adapter aux mouvements lyriques de l'âme, aux ondulations de la rêverie, aux soubre-sauts de la conscience?   (OC I 275–6)]

This is the question with which Baudelaire inaugurates his prose poetry enterprise and, if Baudelaire's prose poetry has attracted increasing atten-tion over the last twenty years and come to rival, in terms of recent schol-arship at least, the verse poetry for which he is best known, then it is in no small part a result of the playful questions that this innovative work raises. Indeed, the questions are legion, not only in the critical studies of *Le Spleen de Paris*, but in the very fabric of the poetry itself. The questions the poems pose are often, like this one about prose poetry, rhetorical inasmuch as they expect no answer from the interlocutor. Real questions are socially man-dating (if we don't answer, we offend): they solicit a response. Rhetorical questions, on the other hand, are duplicitous. They pose as questions, while being declarative assertions, not so much requesting an answer as sponsoring one – and taking the reader's (imposed) silence as their own confirmation. Baudelaire's rhetorical questions take a functional incongruity – the mis-match of form (a question, or the interrogative) to substance (a statement, or the declarative) – to exemplify other sorts of incongruities. The asking of so many questions, and the interrogation of process, form and fact that such questioning implies, point, in other words, to Baudelaire's awareness of, and a deliberate engagement with, the art and devices of rhetoric. Through these he examines questions of poetic form, raises philosophical and social issues and engages the reader in very particular ways – ways, we shall see here, that are intimately connected with the kinds of encounter and exchange the prose poems play out.

The letter to Arsène Houssaye and the questionable status of the text

It is in the letter to Houssaye, a dedicatory letter that serves as a kind of preface, that this question about the nature of prose poetry is asked. The question, though clearly rhetorical, is intended as an open (or public) engagement with Houssaye, a powerful newspaper editor and literary figure of the day, whose own ambitions, Baudelaire notes in another question a few lines later, have led him to 'attempt' something similar:

> Isn't it true that you yourself, my dear friend, have attempted to translate in a *song* the strident cry of the *Glazier*, and to express in lyrical prose all the distressing suggestions that cry sends to the very attics, through the highest fogs of the street? (PP 30–1)

> [Vous-même, mon cher ami, n'avez-vous pas tenté de traduire en une *chanson* le cri strident du *Vitrier*, et d'exprimer dans une prose lyrique toutes les désolantes suggestions que ce cri envoie jusqu'aux mansardes, à travers les plus hautes brumes de la rue? (OC I 276)]

Both the question about the nature of prose poetry and this one about Houssaye's own efforts to respond to the challenge of the form are clearly assertions about the value of prose poetry, although expressed as they are, as questions, they appear more tentative.

The model or precursor Baudelaire invokes for both his own experiment and for Houssaye's – Aloysius Bertrand's *Gaspard de la Nuit* – receives similar treatment when, in a parenthesis, he asks: 'doesn't a book known by you, by me and by a few of our friends have every right to be called *famous*?' (PP 30) ['un livre connu de vous, de moi et de quelques-uns de nos amis, n'a-t-il pas tous les droits à être appelé *fameux*?' (OC I 275)]. The italics here, as in the use of the word *song* to describe Houssaye's own poem, signal another form of indirect communication through which the speaker relies on shared background knowledge, on convention and on our ability as readers to make inferences in order to distinguish within the utterance the literal level from another implied meaning. In other words, the letter to Houssaye relies on irony which, like the rhetorical questions which punctuate it, is a form of duplicity – a form that relies on the same kind of mismatch, too. But while rhetorical questions and irony may be seen to operate in tandem, what is significant is that the questions create, alongside other indicators of tentativeness – such as 'a little piece of work' ['un petit ouvrage'], 'attempting something similar' ['tenter quelque chose d'analogue'] – a sense of hesitancy, uncertainty or humility, while the irony contests that with its barely concealed superiority. The rhetorical question, which looks like a real question, rides with the irony, feigning humility but sponsoring its own view to much the same effect as the duplicitous ironic remark.

In the final paragraph of the letter the temperament behind these forms of duplicity, and a rationale for the discursive strategies, is made clearer:

> But, to tell the truth, I fear my jealousy has not brought me happiness. No sooner had I begun my work than I realized not only that I remained very far from my mysterious and brilliant model, but also that I was doing something (if it can be called something) which was curiously different, an accident in which anyone but I would doubtless take pride, but which can bring only profound humiliation to a mind which considers the poet's greatest honour to lie in accomplishing *exactly* what he planned to do. (PP 31)

> [Mais, pour dire le vrai, je crains que ma jalousie ne m'ait pas porté bonheur. Sitôt que j'eus commencé le travail, je m'aperçus que non seulement je restais bien loin de mon mystérieux et brillant modèle, mais encore que je faisais quelque chose (si cela peut s'appeler *quelque chose*) de singulièrement différent, accident dont tout autre que moi s'enorgueillirait sans doute, mais qui ne peut qu'humilier profondément un esprit qui regarde comme le plus grand honneur du poète d'accomplir *juste* ce qu'il a projeté de faire. (OC I 276)]

The poet's 'profound humiliation' is hyperbolically overturned by his assertion that something in which another might take pride can only be an embarrassment to a poet such as he, and appears especially so since the imitation of Bertrand is obviously a red herring. The 'mysterious and brilliant model' from which Baudelaire's prose poems are derived is not Bertrand's, or for that matter Houssaye's, but his own ('*my* mysterious and brilliant model'); and what is achieved, for all that it falls short of some perfectionist poetic ideal, is 'curiously different' ['singulièrement différent'], with the emphasis here on the work's uniqueness, or originality. It is the reader's concerns, as much as the concerns of the editor, that the poet addresses – and not only the reader's concerns, but also his/her expectations. To diminish the work with false humility is to reduce those expectations in advance – to appeal to the reader's indulgence – only to exceed them in the unfolding of the work itself.

The apparent ambivalence or perhaps, more correctly, the duality expressed through rhetorical questions and ironic discourse, including tendencies towards humility/superiority, is also played out in the title of the work. Like the letter which acts as a preface, the title determines the way the work is read. And this work has two titles. On the one hand, the title *Le Spleen de Paris* points to its content or themes; on the other, *Petits poèmes en prose* defines its form. The doubleness of the titling is a focus for the letter, which not only addresses the specifics of the form, but also the motivation of the city, since the ambition to write prose poetry is born of the city: 'The obsessive ideal springs above all from frequent contact with enormous cities, from the junction of their innumerable connections' (PP 30) ['C'est surtout de la fréquentation des villes énormes, c'est du croisement de leurs innombrables rapports que naît cet idéal obsédant' (OC 1 276)]. As many critics have pointed out, the genre itself, with an oxymoron for a name, speaks of duality; and, as Tzvetan Todorov asserts, these prose poems are 'texts which in their very conception are based on the meeting of opposites'.[1] There is further evidence of this in the titles of individual poems, with their contrasting juxtapositions (for example 'Le Fou et la Vénus', 'Le Chien et le flacon', 'La Femme sauvage et la petite maitresse', 'La Soupe et les nuages', 'Le Tir et le cimetière') or in those poems which present duality in its concrete embodiment (for example 'Le Crépuscule du soir', 'Le Port', 'Le Miroir', 'Laquelle est la vraie?' and 'La Chambre double'). It is not surprising then that a form born of fundamentally opposed discursive modes (poetry and prose) should question its own conjunctions and employ rhetorical strategies which enable the incongruities to subsist. If rhetorical questions, like the prose poem itself, are a kind of trope that propel form in one direction and substance in another, then perhaps we should not be surprised that they are used to such effect in *Le Spleen de Paris*; and perhaps we can look to them, as the titles and the letter to Houssaye lead us to do, as a way of interrogating the poetic processes of the text.

Questioning poetry

The sense of questioning poetry is, of course, twofold: the creation of a new genre clearly questions the limits or limitations of poetry; and these are poems that question, not only through their formal experimentation, but in a very real sense of being interrogative. Nowhere is this more in evidence than in 'L'Etranger', the first poem in the collection; a poem structured by questions which are not directly answered. Here we find evidence of the socially mandating question, for these are questions which expect answers, and which set out to situate socially and ideologically the 'stranger' of the poem. Six questions receive six answers which respond, especially in form (the response is modelled on the question), but without directly offering the interlocutor a satisfying answer. Through this poem, Baudelaire communicates the entrenched difference of the other or outsider (the 'étrange/étranger') and establishes the poet as that other, since his defining, last-word characteristic is his love of the marvellous clouds. The poet in 'La Soupe et les nuages', having been caught 'contemplating the moving architecture that God creates with mists, the marvellous constructions of the impalpable' ['contempl[ant] les mouvements architectures que Dieu fait avec les vapeurs, les merveilleuses constructions de l'impalpable'] is also aggressively referred to by his 'beautiful beloved' (PP 96) ['belle bien-aimée'] as a 'b . . . b . . . of a cloud merchant' (PP 97) ['s . . . b . . . . . de marchand de nuages'] (OC I 350). The exchange is dysfunctional because the speakers come from different places (ideologically); they do not share the same values. Although the questions of 'L'Etranger' are not strictly speaking rhetorical, they nevertheless sponsor an answer or an ideology by speaking of the things on which the bourgeois questioner places value (family, friends, country with implied patriotism, beauty and money) and, because of the refusal of the speaker to enter into the 'game' of question-and-answer here implied, the answers themselves imply further questions in what might be said to be a rhetorical way. It has been argued that this poem extends the kind of dialogue of the letter to Houssaye (with Houssaye cast as the bourgeois questioner and Baudelaire as the intellectually superior outsider). While this might be stretching a point, what is almost certainly the case is that this poem participates in the same sort of rhetoric and through its questions seeks to define the position of the text, both within the new genre of prose poetry and ideologically. What has been called a defining *indefinition* is, then, a result of the rhetorical strategies and the text's divalence. The conflict is, first, semantic.

'La Soupe et les nuages', as we saw above, puts this conflict more directly, situating it within the domestic context and, though the final rhetorical question of the poem – 'Are you going to hurry up and eat your soup, or aren't you, you b . . . b . . . of a cloud merchant?' ['Allez-vous bientôt manger votre soupe, s . . . b . . . . . de marchand de nuages?'] – is clearly intended as an insulting imperative, an exhortation to stop dreaming and eat up, it breaks through the boundary between the two speakers by adopting the private thought of the poet (expressed poetically with the inhabitual anteposition of the adjective) to transform it with a 'husky voice' ['une voix rauque'], 'a hysterical voice, a voice made hoarse with brandy' ['une voix hystérique et comme enrouée par l'eau de vie'] into a chiding aggressive question. The same conflict is played out in 'Le Chien et le flacon', although here there are no questions asked. The principle is the same, though, except that here the poet's worst fears are confirmed. The poet offers something seeking approval; the offer is welcomed, then assessed and found wanting. And, though there may be no questions, the format of the poem is not dissimilar to 'L'Etranger', with its long dashes indicating speech acts, separated only by the canine equivalent of a response: tail wagging ('the sign that, in these poor creatures, represents laughter and smiles' (PP 38) ['le signe correspondant du rire et du sourire'(OC 1 284)]) and reproachful barking. What seems to be lacking in this poem is the duality we have seen operating so far; and it is precisely the apparent exegetical obviousness of this poem and others like it that has led to critics finding poems such as this one (often termed 'poèmes-boutades') wanting. This is, though, to gloss over the subtleties of this text which, while quite different in tone and strategy, nevertheless engages in complex associative symbolism in order to show how problematic direct communication can be. What 'Le Chien et le flacon' does is to emphasise its own nature as prose in an apparent refusal of poetic composition, while all the time relying on the kinds of doubling we have seen elsewhere: poet-narrator/reader, speaker/ interlocutor, perfume/excrement, pleasure/displeasure and indeed prose/ poetry.

This doubling is explored as a polarity in 'La Chambre double', where the spiritual reverie of the dream-space reaches its apotheosis with the asking of multiple questions, counterbalanced, or perhaps counterpointed, with exclamations. The doubleness of the room, announced in the title of the poem, is described and elaborated in its structural dualities. 'La Chambre double' persistently iterates binary opposites, alternations and pairs: the room is 'pink and blue' (PP 34) ['bleuâtre et rosâtre' (OC 1 280)] where the phonetic repetition of '-âtre', meaning '–ish', pairs difference. It is 'pure dream' ['rêve pur'] rather than 'definite art' or 'positive art' ['art défini', 'art positif']. It is 'regret and desire' ['le regret et le désir'] (both past and future). It is 'vegetable and mineral' ['le végétal et le minéral']. It is 'necessary clarity and delicious obscurity' ['suffisante clarté'/'délicieuse obscurité']. It is redolent of 'the most exquisitely chosen perfume combined with a very light humidity' ['Une senteur infinitésimale de choix le plus exquis, à laquelle se mêle une tres légère humidité'] and then of 'a fetid odour of tobacco mingled with an unidentifiable and nauseating mouldiness', 'the stale air of desolation' ['une fétide odeur de tabac mêlée à je ne sais quelle nauséabonde moisissure', 'le ranci de la désolation']. It is 'prodigal in caresses and treachery' (PP 34–5) ['féconde en caresses et en traîtrises' (OC 1 280–1)]. And most significantly, as the two distinct halves of the poem show,[2] it is the experience of timeless spirituality – or what Baudelaire elsewhere describes as the 'surnaturel'[3] – and measured, pressured reality. This spiritual dream-state is contrasted with Time's 'demoniacal train of Memories, Regrets, Spasms, Fear, Anguish,

Nightmares, Rages and Neuroses' (PP 36) ['démoniaque cortège de Souvenirs, de Regrets, de Spasmes, de Peurs, d'Angoisses, de Cauchemars, de Colères et de Névroses' (OC I 281)].

'La Chambre double', as a text, is hinged by a glance which presages the intrusive knock at the door. That glance is issued by the Idol, whose 'subtle and terrible *peepers*' ['subtiles et terribles *mirettes*'] visit fear (of malice) upon the poet-narrator and invite analysis ('I have often studied them' ['Je les ai souvent étudiées']). This mind-altering intervention occurs immediately after a barrage of questions: 'But how does she come to be here? Who brought her? What magic power has installed her on this throne of reverie and pleasure? What does it matter?' (PP 34) ['Mais comment est-elle ici? Qui l'a amenée? Quel pouvoir magique l'a installée sur ce trône de rêverie et de volupté? Qu'importe?' (OC I 280)]. This accumulation of rhetorical questions is dismissed, first, by the last in the series, which echoes the same questions asked more specifically in 'Les Fenêtres': 'What does external reality matter, if it has helped me to live, to feel that I am and what I am?' (PP 87) ['Qu'importe ce que peut être la réalité placée hors de moi, si elle m'a aidé à vivre, à sentir que je suis et ce que je suis?' (OC I 339)]. Then these give way to a final question, in which the poet-narrator is merely expressing (in an exclamatory form immediately mirrored in 'O Bliss!' ['O Béatitude!']) his incredulity at his own good fortune: 'To what benevolent demon am I indebted for being thus wrapped in mystery, silence, peace and perfumes?' (PP 35) ['A quel démon bienveillant dois-je d'être ainsi entouré de mystère, de silence, de paix et de parfums?' (OC I 281)]. The role of these questions is to highlight the sense of excitement generated by the experience; to use rhetorical questions to stir others by the poet's own vehement feeling; an effect that is doubled (as is everything in this 'Chambre double') by the exclamatory negations which follow.

'La Chambre double' explores duality in a number of quite complex ways, underscoring in its semantic and textual couplings and contrasts, rhetorical strategies we have seen to be operating elsewhere. In its opposition of the dream-like experience to the reality of poetic composition – the failure of which is symbolised by 'a newspaper-editor's errand boy come to demand the next instalment of a manuscript', 'manuscripts crossed-out or incomplete; the calendar on which my pencil has marked the ill-starred days' (PP 35) ['le saute-ruisseau d'un directeur de journal qui réclame la suite du manuscrit', 'les manuscrits raturés ou incomplets; l'almanach où le crayon a marqué les dates sinistres!' (OC I 281)][4] – 'La Chambre double' finds an echo in 'Le *Confiteor* de l'artiste', which is also structured as the failure to maintain the expansive lyrical state in a reversal of emotion and sensations resulting in defeat.

And now the depth of the sky fills me with consternation; its clarity exasperates me. The insensitivity of the sea, the immutability of the spectacle revolt me . . . Oh! must one endlessly suffer to be free from beauty? Nature, merciless enchantress, ever-victorious rival, let me be! Tempt no more my desires and my pride! The study of beauty is a duel in which the artist screams with fear before being defeated. (PP 33)

[Et maintenant la profondeur du ciel me consterne; sa limpidité m'exaspère. L'insensibilité de la mer, l'immuabilité du spectacle, me révoltent . . . Ah! faut-il éternellement souffrir, ou fuir éternellement le beau? Nature, enchanteresse sans pitié, rivale toujours victorieuse, laisse-moi! Cesse de tenter mes désirs et mon orgueil! L'étude du beau est un duel où l'artiste crie de frayeur avant d'être vaincu. (OC I 278–9)]

The duel is a significant figure here, for it emphasises opposition, the one-on-one of the duel's combat being suggestive of (and loosely connected to) dual: the contrasting and the contradiction being also combination. In a duel, however, the binary choreography of the conflict finishes with a winner, a prevailing singularity or superiority.

Finally, 'La Chambre double' helps us to grasp other, similarly conceived, textual strategies that question poetry. Like 'Le *Confiteor*', it offers poetic experience mirrored by its real double, here, too, in the form of a dialogue. Comparing the final stanzas/paragraphs of each poem, this becomes clear:

Blue head of hair, tent of spread shadows, you
Give me the azure of the open sky;
In downy wisps along your twisted locks
I'll gladly drug myself on mingled scents,
Essence of cocoa-oil, pitch and musk.

For ages! always! in your heavy mane
My hand will scatter ruby, sapphire, pearl
So you will never chill to my desire!
Are you not the oasis where I dream,
My drinking-gourd for memory's fine wine?
(FM 51–3)

[Cheveux bleus, pavillon de ténèbres tendues,
Vous me rendez l'azur du ciel immense et rond;
Sur les bords duvetés de vos mèches tordues
Je m'enivre ardemment des senteurs confondues
De l'huile de coco, du musc et du goudron.

Longtemps! Toujours! Ma main dans ta crinière lourde
Sèmera le rubis, la perle et le saphir,

Afin qu'à mon désir tu ne sois jamais sourde!
N'est-tu pas l'oasis où je rêve, et la gourde
Où je hume à longs traits le vin du souvenir?
(OC I 27)]

In the blazing hearth of your hair I breathe the scent of tobacco mingled with opium and sugar; in the night of your hair, I see the infinite expanses of tropical skies glittering blue; on the downy banks of your hair how intoxicating are the combined odours of tar and musk and coconut oil.

Let me long bite your heavy black tresses. When I chew your elastic hair, your rebellious hair, I feel as if I am eating memories. (PP 53)

[Dans l'ardent foyer de ta chevelure, je respire l'odeur du tabac mêlé à l'opium et au sucre; dans la nuit de ta chevelure, je vois resplendir l'infini de l'azur tropical; sur les rivages duvetés de ta chevelure je m'enivre des odeurs combinées du goudron, du musc et de l'huile de coco.

Laisse-moi mordre longtemps tes tresses lourdes et noires. Quand je mordille tes cheveux élastiques et rebelles, il me semble que je mange des souvenirs.
(OC I 301)]

Here, then, the 'hemi-' of 'Un hémisphère dans une chevelure' exposes that half of the sphere that is not sublimated by the poetic version, 'La Chevelure', in *Les Fleurs du Mal*. In prosaic form, Baudelaire reworks a lyrical experience, not so much to expose the dream world that is the head of hair as a delusion or hallucination (brought on here by opium and in 'La Chambre double' by the liquefied version, laudanum), but rather to explore the poetry of the banal in an earthy tell-it-as-it-is realism. The kind of doubleness we have seen within poems and in rhetorical strategies is here played out across Baudelaire's poetic texts. The poet maintained that the prose poems should be seen as a counterpart ['pendant'] of *Les Fleurs du Mal*, as 'reciprocal' ['réciproque'] the matching other of a pair. Baudelaire's prose doublets (poems which are prosaic counterparts to verse poems)[5] invite direct comparison in ways which expose the prose–poetry dialogue, its dialectic. In the hair poems, the rhetorical question at the *end* of the verse version, *opens* a dialogue – in a way not dissimilar to Shakespeare's eighteenth sonnet: 'Shall I compare thee to a summer's day?' – that is continued by the prose poem which constitutes a prosaic answer (no questions asked here), and one that seems, like other answers we have examined, to be logically related, or entwined, but somehow distinct and separate.

In an echo of that binary choreography of the duel in 'Le *Confiteor*', the symbol in the title of 'Le Thyrse' brings us to a closer understanding of these issues. Like the letter to Houssaye, it is a dedicated text (to Franz Liszt), and one which asks a question in order to define the object it describes: 'What is a thyrsus?' ['Qu'est-ce qu'un thyrse?']. Like the prose poem, it is double, composed of competing yet complementary forms:

> Straight line and arabesque, intention and expression, firmness of the will, sinuosity of the work, unity of the aim, variety in the means, an all-powerful and indivisible amalgam of genius, what analyst would have the odious courage to divide and separate you? (PP 84–5)

> [Ligne droite et ligne arabesque, intention et expression, roideur de la volonté, sinuosité du verbe, unité du but, variété des moyens, amalgame tout-puissant et indivisible du génie, quel analyste aura le détestable courage de vous diviser et de vous séparer? (OC I 336)]

Here again, the final question (who?) – which follows the sponsored answer to the opening question (what?) – plays a role in modulating the assertion, making it seem more questioning than it is and, therefore, offering a rhetorical pairing (question/answer) to underpin the other dualities of the text itself. Similarly, some bold assertions of the text are punctuated by multiple question-asking. And the questions asked are immediately answered, not merely as a way of reasoning, but as a way of elaborating the difference through binary discursive strategies. In other words, if the thyrsus is composed of both a stick, the straight-line of reasoning (or assertion), and twisting, curvaceous forms, then the arabesques that twist around assertions are the rhetorical questions, 'capricious meanders'(PP 84) ['méandres capricieux' (OC I 335)] that 'pay court to the straight line and dance around it in silent adoration' (PP 84) ['font leur cour à la ligne droite et dansent autour dans une muette adoration' (OC I 336)]. This question–answer strategy, coupled with the dialogue form of the poem, also offers an answer to the question of what constitutes prose poetry, since here there is spirituality (more associated with poetry) and analysis (associated with prose) in 'astonishing duality' ['étonnante dualité'] and 'the all-powerful and indivisible amalgam of genius' (PP 84) ['amalgame tout-puissant et indivisible du génie' (OC I 336)]. Baudelaire uses these terms to describe the dedicatee of the poem, Liszt, but there can be no doubt that he is here talking of his own achievement, for here the humility (if humility there is in Baudelaire's transparently feigned self-deprecation) of the letter to Houssaye is transposed into praise for another's achievement in a similar bivalent enterprise – and, by extension, a confident assertion of the doubleness of this new genre.

Asking the crowd: the possibilities of *flânerie*

At the end of 'Les Fenêtres', the poet-narrator asks 'What does external reality matter, if it has helped me to live, to feel that I am and what I am?'

['Qu'importe ce que peut être la réalité placée hors de moi, si elle m'a aidé à vivre, à sentir que je suis et ce que je suis?'] The question is asked in response to a question the poet imagines the reader might raise about his speculative practice – 'Perhaps you will say to me: Are you sure that that legend is the right one?' (PP 87) ['Peut-être me direz-vous: «Es-tu sûr que cette légende soit la vraie?»' (OC I 339)] – but can be read as a philosophically determined approach to the kinds of duality the prose poems of the previous section explore, especially 'La Chambre double' and 'Le *Confiteor*' (but also, for example, 'Laquelle est la vraie?'). 'Les Fenêtres', like the others we will examine in the remainder of this chapter, explores Paris from the perspective of the 'flâneur', a strolling subject, associated with nineteenth-century Paris, who engages in observation with a representational gaze,[6] so that the city becomes a spectacle, an adventure and a rich source of narrative speculation and poetic inspiration.

Alongside the dialogue with Houssaye about the nature of prose poetry, we saw above that the dedicatory letter asserts (in a way which echoes the divalent title of the work) that their shared poetic ambition is born of a shared experience of the city, and it is to the poems that engage with a particularly Parisian poetics that we should turn next. 'Les Fenêtres' is a particularly significant poem, for as one critic has argued 'the act of looking through a candle-lit window from the street generates a veritable proliferation of some of the major terms of Baudelaire's poetic lexicon . . . in that it opens a space for the productivity of the imagination, supplies a passage from vision into reverie and a release from self into otherness'.[7]

The dynamic of *flânerie* is explored most fully in 'Les Foules', and in a passage from *The Painter of Modern Life* [*Le Peintre de la vie moderne*] (in relation to which it acts as a sort of doublet). In this poem, as in 'Les Fenêtres', Baudelaire explores the experience of having 'lived and suffered in characters other than [his] own' (PP 87) ['avoir vécu et souffert dans d'autres que [s]oi-même' (OC I 339)], of taking 'a plunge into the multitude' (PP 44) ['un bain de multitude' (OC I 291)]. As he describes it in 'Les Foules':

Like those wandering souls in search of a body, he enters, when he so desires, into the character of each individual. For him alone, everything is vacant; and if certain places appear to be closed to him, that is because in his own eyes they are not worth the bother of visiting.   (PP 44)

[Comme ces âmes errantes qui cherchent un corps, il entre, quand il veut, dans le personnage de chacun. Pour lui seul, tout est vacant; et si de certaines places paraissent lui être fermées, c'est qu'à ses yeux elles ne valent pas la peine d'être visitées.   (OC I 291)]

The crowd is energising, kaleidoscopic because of the multiple imaginative configurations it offers; it is 'intoxicating', offering an alternative to the opium-induced dream-states. It is liberating, too, sublimating sexual desires in 'an ineffable orgy' ['ineffable orgie'] 'a holy prostitution of the soul which gives itself entirely, poetry and charity, to the unforeseen which reveals itself, to the unknown which happens along' (PP 44) ['cette sainte prostitution de l'âme qui se donne tout entière, poésie et charité, à l'imprévu qui se montre, à l'inconnu qui passe' (OC 1 291)]. *Flânerie*, then, or this sort of engagement with the other, offers in the prose poems a vehicle for encounter with a range of characters, and an opportunity to engage in an interrogation of those characters, whether through direct questions or not.

In 'Les Projets', for instance, the protagonist catches a glimpse of a woman whom he imagines clothed in finery of his choice and then places himself with her in a palace. Then, prompted by a print in a shop window, he transports himself with her to a suddenly preferred tropical paradise. As he passes an appealing inn, he imagines himself with her, closer to home. In visiting upon the chance (visual) encounter with a woman successive imagined scenarios (each one generated by a new visual encounter with an object), the figure of the poem comes to examine the experience in an echo of the rhetorical question in 'Les Fenêtres':

> And as he went home alone . . . he said to himself: 'Today I have had, in imagination, three homes, each of which has given me equal pleasure. Why force my body to move from place to place, since my soul can travel so nimbly? And why turn plan into reality, when the plan is in itself such sufficient pleasure?'
>
> (PP 65–6)

> [Et en rentrant seul chez lui . . . il se dit: «J'ai eu aujourd'hui, en rêve, trois domiciles où j'ai trouvé un égal plaisir. Pourquoi contraindre mon corps à changer de place, puisque mon âme voyage si lestement? Et à quoi bon exécuter des projets, puisque le projet est en lui-même une jouissance suffisante?»
>
> (OC 1 315)]

Like 'Les Foules' and 'Les Fenêtres', 'Les Projets' engages directly with the question of *flânerie*, poetic inspiration and creation. The rhetorical questions of the latter two poems serve not only to elevate the experience and render it philosophical; they offer a model of the way in which chance encounters of all kinds raise questions and issues in the observer's mind, so that Paris becomes the 'inn of chance encounters' ['l'auberge du hasard'] and the text becomes the space in which these encounters are processed through questioning them.

So it is then, too, that the poet-narrator questions combinations of solitariness, poverty, political principle and the nature of children in 'Les Veuves', 'Le Gâteau', 'Le Joujou du pauvre', 'Les Yeux des pauvres' and 'Assommons les pauvres'; buffoonery and bourgeois wrong-headedness in 'Un Plaisant', 'Les Dons des fées', 'Le Miroir' and 'La Fausse Monnaie'; marital customs and extra-marital relationships in 'La Femme sauvage et la petite maîtresse' and 'Portraits de maîtresses'; the situation of the performer/artist in 'Le Vieux Saltimbanque'; and the obsessive and the monstrous in 'Mademoiselle Bistouri'. This list, although a little reductive, enables us to see the way in which encounters lead to an interrogation of their hypothetical possibilities or intrinsic interest (or, one might say, the way in which situations and issues explored in poems imply encounters).

Like 'La Chambre double', however, what is stimulating can become oppressive, requiring a 'double turn of the key' to lock out its socially demanding perniciousness. Private and public spheres are then seen not to be opposed, but rather each present in the other. 'A une heure du matin' explores such a need to escape the crowd, 'the horrible life and horrible city' (PP 41) ['Horrible vie! Horrible ville!' (OC I 287)] of encounters that the poet-narrator does not want, and that are provided as a cumulatively stupefying list, resulting in the question: 'oof! is that the lot?' (PP 41) ['ouf! est-ce bien fini?' (OC I 288)]. The question is not simply a banal exclamation that brings the list of time-wasting conversations, requests and demands to a close. Rather, in a careful switch-over, the utterly prosaic line ushers in the poetic petitionary prayer in which the poet asks for 'the grace to produce a few lines' (PP 48) ['la grâce de produire quelques beaux vers' (OC I 288)] – and in complex double meaning hinging on 'bien fini', produces those polished lines of verse *in the end*.

In this double-entendre question of 'A une heure du matin', there is, in effect, an answer to the question of 'Les Fenêtres' (what does it matter?) and to those of 'Les Projets' (why? and what's the point?). For, while Baudelaire seems to imply that the collapsing of the distinction between self and other, dream and reality, does not really matter, the writing of poetry (the end result) does, and the questions might be seen to be posturing rhetorical bravado to which the final text gives the lie.

Questioning experience and questionable experiments

If encounters with the other are a way not only of seeking inspiration and expression, then the issues raised by those encounters are, as we have seen, a way of questioning existence, experience and the binary pleasures and trials of dream and reality. They are also, of course, a way of questioning poetic form, appropriate modes and models of self-expression and the reader's expectations. And, therefore, they are a way, too, of raising ethical issues. In 'Les Fenêtres' and 'Les Projets' we saw the way in which the speculative possibilities were derived from (and removed from) the encounters of the *flâneur*. In both cases, windows enabled a fertile imaginative transaction while opening up a gap between the subject and the object, between the observer and what he observes. In other words, like questions, windows 'bring about cleavage rather than communication'.[8]

'Les Yeux des pauvres' opens on a (failed) promise between the narrator and his loved one of shared thoughts and a common soul ('a dream which has nothing original in it, after all, save that, although all men have dreamt it, none has realized it' (PP 67–8) ['un rêve qui n'a rien d'original, après tout, si ce n'est que, rêvé par tous les hommes, il n'a été réalisé par aucun' (OC I 318)]). The failure of the ideal is mediated by gazes: gazes between the couple and through the window of a café; gazes of an impoverished family who look upon the opulence of the newly constructed building and its fortunate clientele. Like the windows of the prose poems, the eyes – often related figures – are the mediators of that 'cleavage'. The window is both an opportunity for looking (as in *flânerie*) and the frame for something the lovers would rather not see. It is a barrier for the poor (who may not enter) and a symbol of the barrier between the lovers, for the woman refuses the narrator's desire for reciprocity: she will not reflect his gaze, his guilt or his self-image. The woman asks for the narrator to have the poor family removed. Her question is reported in direct speech: '"I can't bear those people with their eyes as wide open as coal bunkers! Couldn't you ask the head-waiter to send them on their way?"' (PP 69) ['«Ces gens-là me sont insupportables avec leurs yeux ouverts comme des portes cochères! Ne pourriez-vous pas prier le maître du café de les éloigner d'ici?»' (OC I 319)]. The response that this prompts is presented as a commonplace, a universal truth that widens the gaps by depersonalising the narrator's engagement with the question, while at the same time holding in tension his understanding of the relationship between the personal rift and broader social divisions: 'So difficult is it to understand one another, my dear angel, and so hard it is for thoughts to be communicated, even between people who love each other!' (PP 69) ['Tant il est difficile de s'entendre, mon cher ange, et tant la pensée est incommunicable, même entre gens qui s'aiment!' (OC I 319)].

There is a similar failure of the reflected image in 'Le Miroir'. The narrator witnesses a scene ('A horribly ugly man comes in and looks at himself in the glass' ['Un homme épouvantable entre et se regarde dans la glace']) and raises a question: 'Why do you look at yourself in the mirror, since you can't see your reflection with anything but displeasure? ['Pourquoi vous regardez-vous au miroir, puisque vous ne pouvez vous y voir qu'avec déplaisir?'] The question (which is fundamentally rhetorical and a straightforward insult, expressing incredulity at both the man's ugliness and his desire to contemplate that fact) leads to a pompous answer invoking the 'immortal principles of '89' (in other words, 'it's a free country'). The answer is then measured in an interpretation of weighing-scale equivalence: 'From the point of view of good sense, I was undoubtedly in the right; but from the point of view of the law, he was not in the wrong' (PP 91) ['Au nom du bon sens, j'avais sans doute raison; mais, au point de vue de la loi, il n'avait pas tort'] (OC 1 344). The communication is a failure, as one might suspect it would be, and what emerges from the encounter and the equivalence of response is a truly rhetorical question that leaves a cleavage between the law and common sense.

Taking the rhetorical question seriously leads, too, then, to a caricatural literalism. If the maxim that ends 'Les Yeux des pauvres' is considered alongside the rhetorical mechanics of 'Le Miroir', we can see how the absurdly literal word-playing farce of 'Le Mauvais Vitrier' comes about from the commonplace 'la vie en rose', rose-tinted glass here offering the kind of desired refraction that might have prevented the cleavages brought about by the frames of 'Les Yeux des pauvres' or 'Le Miroir'. The narrator prepares us for the action by building a list of gratuitous acts accomplished by the sort of people that are presented as incomprehensible to the reader, since the poem pivots on the assumed response of the latter (Why?) only to dismiss the question with a frustrated 'Because . . .' and a further narratorial question leading to an inconclusive reason. The narrator calls a glazier up the narrow stairs, asks him for 'coloured panes, 'magic panes', 'panes of paradise' ['des verres de couleur', 'des vitres magiques', 'des vitres de paradis'] (in a rhetorical negative disclosing his anticipation of availability) and then sends him down again, seconds later, to destroy his wares by dropping a flower pot from the balcony in retaliation against the glazier's inability to comply with his request for 'life through rose-coloured glasses' (PP 41) ['la vie en beau' (OC 1 287)]. The request is one that seeks to make the window a fusion of imagination and reality, to artificially combine different possibilities.

The spontaneous experiment inflicted on the glazier, like the others the poem elaborates, might have serious consequences, but the rhetorical question that concludes the poem dismisses these in a way not dissimilar to the questions that close 'Les Fenêtres' and 'Les Projets'. The narrator says:

These nervy pranks are not without peril, and one can often pay dearly for them. But what does eternal damnation matter to one who has found in a second an infinity of pleasure? (PP 41)

[Ces plaisanteries nerveuses ne sont pas sans péril, et on peut souvent les payer cher. Mais qu'importe l'éternité de la damnation à qui a trouvé dans une seconde l'infini de la jouissance? (OC 1 287)]

This is not the only occasion on which a narrator in the prose poems finds himself engaged or implicated in experiments or observation of questionable ethical status. His role in 'Le Gâteau', for example, is far from innocent; and equally his motives in 'Le Joujou du pauvre' are highly questionable. The beating inflicted upon the beggar in 'Assommons les pauvres!', though more deliberate, is careful to measure theory against practice and blow for blow, ensuring that the questionable experiment is resolved by an unquestionable outcome – the beggar wins easily.

To return to the question that concludes 'Le Mauvais Vitrier', it could be said that this is another example of posturing rhetorical bravado. This would be consistent with the characterisation of those who engage in such behaviour, based on the examples given. There is a sense, though, that the orchestrated farce and the question refer us to something other than the conflict played out over some panes and a balcony. The encounter with the glazier is, to be sure, a way of exploring prevalent literary ideas about the world and its reflection/refraction, and associated ideological questions, but it is also an interrogation of very specific poetic form: Houssaye's own glazier, the glazier of the '*Song*' ironically invoked in the dedicatory letter. In the final question, then, what is at stake is as much potential editorial prosecution as criminal; a question of a place in literary posterity rather than eternal moral condemnation; and the 'infinity of pleasure' that is art – not to mention the satisfaction of putting the powerful Houssaye in his place by a destructive and covert literary attack.

A question of motive?

In 'A une heure du matin', the poet-narrator lists his day's activities and at one point questions his own motives: 'boasted (why?) about several scurrilous acts I've never committed and pusillanimously denied several other misdeeds I performed with joy' (PP 41) ['m'être vanté (pourquoi?) de plusieurs vilaines actions que je n'ai jamais commises, et avoir lâchement nié quelques autres méfaits que j'ai accomplis avec joie' (OC 1 288)]. Although the question of motive is raised only once, the entire list is effectively subjected to the same *post hoc* scrutiny. 'Le Mauvais Vitrier' too, as we have seen, brings to the fore questions of motive. At one level the poem explores why certain individuals are motivated to accomplish certain acts; on another, it takes up the cause of the ironically motivated letter of dedication. Indeed, questions of motive are legion. Why does the majestic widow of 'Les Veuves' 'remain, of her own free will, in surroundings where she is obviously out of place?' (PP 47) ['Pourquoi donc reste-t-elle volontairement dans un milieu où elle fait une tache si éclatante?' (OC 1 294)]. Why does the narrator of 'Le Vieux

Saltimbanque' resist the act of human charity he claims moved to perform? Why, in 'Le Gâteau', describe 'a hideous struggle which in truth lasted longer than their childish strength seemed to promise?' (PP 51) ['une lutte hideuse qui dura en vérité plus longtemps que leurs forces enfantines ne semblaient le promettre?'(OC I 298)]. Why pass on a counterfeit coin to a beggar? Perhaps, as the narrator in 'Le Mauvais Vitrier' speculates: 'to see, to know, to tempt fate . . .' (PP 39)['pour voir, pour savoir, pour tenter la destinée . . .' (OC I 285)].

Nowhere is there more questioning of motives than in 'Une mort héroïque'. Why did Fancioulle become involved in the political conspiracy? To what end was the Prince allowing him to perform one last time, watched by the condemned noblemen? '[Was] there in his soul a more or less clearly defined intention to be merciful?' (PP 70) ['existait-il dans son âme une intention plus ou moins arrêtée de clémence?'(OC I 320)]. As Fancioulle acted out his role so perfectly, did the Prince 'feel defeated in his power as despot?' ['se sentait-il vaincu dans son pouvoir de despote?' (OC I 322)]. Did he feel humiliated or frustrated? Did the whistle kill Fancioulle? And did the Prince command it in the knowledge that it would? Did he subsequently regret the loss of his favoured actor? The narrator raises all these questions, but answers, with conjecture, only some of them, leaving the reader to continue the speculation. 'Une mort héroïque' questions the tendency to see the world in terms of contrasts (political power versus the power of art) through a range of rhetorical questioning devices we have seen in operation elsewhere. It asks questions to affirm, to reason, to express grief; it multiplies questions; it raises questions to stir the reader as Fancioulle stirs his audience. But what the accumulation of questions also discloses is the poem's narrative framework (the act of *writing* the performance), and the somewhat questionable perception of the narrator-spectator. In other words, what the rhetorical questions again serve to do is to underscore the duality of the text, to highlight potentially meaningful formal differences, to combine speculation with analysis, and to hold in tension the world of political (despotic) reality and creative genius or artistry.

Finally, the question of motive brings us back to the question of Baudelaire's own art, the art of the prose poem, to his motivated act of dedication (a political move) and to the rhetorical strategies we have seen to be operating in both. The showing and telling of 'Une mort héroïque' – the performance itself doubled by the performance of writing – discloses and underscores the dualities that the text plays out through rhetorical questions of motive. Similarly, in the letter to Houssaye, Baudelaire out-performs the uncertainties and humilities he explores there, and further elaborates that performance, as we have seen, in the divalent play of the prose poems themselves, and especially in that of 'Le Mauvais Vitrier'. Rhetorical questions in the prose poems, like the irony they accompany and sponsor, turn or transfer meaning in a consistent interrogation of the relationship of language to a reality, of poetry to prose. They unfix the stable realities even of grammar and show language, like the windows of (and indeed that are) the prose poems, to be a far from transparent medium.

NOTES

I take this opportunity to acknowledge the support of the University of Connecticut. It was during the tenure of a fellowship at the Humanities Institute there that the research and writing of this chapter were undertaken.

1. Tzvetan Todorov, 'Poetry Without Verse', in *The Prose Poem in France. Theory and Practice*, eds. Mary Ann Caws and Hermine Riffaterre (New York: Columbia University Press, 1983), p. 64.
2. There are nine paragraphs of dream, nine of reality, separated by the paragraph containing the intrusive knock.
3. The 'surnaturel' is defined, in *Fusées*, as

   comprising both the general colour and tone, that is to say intensity, sonority, clarity, vibrativity, depth and repercussion in both space and time. There are moments of existence when time and expanse are deeper and the sense of existence immensely heightened.

   [Le surnaturel comprend la couleur générale et l'accent, c'est-à-dire, intensité, sonorité, limpidité, vibrativité, profondeur et retentissement dans l'espace et dans le temps. Il y a des moments de l'existence où le temps et l'étendue sont plus profonds, et le sentiment de l'existence immensément augmenté.

   (OC I 658, my translation)]

4. These references to the failure of composition also recall the anxieties of 'Le Chien et le flacon', and the letter to Houssaye, with its apparently pragmatic publication concerns, and the spectre of literary power and authority.
5. Poems in this category include the poems entitled 'Le Crépuscule du soir', 'L'Invitation au voyage' 'La Chevelure' and 'Un hémisphère dans une chevelure'; and 'L'Examen de minuit', 'La Fin de la journée' and 'A une heure du matin'. A general discussion of the doublets can be found in J. A. Hiddleston, *Baudelaire and 'Le Spleen de Paris'* (Oxford: Clarendon Press, 1987), pp. 66–75 and in Barbara Wright and David Scott, *'La Fanfarlo' and 'Le Spleen de Paris'* (London: Grant and Cutler, 1984), pp. 52–8, and detailed comparisons (in French) in Barbara Johnson, *Défigurations du langage poétique: la seconde révolution baudelairienne* (Paris: Flammarion, 1979), pp. 31–55 and 103–60.
6. *Flânerie* is a complex phenomenon, explored in detail in Keith Tester, ed., *The Flâneur* (London: Routledge, 1994). A significant aspect of the phenomenon is the way it emphasises the individual within the crowd, elevating his/her idiosyncrasies, and privileging his/her perspective or point of view.
7. Christopher Prendergast, *Paris and the Nineteenth Century* (Oxford: Blackwell, 1992), p. 36.
8. *Ibid.*, p. 37.

6

EDWARD K. KAPLAN

Baudelairean ethics

For it is truly, Lord, best witness in the world
That we might give to you of human dignity,
This ardent sob that rolls onward from age to age
And comes to die at the brink of your eternity!
'Beacons' (FM 25)[1]

[Car c'est vraiment Seigneur! le meilleur témoignage
Que nous puissions donner de notre dignité
Que cet ardent sanglot qui roule d'âge en âge
Et vient mourir aux bords de votre éternité!
'Les Phares' (OC I 14)]

It might surprise readers who know only Baudelaire's dubious reputation as a sadist, a blasphemer, an addict or a poet of depravity that his literary and critical works are motivated in large part by a passionate ethical commitment. While his masterpiece, *Les Fleurs du Mal*, appears to overturn the conventional hierarchy of good and bad, his poetry does not literally celebrate criminals or prostitutes, nor does he truly condescend to women, the poor and the infirm. A closer look reveals that the poet frequently demonstrates compassion for people in the corrupt city of Paris, which he calls 'the gigantic whore' ['l'énorme catin' (OC I 191)]. The rebellious and afflicted are Baudelaire's beloved brothers and sisters, but he cannot state so directly.

In his essay on Edgar Allan Poe, Baudelaire bluntly denounces 'the great heresy' ['la grande hérésie'] of didacticism, art in the service of 'direct usefulness' ['l'utilité directe' (OC II 263)]. He rejects the idealised characters and moralistic lessons of the great Romantic poet and novelist Victor Hugo, while admiring his imagination (OC II 217–24). In his essay 'Conventional Plays and Novels' ['Les Drames et les romans honnêtes'] Baudelaire asserts that the artist or writer must study vice as would a physician seeking to cure a disease: 'Vice is seductive, it must be painted as seductive' ['le vice est séduisant, il faut le peindre séduisant' (OC II 41)]. Unfortunately, the government prosecutor read *Les Fleurs du Mal* literally as promoting corrupt behaviour, and the court condemned the poet for outrage against public morality (see OC I 1176–224).

Yet Baudelaire's own ethical standards were noble, in spite of his personal difficulties in maintaining loving relationships and completing his manuscripts on time. He also admitted that the quest for ideal beauty was more compelling than moral responsibility. Above all, he was tempted by the 'voluptuous pleasures' of beauty, reverie and artificial stimulants. He summarised his devotion to the arts in *My Heart Laid Bare [Mon Cœur mis à nu]*: 'Glorify the worship of images (my great, my only, my primitive passion)' ['Glorifier le culte des images (ma grande, mon unique, ma primitive passion')' (OC I 701)].

The generative tension of Baudelaire's entire work can be understood as a struggle to maintain both compassion (ethics) and a fervent aestheticism, an intense inner experience. In his first reflections on imagination, 'On Wine and Hashish' ['Du vin et du haschisch'] (1851), he firmly distinguishes between the 'good' intoxication of wine, which makes one sociable, from the 'bad' ecstasies of hashish, which enfeeble the dreamer. Years later, he devoted an entire section of *Artificial Paradises [Les Paradis artificiels]* (1858–60), entitled 'Morality,' to the undermining effect of drugs on free will and the reality principle: 'Indeed, any person who does not accept life's conditions is selling his soul' ['En effet, tout homme qui n'accepte pas les conditions de la vie, vend son âme' (OC I 438)]. Writing in 'The Pagan School' of the movement of art for art's sake, he denounced

> [t]he excessive taste for form [which] induces unknown and monstrous disorders . . . The frenzied passion for art is an ulcer which devours the rest; and, as the clear absence of the accurate and true equals the absence of art, the entire person vanishes.

> ['Le goût immodéré de la forme pousse à des désordres monstrueux et inconnus. . . . La passion frénétique de l'art est un chancre qui dévore le reste; et, comme l'absence nette du juste et du vrai dans l'art équivaut à l'absence d'art, l'homme entier s'évanouit. (OC II 48–9)]

Baudelaire defined his personal values, what he called the 'eternal rules of my life' ['règles éternelles de ma vie'] in his *Intimate Journals [Journaux intimes* (OC I 673)]. There he confessed his most pressing problems and invoked the people he loved the most: 'Every morning *pray to God, reservoir of all strength and all justice, to my father, to Mariette and to Poe*' ['Faire tous les matins ma *prière à Dieu, réservoir de toute force et de toute justice, à mon père, à Mariette et à Poe*'] (Baudelaire's emphasis). He continued with valiant resolve to accept responsibility, all the while recognising his limitations:

to work all day long, or at least *according to what my strength allows*; to entrust to God, that is to say, to Justice itself, the success of my plans; every evening make a new prayer, to ask God for life and strength for my mother and for me . . .

[travailler toute la journée, ou du moins *tant que mes forces me le permettront*; me fier à Dieu, c'est-à-dire à la Justice même, pour la réussite de mes projets; faire tous les soirs une nouvelle prière, pour demander à Dieu la vie et la force pour ma mère et pour moi . . .]

He then supplemented faith with a practical strategy of self-control: 'to obey the strictest principles of sobriety, the first of which is to eliminate all stimulants, whatever they may be' ['obéir aux principes de la plus stricte sobriété, dont le premier est la suppression de tous les excitants, quels qu'ils soient'].

This admittedly moralistic confession embraces the values of family, friendship, love and fiscal responsibility. In private, Baudelaire thus affirmed free will and social duty as values higher than beauty, intoxication and ecstasy.

Baudelaire's ethical irony

Such goals, however, as inspiring as they might be, and pathetic in their frustration, are not the stuff of great literature. Baudelaire disguised his ethical positions with what I call 'ethical irony'. His narrators express negative and destructive moods, or feign to admire the depraved, in order to provoke outrage against the manifest immorality. What Victor Hugo named as Baudelaire's 'new shudder' ['un frisson nouveau'] points to what Baudelaire himself called his 'horrifying morality' ['terrible moralité'], that screen of ethical ambiguity around his poetry, prose poems and some critical essays.[2]

Baudelaire's ethical irony challenges conventional moral dualities and confronts the complexity of good and evil, far beyond the simplistic ideologies of God, family and nation that dominated his era. Like Socrates, who pretends to be ignorant, or stupid, Baudelaire undermines the complacency and self-satisfaction of his public. As a rhetorical strategy, ethical irony incites readers to question the polar opposites that structure Baudelaire's literary universe: beauty and horror, old and young, fantasy and reality, disillusion and the ideal, and of course good and evil, the two 'simultaneous postulations, one toward God, the other toward Satan' ['deux postulations simultanées, l'une vers Dieu, l'autre vers Satan' (OC I 682)]. Far from being absolute, in actual life these contraries are mixed, sometimes confused.

Baudelaire's ethical irony includes a harsh ideological critique, as it exposes the hypocritical standards which the rich and powerful use to justify and to camouflage their authority. His notorious preface to the *Salon of 1846*, addressed with apparent sincerity 'to the bourgeois', appears to glorify this class which he associated with stupidity, callousness, abuse of power and self-deception. He declares that this 'majority' enjoys the best taste in art *because* it possesses the most power. By indirection he protests against the tyranny of wealth; yet amidst the contradictions, he states his true position: 'You can live for three days without bread; without poetry, never' ['Vous pouvez vivre trois jours sans pain; – sans poésie, jamais' (OC II 415)]. Baudelaire the art critic clearly values spirit over cash and comfort.

A poetry of affliction

Read in sequence as a spiritual autobiography, *Les Fleurs du Mal* maintains a pervasive atmosphere of sin and corruption. From the opening poem, 'Au lecteur', to the last, 'Le Voyage', the poet appears to rebel against cherished social ideals while surrendering to disillusion and wallowing in despair. An ethical reading of the collection, however, highlights the positive values that coexist with the cynicism and negativity.

We interpret the collection's ethical developments in two ways: (1) through its overall structure, following the six sections in sequence: Spleen and the Ideal, Parisian Scenes, Flowers of Evil, Revolt, Death; (2) by examining individual poems or clusters of poems.

These textual analyses are confirmed historically by the substantial changes Baudelaire made to *Les Fleurs du Mal* between the first (1857) and second (1861) editions.[3] Baudelaire added thirty-two poems and a new section, 'Parisian Scenes' ['Tableaux parisiens'] to the second edition, which remained definitive. Briefly put, the first edition seeks to escape from the ugly world and to grasp a perfect, transcendent ideal, while the second edition sanctifies finite, imperfect existence. Both editions confront the challenge of despair, wrongdoing and personal responsibility.

The second edition advances Baudelaire's ethical orientation. The opening poem, 'Au lecteur', introduces the poet's ethical irony. Human beings are controlled by Satan, appearing to delight in vices, among them stinginess, folly and 'tame remorse' ['aimables remords'] and attracted by 'repugnant objects' ['objets répugnants' (OC I 5)]. The poet deplores the loss of human freedom as Satan 'vaporizes . . . the rich metal of our will' (FM 5) ['le riche métal de notre volonté est vaporisé par ce savant chimiste' (OC I 5)], pulling our strings as if we were marionettes. The worst vice, however, is not an evil initiative but moral passivity, *Ennui*, variously translated as boredom or apathetic despair.

At the end, the poet defines his multiple attitudes towards the reader in the famous line quoted by T. S. Eliot in *The Waste Land*: '– Hypocrite reader, – fellowman, – my twin!' ['– Hypocrite lecteur, – mon semblable, – mon frère!']. He first attacks; then he associates himself, compassionately, with his troubled readers, finally identifying with them as a brother. Ethical irony brings out the full meaning of 'hypocrisy' which the poet shares: it refers both to deliberate dishonesty and to self-deception.

The spiritual itinerary of *Les Fleurs du Mal* begins with the largest and most complex section, 'Spleen and the Ideal'. Groups of poems typify the changes Baudelaire made between the first two editions. The contrast is marked by differing representations of women as symbols of the ideal. The famous sonnet 'La Beauté', which depicts transcendent perfection as a cold statue, gives way to 'Le Masque', added in 1861. There the poet first savours a woman's youthful athletic body; he then discovers her 'two heads', one of which is a mask representing false art, a denial of time, and the other her real, anguished face. At the very end, a reader asks the poet why she suffers; he answers directly by expressing compassion for the real woman with a surprising pathos:

> What makes her tremble even to her knees,
> Is that tomorrow she'll be living still!
> Tomorrow, every day! – And so will we!
>
> (FM 43)

> [Ce qui la fait frémir jusqu'aux genoux,
> C'est que demain, hélas! il faudra vivre encore!
> Demain, après-demain et toujours! – comme nous.
>
> (OC I 24)]

The dialogue format thus leads to the poet's explicit identification with his fellow mortal.

The ethical dimension of art shares this assumption of common mortality. The poem which directly follows, 'L'Hymne à la Beauté', further undermines the cruel idealism of 'Beauty' by insisting upon art's ameliorative function, to make '[t]he world less dreadful, and the time less dead' (FM 45) ['l'univers moins hideux et les instants moins lourds' (OC I 250)]. Art may reflect the infinite but it does not have to be perfect.

Baudelaire added the next section, 'Parisian Scenes', in 1861 to consolidate his acceptance of mortal life as a vital source of poetry. Historically speaking, this urban poetry was one of Baudelaire's greatest innovations, and his most salient contribution to our modernity.[4] Some major new poems depict our inevitable ageing and death with sadness and anger, but also with love.

Political exile serves as a metaphor for the alienated condition of modern city dwellers. A cluster of three poems dedicated to Victor Hugo, in self-exile as an act of opposition to Napoleon III, exemplifies how temporality, the very fact of inescapable time, can inspire poetry. In 'Le Cygne' the poet associates his grief at the urban renewal that destroys 'the old Paris' (FM 175) ['le vieux Paris' (OC 1 85)] with the grieving of Andromache, the exiled widow of Hector. A swan escaped from its cage recalls a number of other exiles as well, 'a Negress, thin and tubercular', 'sailors forgotten on an isle / captives, the defeated . . . and many others more!' (FM 177) ['la négresse, amaigrie et phtysique', 'matelots oubliés dans une île, / Aux captifs, aux vaincus! . . . à bien d'autres encor!' (OC 1 87)]. The poet's identification with these wanderers, immigrants and political prisoners stimulates a multitude of other images of moral courage.

The two following poems, 'Les Sept Vieillards' and 'Les Petites Vieilles', suggest the fragility of life while recognising its horrors. Baudelaire conveys the ambiguity of his ethical inspiration as he admits, 'With tenderness, and restless eye intent . . . / Unknown to you I taste a secret joy' (FM 187) ['moi qui de loin tendrement vous surveille, / l'œil inquiet . . . / Je goûte à votre insu des plaisirs clandestins' (OC 1 91)]. Compassion again becomes a source of aesthetic pleasure. Then must we collapse his ethical generosity, transitive concern, into selfish inspiration? They are not exclusive; this ambiguity of the ethical and the aesthetic includes a mixture of anxiety, moral outrage and loving-kindness.

The next three sections explore ways in which people can either embrace the finite life or evade personal responsibility. The five pieces of 'Wine' deal straightforwardly with escapism in various social types, from the ragman, the assassin, the solitary, to lovers, implying a moral equivalence – the very fact of being human.

The section 'Flowers of Evil', which echoes the collection's title, defies conventional norms of love, sexuality and gender with compassion for suffering individuals. 'Une Martyre', for example, depicts an apparently lascivious teenager who is murdered, decapitated by her lover. The 'marriage' evoked at the end is tragically ironic, emphasising the despair that exacerbated this crime:

> Did her sickness of soul
> And her senses gnawed by ennui
> Open to her that depraved pack of lusts
> And encourage them willingly?
>
> (FM 233)

[Son âme exaspérée
Et ses sens par l'ennui mordus
S'étaient-ils entr'ouverts à la meute altérée
Des désirs errants et perdus?
(OC I 113)]

Lesbian love in 'Femmes damnées' manifests a similar frustration of infinite desire. Without shame, the poet willingly identifies with his

poor sisters . . .
For all your leaden griefs, for slakeless thirsts,
And for your hearts, great urns that ache with love!
(FM 247)

[Pauvres sœurs . . .
Pour vos mornes douleurs, vos soifs inassouvies,
Et les urnes d'amour dont vos grands cœurs sont pleins!
(OC I 114)]

At this point in a sequential reading of *Les Fleurs du Mal*, it becomes clear that we might translate the title as *The Flowers of Affliction*. Inspired by the French philosopher Simone Weil's reflections on existential *malheur* (misfortune or suffering) as a parallel to original sin, we might restore the ambiguity of the French word *mal*, which can signify evil, sickness or pain. According to this reading, people are not essentially 'evil' or malicious but rather 'fallible', as Paul Ricoeur uses the term, that is, depraved only in potential and thus responsible for their actions.

Sin is separable from the sinner, and religion has a basic ethical function. In Baudelaire's view, the Catholic Church, which defined 'religion' in his time, played a significant role in fostering despair. In 'Un voyage à Cythère' the poet comes upon a dead man punished by Christians for his pagan cult to Venus; the victim hangs on a gallows and is castrated by birds. With irony he calls this cadaver 'ridiculous' as he describes how it becomes an 'allegory', how the image gives meaning to his own self-disgust. At this point of extreme tension he cries out to God, as did Baudelaire in his private prayer, beseeching the Almighty to give him 'the courage and the strength / To take without disgust my body and my heart!' (FM 259) ['la force et le courage / De contempler mon cœur et mon corps sans dégoût!' (OC I 119)]. Rising above the shocking imagery, without bitterness he prays for a harmony of body and spirit denied by conventional Christian dualism.

Baudelaire judges Christendom according to ethical standards in the three poems of the penultimate section, 'Revolt'. Their apparent blasphemy dismayed his contemporaries, who confused the official religion with its ideals.

Here the poet appears to repudiate Christianity, but he does so in the name of social justice, thus affirming the essential humaneness of Jesus.

The ultimate ethical category is arguably life itself (in Christianity, suicide is a sin against the Holy Spirit). The poet and critic Yves Bonnefoy suggested that Baudelaire 'invented death', meaning that he made of our mortal nature the very heartbeat of his poetry. The final section of *Les Fleurs du Mal*, 'Death,' ['La Mort'] juxtaposes three poems that depict illusory images of the afterlife, and three poems, added in 1861, that assume death's finality. This juxtaposition of opposing views affirms the ultimate value of the here and now.[5]

The ambiguous ending of 'Le Voyage,' the collection's grand finale, provides a decisive test of ethical irony. Its several journeys rehearse the breakdown of all illusions, while the last two stanzas force us to face life's ambiguity: 'O Death, old captain, time to make our trip!' (FM 293) ['O Mort, vieux capitaine, il est temps! Levons l'ancre!' (OC I 134)]. Is 'death' here literally suicide or the acceptance of our finite condition? We can interpret the ending as implying two contradictory solutions: either suicide or a heroic embrace of chance. Interpreted in terms of its ethical affirmations, 'Le Voyage' confirms that death has been integrated into a courageous passion for living, beyond good and evil: 'plunge to depths of Heaven or of Hell, / To fathom the Unknown, and find the *new*!' (FM 293) ['Plonger au fond du gouffre, Enfer ou Ciel, qu'importe? / Au fond de l'Inconnu pour trouver du *nouveau*!' (OC I 134)].

Fables of self-awareness

Baudelaire's collection of fifty 'prose poems' was first published together under the title *Le Spleen de Paris, Petits Poèmes en prose*, in 1869, the year after his death. (While he was alive, he published most of them in periodicals.) Baudelaire invented this new genre as a parallel to his poetry, which I prefer to call 'fables of modern life' (as in 'The Painter of Modern Life' ['Le Peintre de la vie moderne']) that capture the complexities of urban consciousness. In *The Critical Difference* Barbara Johnson has shown how some of these self-reflective fables function as a 'critical poetry', providing deconstructive or ironic parallels to poems added in 1861 to *Les Fleurs du Mal*; I find that the prose collection as a whole provides a global interpretation of Baudelaire's entire work. The narrator of the prose poems is a dreamer and city stroller (a *flâneur*, whom I call 'the Parisian Prowler') who repeatedly struggles between his aesthetic and his ethical drives.[6] A sequential reading of this collection reveals a progression towards an acceptance of reality similar to that of *Les Fleurs du Mal*.

The first two fables, 'L'Etranger' and 'Le Désespoir de la vieille', brief and prosaic, provide a model for an ethical reading. Their main characters – one a man, the other a woman – seek to alleviate their alienation, the first through daydreaming, the other through gestures of tenderness. Both depict the impossibility of dialogue and affection. The enigmatic man of the first fable, and the good decrepit woman of the second represent aspects of the narrator, who himself seeks to reconcile truth and beauty, reality and imagination, the ethical and the aesthetic.

'Le Mauvais Vitrier' typifies the narrator's pretence of sacrificing common decency for the purpose of experiencing beauty. Here he is a depressed artist (really the 'bad' one) who sadistically smashes the glass of an itinerant peddler because the 'bad' glazier does not have pink panes ('panes of paradise' (PP 40) ['des vitres de paradis' (OC I 287)]) that transform sordid reality. The poem concludes with a rhetorical question, usually answered in favour of immoral, aesthetic delight: 'What does eternal damnation matter to one who has found in a second an eternity of pleasure?' (PP 41) ['Mais qu'importe l'éternité de la damnation à qui a trouvé dans une seconde l'infini de la jouissance?' (OC I 287)].

Ethical irony restores two possible answers: a 'moral' one expressing compassion for the impoverished worker, and the other a hedonistic contempt for the victim. Able to have both within literature, the reader is faced with a primal choice, one which may be impossible to resolve.

Another form of ethical irony involves the ideology of 'democracy' and the intellectual supporters of a 'republic'. The topics of poverty and social injustice appear in several pieces, among them, 'Les Foules', 'Les Veuves', 'Le Vieux Saltimbanque', 'Le Gâteau', 'Le Joujou du pauvre', 'La Belle Dorothée', 'Les Yeux des pauvres', 'La Corde', 'Les Fenêtres', 'Mademoiselle Bistouri' and 'Assommons les pauvres!'. Virtually none of these pieces promote equality and justice with a didactic or moralistic tone. Baudelaire's usual strategy is ironic, a pretence of cynicism that masks his tenacious commitment to kindness, respect and compassion.

Two of these in particular remind readers that democratic ideals, even if sincere, demand realistic self-critical examination. Liberty, Equality and Fraternity are worthy goals, but their implementation requires far more than dreams and good will. 'Le Joujou du pauvre', for example, depicts a rich boy and a poor boy on opposite sides of a symbolic fence, both of whom are delighting in their 'toy,' a living rat. ('The parents, no doubt as a means of saving money, had found the toy in life itself' (PP 56) ['Les parents, par économie sans doute, avaient tiré le joujou de la vie elle-même' (OC I 305)]). The last line lifts the social evil of poverty to a higher theoretical plane, but only indirectly: 'And the two children laughed at one another fraternally, with teeth that were *equally* white' (PP 56) ['Et les deux enfants se riaient l'un à l'autre fraternellement, avec des dents d'une *égale* blancheur' (OC 1 305)]. The italicised word *égale* signals ethical irony, as he recognises that *inequality* fostered by economic and political facts may be irremediable. The boys' transient 'equality' is a figment of desire, as is the 'beauty' of the amusing rodent. This conclusion suggests by indirection that class warfare is not 'natural'.

Baudelaire's use of italics to signal ethical irony recalls 'Le Gâteau', in which two impoverished boys violently fight each other for a crust of bread, which they call 'cake'. The narrator, who had been daydreaming of human perfection, concludes with a caustic observation: 'So there is then a superb country where bread is called *cake* and is so rare a delicacy that it is enough to cause a war which is completely fratricidal!' (PP 51) ['Il y a donc un pays superbe où le pain s'appelle du *gâteau*, friandise si rare qu'elle suffit pour engendrer une guerre parfaitement fratricide!' (OC 1 299)].

The penultimate fable, 'Assommons les pauvres!', questions the dogma of equality by demystifying theory as such. The narrator has been reading utopian books; he has 'swallowed . . . all the lucubrations of all those entrepreneurs of public happiness' (PP 103) ['avalé . . . toutes les élucubrations des tous ces entrepreneurs de bonheur public' (OC 1 357)] who promote imaginary solutions to social injustice. He then goes out to get a drink and to test his theory. Referring to the demon of Socrates, he explains that an impulse caused him to beat an old beggar, until 'the decrepit brigand' ['malandrin décrépit'] turned around and pummelled him. The worthy goal was reached: 'Through my energetic medication I had, therefore, restored to him both pride and life' (PP 104) ['par mon énergique médication, je lui avais donc rendu l'orgueil et la vie' (OC 1 359)]. The delighted narrator exclaims: 'Oh miracle! oh the joy a philosopher feels when he has confirmed the excellence of his theory!' ['O miracle! ô jouissance du philosophe qui vérifie l'excellence de sa théorie!' (OC 1 359)]. This pedagogy of self-esteem is admirable, but the means of inciting it are absurd, dangerous if taken too literally. That is the point of ethical irony. 'Assommons les pauvres!' parodies egalitarian propaganda, but not democratic values as such.

Truth, injustice and compassion

As do many of the poems added in 1861 to *Les Fleurs du Mal*, Baudelaire's prose poems highlight the reality principle as over against hedonistic constructions, many of which may require other people to suffer. The conflict between the aesthetic and the ethical can be summarised as the dialogue of solipsism and truth. 'Les Fenêtres' explicitly raises the question of the artist's responsibility to reality.[7] The fable begins by vaunting creative privilege, in this case, a writer imagining the lives (the 'histories' or 'legends') of women, or men, seen through an open window. At the end a dialogue with the reader occurs: 'Perhaps you will say to me: "Are you sure that that legend is the true one?" What does external reality matter, if it has helped me to live, to feel that I am and *what* I am?' (PP 87) ['Peut-être me direz-vous: «Es-tu sûr que cette légende soit la vraie?» Qu'importe ce que peut être la réalité placée hors de moi, si elle m'a aidé à vivre, à sentir que je suis et *ce que* je suis?' (OC I 339)] (Baudelaire's italics).[8] What he is is a writer. How do we answer the question of reality?

Baudelaire introduces a reflective reader within his fable to challenge the truth of literature as such. The concluding question is ambiguous. The narrator appears to affirm solipsism, the priority of mind over reality. However, the ethical voice behind the irony affirms truth over beauty: reality external to the mind does count. The reader must find a way to reconcile both, the 'true' and the 'legend'.

The conflict of wish and fact which energises 'Spleen and the Ideal', the first section of *Les Fleurs du Mal*, remains a powerful force in the prose poems. Women, actual or symbolic, again provide a locus for the poet's struggle with ambivalence. The fable, 'Laquelle est la vraie?', acknowledges the necessity of accepting reality only by its antithesis: 'like a wolf caught in a trap, I remain attached, perhaps forever, to the grave of the ideal' (PP 90) ['comme un loup pris au piège, je reste attaché, pour toujours peut-être, à la fosse de l'idéal' (OC I 342)]. These contradictions are almost resolved in 'Un cheval de race', which directly follows. The woman of this fable, who is described as both ugly and delicious, reconciles the poet with the impossibility of his quest for the ideal; she is both mortal and loving:

> She loves as one loves in autumn; it seems that the approach of winter kindles in her heart a fresh fire, and the servility of her tenderness has nothing in it that is wearying. (PP 90–1)

> [Elle aime comme on aime en automne; on dirait que les approches de l'hiver allument dans son cœur un feu nouveau, et la servilité de sa tendresse n'a jamais rien de fatigant. (OC I 343)]

Unrelentingly sceptical, Baudelaire cannot simply admire this ageing bearer of love, as he ends by tainting the purity of her 'fresh fire' with suggestions of 'servility'.

Baudelaire's most advanced fable of modern consciousness, 'Mademoiselle Bistouri', faces the ultimate ethical dilemma, the mystery of unjust human suffering.[9] The narrator meets an ageing woman whose nickname is '*bistouri*' (meaning surgical knife), whose obsession with attending bloody operations serves no apparent purpose, although he suggests that his own 'taste for horror' ['goût de l'horreur'] should 'convert [his] heart, as a cure at the tip of a blade' (PP 101) ['convertir mon cœur, comme la guérison au bout d'une lame' (OC I 356)]. Unable to convince her rationally to accept his version of reality, he cries out to God:

> Lord, have pity, have pity on the madmen and the madwomen! Oh Creator! Can there exist monsters in the sight of Him who alone knows why they exist, how they *made themselves*, and how they would have been able *not to make themselves*? (PP 101)

> [Seigneur, ayez pitié, ayez pitié des fous et des folles! O Créateur! peut-il exister des monstres aux yeux de Celui-là seul qui sait pourquoi ils existent, comment il *se sont faits* et comment ils auraient pu *ne pas se faire*? (OC I 356)]

The narrator has become a moral philosopher who experiences, in his marrow, metaphysical absurdity, the inaccessibility of divine justice. Overwhelmed, he questions the raw, brute mystery of existence, facing the alternative of despair or faith – unable to embrace either.

Evil is an irresolvable mystery. Miss Scalpel is vicariously sadistic as she is attracted to surgeons; but she is innocent, because she is insane. The narrator surrenders his pride as he acknowledges that, perhaps, God might hold the answer. Yet we do not know if Baudelaire the author, interpreting his own fable, would ratify the existence of a God who listens and cares. Within the fable, however, as we read it ethically, he struggles to penetrate the meaning of undeserved suffering and irremediable injustice in a radically new manner: from God's perspective. As did his contemporary, the Danish existential philosopher Søren Kierkegaard, Baudelaire asserted that the ethical questions of good and evil, and ultimate meaning, are incommensurable.

Baudelaire concludes *Le Spleen de Paris* by returning to the ethical. His final fable, 'Les Bons Chiens', assumes human limitations as he 'sings' of the downtrodden. Various canines are stand-ins for the alienated or afflicted characters who populate the prose poems: 'I sing of the muddy dog, the poor dog, the homeless dog, the wandering dog, the acrobat dog' (PP 106) ['Je chante le chien crotté, le chien pauvre, le chien sans domicile, le chien flâneur, le chien saltimbanque' (OC I 361)]. The narrator exchanges his poem for a painter's vest, symbolising the realisation of friendship through art, or the harmony of imagination and humane reality. A rhythmical refrain, repeated in the final lines, evokes his deepest values: 'And every time the poet dons the painter's waistcoat, he is obliged to think of the good dogs, the philosophical dogs, of Indian summers and the beauty of very mature women' (PP 108) ['et toutes les fois que le poète endosse le gilet du peintre, il est contraint de penser aux bons chiens, aux chiens philosophes, aux étés de la Saint-Martin et à la beauté des femmes très mûres' (OC I 363)]. These images of transition combine in older women ('quite mature') who have lived and who have conquered time. Whether or not they represent Baudelaire's widowed mother, or the forty-five-year-old greying author (truly at the autumn of his own life), he makes of mortality – and the acceptance of human fallibility – the seal of his wisdom and his art.

Baudelaire succeeded in reconciling the relentless search for absolute beauty, justice and truth with an anguished recognition that such aspirations cannot be fulfilled. He acknowledged the pervasiveness of malice and despair, but found in the inner life of social outcasts and rebels tokens of his own noble yearnings. *Les Fleurs du Mal* and *Le Spleen de Paris* undermine the idealistic ideologies of Romanticism, which they also encompass, as they announce the paradoxes of our post-modernity.[10] Baudelaire's prose and verse masterworks, directly or through irony, strive to liberate men and women from affliction, be it economic, political or self-imposed. Radically life-affirming, his art sanctifies the here and now as it stands at the brink of the divine.

NOTES

1. Translation of final line slightly revised.
2. In a letter to Baudelaire on 6 October 1859, Victor Hugo praised the poet by saying, 'You are bestowing on art's sky some strange macabre ray of light. You are creating a new shudder' ['Vous dotez le ciel de l'art d'on ne sait quel rayon macabre. Vous créez un frisson nouveau'], Claude and Vincentte Pichois, ed., *Lettres à Baudelaire* (Geneva: A la Baconnière, 1973), pp. 188–9. Baudelaire introduced the complexity of his moral perspective at the beginning of his notes for his lawyer: 'The book must be judged *as a whole* and then there arises from it a terrible moral lesson' ['Le livre doit être jugé *dans son ensemble*, et alors il en ressort une terrible moralité' (OC I 193)].
3. See J. R. Lawler, *Poetry and Moral Dialectic: Baudelaire's 'Secret Architecture'* (Madison, NJ: Fairleigh Dickenson University Press, 1997), pp. 182–8; Edward K. Kaplan, 'Baudelaire and the Battle with Finitude: "La Mort," Conclusion of *Les Fleurs du Mal*', *French Forum* 4, 3 (September 1979), pp. 219–31, and Kaplan, 'Baudelaire and the Vicissitudes of Venus: Ethical Irony in "Fleurs du Mal",' in *The Shaping of Text: Style, Imagery, and Structure in French Literature*, ed. Emanuel Mickel (Lewisburg, PA: Bucknell University Press, 1993), pp. 113–30.
4. See Walter Benjamin, *Charles Baudelaire: A Lyric Poet in the Era of High Capitalism*, trans. Harry Zohn (London: NLB, 1973).
5. See Lawler, *Poetry and Moral Dialectic* and Kaplan, 'Baudelaire and the Battle with Finitude'.
6. See Barbara Johnson, *Défigurations du langage poétique. La seconde révolution baudelairienne* (Paris: Flammarion, 1979); J. A. Hiddleston, *Baudelaire and 'Le*

Spleen de Paris' (Oxford: Clarendon Press, 1987); and Sonya Stephens, *Baudelaire's Prose Poems: The Practice and Politics of Irony* (Oxford: Oxford University Press, 1999). Several of my formulations are taken from my integral study of the prose poems, *Baudelaire's Prose Poems: The Esthetic, the Ethical, and the Religious in 'The Parisian Prowler'* (Athens and London: University of Georgia Press, 1990). See my translation, *The Parisian Prowler* (Athens: University of Georgia Press, 1997; second edition with new preface).

7. See Sima Godfrey, 'Baudelaire's Windows,' *L'Esprit Créateur* 22, 4 (Winter 1982), pp. 83–100 and Kaplan, *Baudelaire's Prose Poems*, pp. 122–5.

8. I have added to the Lloyd translation Baudelaire's italics and changed 'the right one' to 'the true one'. The 1863 *Revue nationale* publication italicises 'ce que'; see Robert Kopp's edition of the *Petits Poèmes en prose* (Paris: José Corti, 1969), p. 111.

9. Kaplan, *Baudelaire's Prose Poems*, pp. 145–51.

10. As he wrote in the *Universal Exposition* of 1855: 'And always a spontaneous unexpected product of universal vitality would come to give the lie to my infantile and obsolete knowledge, the lamentable daughter of utopias' ['Et toujours un produit spontané, inattendu, de la vitalité universelle venait donner un démenti à ma science enfantine et vieillotte, fille déplorable de l'utopie' (OC II 577)].

7

ROSS CHAMBERS

Baudelaire's Paris

Around me the street deafeningly screeched.

La rue assourdissante autour de moi hurlait.
                    – 'A une passante' (translation modified)

The development of large cities in the nineteenth century presented a major challenge to poetry which, in the era of Romanticism most particularly, had been severely addicted to nature: nature as context, but often too as object, of lyric emotions. It is Baudelaire, preceded by Poe contemporaneously with Whitman,[1] who 'first' saw that poets needed to find a way of accommodating the making of poetry to the sometimes exhilarating, but mostly prosaic and alienating, mode of existence now led by the inhabitants of cities. Baudelaire saw too that this effort held a crucial clue to the significance of modernity itself. Since 1848, the theological orientation his sensibility then took had led him to define the problem of poetic modernity as a search for the beauty in *le mal* (whence the title of *The Flowers of Evil*). But following the 1857 censorship trial of this volume of verse, the question was significantly modified and its orientation shifted, as he began to work on a new edition that in 1861 was to include the section entitled 'Parisian Scenes', and laboured at inventing a new poetic genre, the prose poem.

During these last years of his life, Baudelaire's attention focused strongly on urban reality, and concomitantly his writing comes to seem less concerned with creating beauty in any conventional sense. Rather it becomes a critical practice, a clinical or diagnostic activity, responding in particular to *le mal* as the phenomenon of social alienation, understood as the sign of an unhealthy society and most evident in city life. Not that he abandons the problem of beauty and *le mal*. But the aesthetic theory that is implicit in his poetic texts, which now become increasingly ironic and allegorical, tends to make of the poet, as a denizen of the city, a kind of engaged (better: embattled) social observer, one who is concerned on the one hand to seek out and report on the symptoms that betray the pathological character of the city as a social formation, while somewhat troubled, on the other, by what it might mean for a poet to play such a role.

For isn't the ironist/allegorist also an actor on the same stage as those he observes? May not the very critical distance his new poetry requires – the distance of irony and allegory – draw him uncomfortably close, as itself a sign of social alienation, to the various actors whose estrangement his texts pitilessly display? The 'lyric I' had always been a privileged figure. Suddenly, in late Baudelaire, the 'I' who speaks (in) a poem becomes a more dubious and even problematic authority: a 'Parisian prowler' and 'man of the crowd' whose aloofness and melancholia, which enable him to *see* the problem that escapes others, also make him *part* of the problem he sees: an observant 'eye' indistinguishable from a socially embattled 'I'.

During Baudelaire's short lifetime, the city of Paris grew exponentially in size and population, and its character was radically transformed under the impact of the new historical forces we call industrialism and capitalism. Preoccupied with a political revolution that merged into the Europe-wide Napoleonic adventure, France didn't begin to industrialise until well into the era of the Restoration (1815–30), and it was really only under the reign of the 'bourgeois monarch' Louis-Philippe (1830–48) that some new facts of social life in the capital became evident. Immigrants had been flooding the city from the impoverished provinces in search of employment, so that France's large population of peasants was fast becoming an urban proletariat: workers laboured for pittances under the cruellest conditions of laissez-faire capitalism. Simultaneously, the small but increasingly wealthy and educated class of property owners had acquired social authority and at least indirect political power, as birth (the *ancien régime*'s sole criterion of social status) was replaced by the new universal social signifier, money. Now wealth and poverty, on the one hand, and on the other issues of what Marx was to call exchange value, became something like social obsessions – not least in the writing of the poet who gave us texts like 'Les Yeux des pauvres' and 'La Fausse Monnaie'. Thus the social value of 'distinction' came to be opposed to the also new sense of the undistinguished majority as the unwashed and socially dangerous 'masses'.

However, early modern France had had a more informal, yet highly efficacious, alternative social signifier, which for brevity's sake I'll call sexuality. Sexual attraction had operated for a long time as the wild card in social relations; and if anything the unprecedented conditions of nineteenth-century urban life – notably the new anonymity people came to have in big cities – worked to intensify this role of the sexual in collective life. Many of Baudelaire's later poems (for example in verse, 'A une passante', and in prose 'Mademoiselle Bistouri') crackle with the sexual electricity generated by urban encounters. And finally, to the extent that the money economy fused with sexual supply-and-demand to produce a sort of parallel marketplace called prostitution, the poet was offered a facile but nevertheless irresistible overall metaphor, one that was applicable, as many observers noticed, to social relations in general under the July Monarchy (1830–48) and especially the Second Empire (1851–70), but also, as Baudelaire more specifically saw, to what the practice of art had become now that, with the disappearance of the *ancien régime* institution of patronage, it too was forced to compete in a kind of intellectual and cultural market. (Whence also Baudelaire's ambivalent interest in crowd-pleasers of every stripe: popular theatre in all its manifestations, mountebanks, strolling musicians and fairground entertainers, clowns and court jesters.)

At the same time, and as if to underline these transformations, city-planners – a bit timidly prior to 1848 but on a very large and dramatic scale under the Second Empire – set about transforming the very face of the city, inventing the form of make-over we now call urban renewal. In 1850s Paris it was called Haussmannisation, after the Prefect broadly responsible for sweeping away the higgledy-piggledy old city, with its maze of narrow, winding streets, and replacing them with the pattern of broad boulevards, large open squares and long vistas we associate with Paris today. Haussmannisation was part real-estate bonanza and part what contemporaries wryly called 'strategic beautification', since it was clear that if the boulevards were designed to extend the new railways by facilitating access to the city's centre, they would also make it very much harder for the discontented to set up street barricades while it correspondingly became easier for the 'forces of order' to bring in heavy weaponry with which to control urban mobs. The more so as rising rents in the inner city now forced a mass evacuation of the working-class population towards the city's outskirts, producing the segregated social topography evident today, with wealthy *beaux quartiers* (smart neighbourhoods) in the centre and to the west, and working-class *arrondissements* and the suburban *banlieue populaire* relegated to the east and the north.

Haussmann's new boulevards, clean and paved, quickly became the showcase of the new city. There 'distinguished' folk strolled or lounged in cafés that could now, for the first time, spread on to the street; theatres sprang up and a rather glitzy commercialism prevailed – the culture of 'gay Paree' was ready to take off. Nevertheless, much as today you can meet crowds of kids from the *banlieue* on a spree in the heart of Paris, so then the boulevards became one of the very few remaining places where the socially dominant beautiful people and the newly evicted poor and labouring classes could actually, not really meet, of course, but at least catch sight of one another. The mutual eyeing that went on, cross-class sometimes but also cross-gender (and in the case of prostitution both), furnished Baudelaire with another metaphor for urban experience that became one of his key motifs. For what French calls an *échange de regards*, even though it may be erotically or otherwise a highly charged experience, is also an experience of distance. It doesn't neces-sarily imply – as perhaps English 'eye-contact' does – a meeting of minds or mutual understanding. It bespeaks separateness more fundamentally than it concerns communication.

And indeed, the then-novel, now-everyday experience of being in close proximity, spatially, with people whom, socially, one didn't and probably couldn't know – an experience of encounter without an actual meeting – is something that was much commented upon, notably by visitors to Paris from the provinces. In a small town, one may well not know the names of people one sees, but there is every chance of their being perfectly familiar, or alternatively of their becoming so. By contrast, what came to be called urban solitude – the anonymity of the crowd – is close to the definitional heart of the word 'alienation', precisely because in it the element of familiarity, both actual and potential, is lacking. That element is replaced in the crowded city by a sense of singularity. People one glimpses in the street seem strange or bizarre – they resist one's interpretive skills – not just because one doesn't know them but more particularly because there is so little chance of one's ever encountering them again.

The prime association with the idea of the crowd in this period isn't so much the idea of a multiplicity of people, then, as it is the combined sense of stimulus and novelty, but also of oppression and estrangement, that arises in the street. And not surprisingly a genuinely new mode of writing sprang up and flourished in the first half of the nineteenth century in response to this phenomenon, its function being largely that of cultural reassurance. Here the strangeness of the streets is partly celebrated and partly explained away, as readers – pretty much by definition middle-class – were provided with entertaining accounts of urban types and social milieus they might well glimpse in their daily lives, but would never consider approaching in the flesh.

This *flâneur* writing, as it was called, furnished a steady and welcome livelihood to a new breed of semi-journalistic writers paid by the column of print, and simultaneously gave birth to the sort of modern myth that Surrealism was to inherit: the myth of the city as a place of wonderment. Baudelaire's city writing, in turn, owes a clear debt to this same, very recent, tradition of *flânerie*, and many of his city poems, at first sight, could be confused with it. His interest in the category of the bizarre, which in 1855 he declared an essential component of the beautiful,[2] is clearly in line with, although equally clearly not fully identical with, the oddities that provided *flâneur* writing's stock-in-trade. 'What bizarre things we find in a big city when we know how to stroll about looking' he writes in 'Mademoiselle

Bistouri'. But he adds, more pointedly: 'Life swarms with innocent monsters' (PP 101) ['Quelles bizarreries ne trouve-t-on pas dans une grande ville, quand on sait se promener et regarder? La vie fourmille de monstres innocents' (OC 1 355)]. This is *flâneur* prose with a sting in its tail.

For unlike most such writing, Baudelaire isn't interested in making his readers feel comfortable with the strangeness of city experience, and in his work even the thematics of urban wonderment (as in 'Les Sept Vieillards') is less inspiriting than it is deeply troubling. The alienation that most *flâneur* writing existed to exploit, to mitigate or to deny is what he persistently draws attention to, and he does so with an eye to pointing up what is pathological in the social reality it bespeaks: the ill or evil (*le mal*) that modern life exemplifies, but also diverts us from grasping or coming to grips with. In other words, he takes up the thematics of *flâneur* writing, but with a view to giving it a critical edge. The theme of urban encounter, in that respect, is exhibit A. Baudelairean encounters aren't simply occasions for the exercise of idle curiosity or mild bewilderment, let alone smug enjoyment of modern life's bizarreries. They're awkward and troubling cases of mutual ignorance producing instances of double, sometimes multiple, misprision. People who don't know one another – and so can't understand one another – become 'monstrous' in their alienated relations, one to the other. That they may be innocent in/of their monstrosity – can't perceive or acknowledge it – doesn't cancel the monstrosity, but exacerbates the problem.

So urban encounters in Baudelaire are always intersections, temporary and usually mystified, of individual trajectories that cross, as in an exchange of glances, even as their participants go their separate ways along what Deleuze and Guattari might call 'lines of flight' – the flight-lines that guarantee the unlikelihood of their intersecting again.[3] As the penultimate line of 'A une passante' has it: 'neither one know[s] where the other one goes'. In its original French this line is a kind of flawed chiasmus – chiasmus (from the Greek letter *chi*) being the figure of intersection: 'Car j'ignore où tu fuis, tu ne sais où je vais' (OC 1 93). Intersection, then, implies flight-lines and flight-lines in turn can and do intersect because the *law* of this universe is that meeting, because it entails mutual distance, can only ever be encounter, while distance does not preclude encounter, but tends rather, in the crowded space of cities, to guarantee that it will occur.

There are two sets of comments to be made about this law of intersection. The first is that, if urban intersections are symptomatic events, they have the particular character of a *syndrome*, because what such intersections demonstrate is the con-currence (cf. syn-drome) of two or more symptomatic manifestations. Such a concurrence of manifestations – say wealth on the one hand and poverty on the other, or more concretely rich people and poor people – points to an underlying pathology that generates it.[4] In the old, pre-capitalist, pre-Haussmann Paris that people of Baudelaire's age remembered well, rich and poor shared the same neighbourhood and even the same apartment-houses (the rich on the lower floors, their poor neighbours above, below the roof). Despite the obvious differences in living conditions, each group was familiar with (and to) the other – they were able to know something of one another's lives. On the new boulevards, however (the construction of which had entailed a spectacular boom in property values, accompanied by an undignified speculative scramble and much graft and chicanery), on the boulevards *as a specifically capitalist site*, then, rich people and poor people could still be found within the same space. But they were now like, for example, the various specific opportunistic infections that beset a patient and in doing so signal the syndrome of AIDS: although they co-occurred, they were not in direct interrelation except insofar as their unrelated co-occurrence was itself the sign of a new historical problem. By comparison with the old, harmonious state of affairs, their disjoined presence on the same scene pointed to something that had changed, and not for the better: an underlying evil or ill that now defined the modern way of living as pathological. And that evil/ill was none other than the historically new mode of production called capitalism, which (as Marx was to point out) generated the phenomenon of stand-off that is commonly called class warfare.

It's here that things get tricky, however. A familiar adage has it that the more things change the more they stay the same, and the phenomenon called modernity has just that paradoxical structure. Modernity arises as an awareness that a crucial change has occurred (for example the classes now interact only in stand-off mode). But that awareness is accompanied by the disabused knowledge that, this 'shock of the new' (Walter Benjamin's expression) notwithstanding, nothing essential has altered. Despite those harmonious living arrangements of old, the rich and the poor have always been around and have always lived on opposite sides of a certain fence – the fence, one might say, that has eternally divided history's winners and history's losers. And if that is the case, the alleged harmony of the old living arrangements is itself just a modern illusion, born of the visible contrast between 'the way we live now' (the rich segregated from the poor) and 'how they lived then' (together). The actual reality will have *always* been syndromic in character, and the separateness of the lives of rich and poor wasn't much mitigated by their living in daily proximity and mutual familiarity. What is modern, then, boils down to the fact that the way we live now has given us a framework for viewing the past that brings the continuity of past and present into unprecedented visibility; it's the modern concept of class war, for example, that makes it possible to speak, in a new sense, of history's eternal 'winners' and 'losers'.

For a modern to regret the past as having been crucially different from and preferable to the present is to fall victim, therefore, to a form of illusion, specifically the form of self-deceit known as nostalgia. A truly modern consciousness – one that has been jolted into a diagnostic disposition by experiencing the shock of the new – is one for which nostalgia is made impossible by the knowledge that no essential difference separates past from present even though a crucial change has taken place. The alienations of the present existed also in the past, albeit under a different historical form. Baudelaire's word for such diagnostic lucidity will be, not nostalgia therefore, but melancholia.

This we learn from his great poem of urban modernity, 'Le Cygne', in which the 'I' of the poem reflects on the way history – history understood in light of the adage that the more things change the more they stay the same – produces winners and losers, whose lives intersect without meeting because their experience of that history differs radically, the winners being optimists, celebrating change as good, while the losers are in the grip of a paralysing nostalgia for former times, even as they survive painfully among the ruins of the present. This vision of history is worked out, from the vantage-point of modern, post-Haussmann Paris, in terms of the long history of Western civilisation (understood by Baudelaire as more or less equivalent to world history). This story is a history of cities, viewable on the one hand as a history of change and progress, as ancient Troy yields to Greece, then to Rome and finally to Paris, but on the other as a narrative of exclusion and suffering that in its essentials has never changed since the sack of Troy. It's in view of this latter history that a bedraggled swan in a Parisian gutter can be associated with Andromache, proud Hector's widow exiled in Epirus after the fall of Troy, while simultaneously – albeit more discreetly, given the Second Empire's apparatus of formal and informal censorship – the same bird symbolises the fate of the workers in 1848, who in June of that year were treacherously betrayed by the bourgeois, massacred and eventually, by means of strategic beautification, excluded from the consciousness if not the sight of their supposed betters by being evicted from the old city centre.[5]

There's no real doubt where the sympathies of the poem's 'I' lie in this account of 'human' history since the Trojan horse. But it's also clear that, if the unified disjunction of winners and losers forms an endlessly repetitive syndrome, the diagnostic consciousness 'I' has of the double component of this syndrome distinguishes him from each of the groups whose history his vision embraces. As the allegorist aware of the humiliating relevance of the most ancient past to the most recent present ('new palaces, blocks, scaffoldings / Old neighbourhoods are allegorical *for me*') (FM 175) ['palais neufs, échafaudages, blocs / vieux faubourgs, tout pour moi devient allégorie' (OC 1 86)], he can scarcely share the winner optimism of belief in progress. But neither is he nostalgic, like the exiled figures in the poem. Rather his 'mood' is melancholy: 'Paris is changed, but in my melancholy mood / Nothing has budged!' (FM 175). A mood that doesn't budge, though, is more than a mere mood. It's a permanent mental disposition, as the line in French suggests: 'mais rien dans ma mélancolie / N'a bougé!' (OC 1 86).

This poem, then, provides some analytic tools for grasping the tricky character of Baudelairean modernity, and at the same time it offers evidence of the traumatic impact on Baudelaire himself of the events of June 1848, the moment when the Republic's fate was sealed and the heady, utopian and 'harmonian' dreams of the 1830s and 1840s, in which the whole intellectual class (Baudelaire included) had indulged, were suddenly and irrevocably dispelled, rendered null and void, by the revelation that the property-owning class would defend its own interests against those of the workers, if necessary to the point of bloodshed. 'Traumatic' is not too strong a word if we measure the violence of the disenchantment, and understand the melancholia of aftermath that's expressed in the poem as an indicator of what we now call post-traumatic stress. But 'Le Cygne' is interesting too because it shows us the kind of urban landscape that Baudelaire finds particularly expressive of the modern predicament, the cityscape he associates with the swan and thus with both the syndromic, intersectional character of social relations in the present, and the melancholic historical experience that is indistinguishable from modernity. I'll call such an urban landscape the 'urban jumble', the play on the more recent metaphor of 'urban jungle' being very much intended.

Cities are notoriously stratified, in historical terms, in that evidence of the past, both recent and remote, always remains apparent to those with eyes to see it, even as the city continues to change and grow, altering its historical and sociological character as it does so. This is never more the case than at times of intensified and accelerated change, such as Haussmann's makeover of Paris. At such times, it can seem that the past, the present and even the future are co-present and commingled. Rubble, rubbish, ruins and other residua can acquire great pathos and significance, as can new but unfinished structures that are like ghosts visiting from the future. Such, then, is the context in which the 'I' of 'Le Cygne' recalls encountering the bird:

I picture in my head the busy camp of huts,
And heaps of rough-hewn columns, capitals and shafts,
The grass, the giant blocks made green by puddle-stain,
Reflected in the glaze, the jumbled bric-a-brac.

(FM 175)

[Je ne vois qu'en esprit tout ce camp de baraques,
Ces tas de chapiteaux ébauchés et de fûts,
Les herbes, les gros blocs verdis par l'eau des flaques,
Et, brillant aux carreaux, le bric-à-brac confus.

(OC 1 86)]

These lines are a snapshot of central Paris in mid-Haussmannisation, and the jumble of residuality but also of ('rough-hewn') imminence that they picture signifies what I'll call the untimeliness of modernity, understanding the word in its two senses. For modernity comes upon us unexpectedly, takes us by surprise; it's the shock of the new. But it comes also as a strange disruption of the categories we habitually use in order to reflect on history and time, those of past, present and future.

That disruption, I suggest, is Baudelaire's crucial subject-matter; and it brings us to my second set of observations on the intersectional or syndromic character of urban social relations in general and urban encounter in particular. It brings us to the topic of noise and the noisy city, but also to the issue of modern poiesis as the making of noisy texts.

Less than a generation after Baudelaire, Mallarmé and others would be insulating poetry from the contamination of everyday transactions by promoting it as a mysterious, semi-sacred practice of obscurity. But there is nothing hermetic about Baudelaire's city writing, and its character, he once suggested (speaking of prose poetry in a letter to Houssaye), actually derives from 'frequenting' great cities ('frequenting' is a carefully chosen word). A casual reader may find these texts clear, then. Nevertheless, the more attentively one pieces them together in pursuit of their textual unity, the more they tend to fall apart and fail to coalesce into a fully coherent statement. They're traversed by noise, in the sense the word has in information theory, where it refers to the impediments introduced into communication by the medium or 'channel' employed.

These late texts have a looser texture, one that derives from the unity-defying principle of intersection which – as we've seen – brings elements together only for them to cross and split apart again along their own lines of flight. Not, as in 'Parfum exotique', in which 'the warm scent of your breasts' ['l'odeur de ton sein chaleureux'] equals 'inviting shorelines' ['des rivages heureux'] equals 'an island where . . . etc.' (FM 49) ['Une île paresseuse où' (OC I 25)]. But texts whose texture is like certain kinds of pastry (a croissant, say, or a baklava) whose consistency derives from superimposed layers of dough – segments of text – that fail to cohere. Such texts are called *feuilletés*, or flaky, by Deleuze and Guattari (the official translation is 'striated'); they contrast with the kind of texts whose (smooth) authority derives from iron-clad self-consistency and coherence.[6] They're noisy and unsettling to read, much as the urban jumble – both the social and the historical jumble – resists attempts to read *it* as unified, because like the past, the present and the future, people too coincide and intersect in the city, but don't cohere.

Nevertheless, just as urban dwellers may believe, even as they intersect, that they understand one another implicitly or can correctly read the messages in one another's eyes, so too Baudelaire's texts make all the gestures of communicating conventionally and can be taken, therefore, as mentioned above, to be telling a grammatical story or making a straightforward – non-ironic, non-allegorical – statement. If they make readable the metaphoric noisiness of the city, then, they do so only for readers willing to engage them more carefully and reflectively – to be detained by them in a less hasty intersection. They derive from frequenting the crowd, but they're not necessarily *for* the crowd.

The letter about prose poetry I quoted earlier doesn't talk about flaky poiesis. Written in 1862, this letter is a tricky document for a number of reasons, one of which is that Baudelaire is simultaneously describing the heterogeneity of a group of texts he is submitting to Arsène Houssaye for publication, and the flaky quality of their prose.[7] Still, in order to do this, he comes up with a homely image of his own. His texts, he says, are like a snake that can be chopped into pieces that are viable on their own or alternatively can recombine in new ways despite their missing 'vertebrae'. (Let's not look too closely into his knowledge of natural history – in this, too, he is a city poet.) It's when he moves from this metaphor into something more like analysis that we can see him struggling to use the only vocabulary available to him – which is that of a traditional, subject-centred understanding of lyric 'expression' – to describe his own very different practice. 'Who among us', he asks, 'in their more ambitious moments hasn't dreamed of the miracle of a poetic prose that would be musical without recourse to rhythm and rhyme' ['Quel est celui de nous qui n'a pas, dans ses jours d'ambition, rêvé le miracle d'une prose poétique, musicale sans rythme et sans rime'], – without recourse, that is, to the principle of harmony. Such prose, he goes on, would be 'supple enough and abrupt enough to adapt to the lyric motions of the soul, the undulations of reverie, and the somersaults of consciousness'

(PP 30: translation altered) ['assez souple et assez heurtée pour s'adapter aux mouvements lyriques de l'âme, aux ondulations de la rêverie, aux soubre-sauts de la conscience?' (OC I 275–6)]. This last word, *conscience* in the French, signifies both moral conscience and awareness of self. So if we take that final list (lyric motions, reveries, somersaulting consciousness) to be a catalogue of the different kinds of poem Baudelaire is offering the editor Houssaye, it's the somersaulting consciousness that best describes the flaky texts of city life, as opposed to those of lyric (e)motion and of reverie; texts in which the intersecting encounters of the urban jumble keep a poet's self-awareness *and* his moral judgment (and with them, of course, the reader's corresponding judgments and interpretive efforts) constantly on the hop. Texts, then, that destabilise us, as readers, rather than gratifying or reassuring us in the manner of, say, *flâneur* writing.

In this brief essay a single example, that of 'Les Yeux des pauvres', will have to suffice (PP 67–9: OC I 317–19). The scene is a café situated at an intersection on a brand-new boulevard, one that's still 'full of rubble but already showing the glory of its unfinished splendours' ['encore tout plein de gravois et montrant déjà glorieusement ses splendeurs inachevées']. The male narrator and his mistress have spent their day 'promising' ['nous avions bien promis'] each other always to think in common and to share a single soul – this despite the fact that the same narrator has just told us unequiv-ocally to expect the subject-matter of the text to be the 'impenetrability' ['imperméabilité'] of women to men. The lady being 'somewhat weary' ['un peu fatiguée'], they've seated themselves outside the brightly lit café whose sparkling mirrors, gilt trim and exuberant mural decorations – a jumble of aristocratic and mythological figures offering fruit, pâtés, game, pastries and ices – are described for us at some length (and as it were with raised eyebrows) by an amused narrator who sums it all up as the usual Second Empire kitsch: 'all history and all mythology pressed into the service of sheer gluttony' ['toute l'histoire et toute la mythologie mises au service de la goinfrerie']. His raised eyebrows turn to condescension, though – another form of superciliousness – as he shifts his attention to the street. There a 'good chap' ['un brave homme'] in his forties stands with his two young children, one of whom he carries in his arms. With his greying beard and weary features (he's not just 'somewhat weary', like the mistress) the father is presented as 'performing the function of a nanny and taking his children for an evening stroll' ['Il remplissait l'office de bonne et faisait prendre à ses enfants l'air du soir']. Such a comment can only be a joke, and an unfeel-ing one at that, since the three are manifestly *not* of the nanny-employing class. You and I might guess that their wide-eyed stare, which the narrator understands to be a sign of profound admiration for the gimcrack café, is

more likely to express fatigue, hunger or a sense of exclusion. For it's clearly poverty that keeps them at a respectful distance. Perhaps indeed they've been evicted and have spent *their* day trudging the streets of this now inhospitable neighbourhood where they're unlikely to find an affordable scrap to eat. Of all such likelihoods, however, our narrator, intent on his own interests and train of thought, seems blithely unaware.

Although we've been told to expect a poem about the impenetrability of women, the text is shaping up, then, as more an ironic comment on the limited vision of its male narrator, whose assured judgments about his class and others seem dubious while his insensitivity is plain. The poem has begun to show us that there's another side to 'impenetrability', and that things like judgment and sensitivity, the prerequisites for an empathetic understanding of others, are relative to one's own social situation. The narrator can literally *afford* to immerse himself in aesthetic issues, waxing critical of the café's glitz and assuming condescendingly that the poor family is admiring its tawdry splendours, but failing to notice the gap that divides him from them or to reflect that, to middle-class eyes, a poor family's thoughts may be as 'impenetrable' as he thinks women are to men. Indeed, he goes on to compound his error by insisting that he can even discern different forms of admiration in the trio according to their age. The father's eyes, he tells us, say: 'How beautiful it is! You'd think all the gold in the whole weary world had come together on these walls' (translation modified) ['Que c'est beau! que c'est beau! on dirait tout l'or du pauvre monde est venu se porter sur ces murs']. The boy's eyes are envious: 'How beautiful it is! But it's a house you can go in only if you're not like us' ['Que c'est beau ! mais c'est une maison où peuvent seuls entrer les gens qui ne sont pas comme nous']. The baby has eyes 'too bewitched to express anything but a boundless and mindless joy' ['trop fascinés pour exprimer autre chose qu'une joie stupide et profonde'].

Oddly, these judgments carry a certain weight, provided we accept their premise that the family is wide-eyed with admiration. To the extent that the text appears to have endorsed the idea of a gender-gap with respect to the readability of thoughts, the idea of there being a difference of thinking according to age has a certain plausibility; judgments do change as people mature. On the other hand, however, in that case the probability of there being a class-gap also – something the narrator never considers – is likewise confirmed. And how can a man who misreads hunger as aesthetic emotion be correct, then, in attributing distinct, if equally unsophisticated, opinions to the different members of an anonymous working-class family passing by at some distance, whose eyes he claims to be able to read? Our suspicion that he is fantasising, projecting on to them his own interest in the nature of the beautiful, returns. And that being so, why in turn should we trust his idea of a gender-gap, since it too may well be a function of class, given that a mistress willing to exhibit herself on a 'terrasse de café' in the 1860s can only be a demi-mondaine, i.e. a high-class tart – not a street prostitute but an actress or an artist's model, say, and a woman, therefore, very probably of working-class origin herself, putting on airs for her own pleasure and/or the good of her trade? The notion that the impenetrability of the eyes of the poor, unrecognised by the narrator, is of a piece with the impenetrability of women, an article of faith in his book, acquires some substance. But by the same token we can see that the text, as opposed to its narrator, is redefining impenetrability: the opaqueness of others isn't a function of their nature, but of social realities; it's evidence of alienation.

So this noisy text has our consciousness somersaulting, even as its protagonists' criss-crossing looks volley back and forth, intersecting but (given in particular that the narrator and his beloved are watching the family which itself is looking at the café) failing to meet. And it continues to somersault. For now, 'feeling a trifle ashamed of our glasses and our jugs, which were bigger than our thirst' ['un peu honteux de nos verres et de nos carafes, plus grands que notre soif'] the narrator – while we quickly revise our judgment as to his insensitivity – turns finally to his beloved. He expects – with the same unexamined sense of inevitable rightness with which he (mis)read the eyes of the poor – to see in *her* eyes an expression of a discomfort similar to his own. The glasses, carafes and thirsts are 'ours', we have them in common, so presumably the 'thoughts' – the moral discomfort, our *conscience* – are also shared . . . But no. Here the narrator reaches the moment of truth we've – perhaps – been expecting. The lady snaps: 'I can't bear those people with their eyes as wide open as carriage-entrances. Couldn't you ask the head waiter to send them on their way?' (translation modified) ['Ces gens-là me sont insupportables avec leurs yeux ouverts comme des portes cochères! Ne pourriez-vous pas prier le maître du café de les éloigner d'ici?']. No possible community of souls there, one thinks (and so also no trusting the narrator's judgment when it comes to the poor, or the décor of a café). Women's impenetrability seems to sanction the idea of the universal impenetrability – aside, that is, from some niggles of conscience – of one's social others. Case closed.

Or is it? Can it be, I ask myself, that the narrator is wrong again? For perhaps the lady's dismissiveness is *not* the opposite, but actually a counterpart, of his own comfortable sense of shame? She's simply more honest than he, perhaps, in wishing the poor would go away and not spoil the pleasures of the café? And if so, there's a certain solidarity, a complicity even, a commonality of soul, between the high-class pro and the middle-class aesthete, a complicity or commonality not anchored in class origins so much as it's grounded in the privileges that attach, in Second Empire society, to the possession of money. That is, in innocent monstrosity. For we've just learned that, for the narrator who is so critical of the café's decoration, it's the lady's beauty, notably that of her eyes, that exemplifies the truly beautiful. And the eyes, 'so lovely and so strangely gentle' ['si beaux et si bizarrement doux']' but also (the beautiful is always bizarre!) 'inhabited by Caprice and inspired by the Moon' ['habités par le Caprice et inspirés par la Lune'], are impenetrable in that they resist coherent reading. Perhaps, then, the poem we took for an ironic comment on social incompatibilities (to which the narrator's interest in aesthetic questions is subsidiary) can be better read as an allegorical exploration of modern beauty. A form of beauty to which it's the enthralled relation of the poet to his mistress's unreadable eyes under the supposedly admiring but also troubling gaze of the poor that is relevant . . . In that case, the poem can be taken to endorse the proposition that a poem, say, that doesn't *baffle* us – doesn't set our consciousness somersaulting by its capricious failure to cohere – doesn't have the quality of flaky impenetrability, of noisy (un)readability, that is the hallmark of the kind of modern beauty that arises from 'frequenting' the urban jumble.

But if that is so, the text's endorsement of modernity in art comes at a price. For art, we must conclude, can be diagnostic in relation to the modern social formation, but its diagnostic stance doesn't prevent it from being itself part of the deplorable social conditions it diagnoses, in the way that the narrator, here, in thrall to the impenetrable beauty of his mistress's eyes, is led by that thraldom into complicity with her whoreish soul, and thus into betrayal of the eyes of the poor and all that they might express. Complicity doesn't necessarily entail an identity of viewpoints, but it does presuppose some convergence of interests, ambitions or desires: a community of the soul. Describing an intersection of interests that doesn't amount to a meeting of minds, its relational noisiness makes complicity the moral counterpart of intersecting eyes, as the verse poem 'A une passante' makes clear. The question here, then, is whether art is different from (i.e. better than) society as the narrator and his mistress differ in their responses to the eyes of the poor; or whether their apparent difference only underscores the fact, ironically foreshadowed at the outset, that they have in common a tarnished soul, in the way that he, with his guilt and 'bad faith', is as socially irresponsible as she, with her casual indifference, and a flaky text part and parcel of a noisy city. The undecidability is maddening; but it explains why it has become impossible for Baudelaire to believe, as before 1848 French intellectuals unanimously believed, in the redemptive role of art, or even its therapeutic or ameliorative capacity. Post-1848 art is, at best, critical. And like all criticism it is, inevitably, at least half in love with its object: the city.

Therein lies a more private source of Baudelaire's melancholia, which is perhaps not quite so unmixed with nostalgia as I suggested earlier. It's not for nothing that in 'Le Cygne' (FM 173–7; OC 1 85–7), the poem that explicitly names melancholia as the disease of lucidity and of a modern urban consciousness, the stanza following the lines portraying the urban jumble concerns a noisy, early-morning street, and evokes both what I believe Baudelaire views as the only antidote to melancholia, namely, work, and – again, of course very discreetly – the moment in 1848 from which he dates poetry's fall into modernity: its own Trojan horse.

This means that the ambiguous moment of jumble, when the present is continuous with both the past and the future, is matched by the ambiguous sense that attaches to dawn, the crepuscular morning hour, neither night nor yet day, when 'Labour awakes' ['le Travaille s'éveille']. As a figure of modernity, noisy dawn refers us variously to (a) the time of day when workers throng the streets on their way to work; to (b) the hopeful awakening of the proletarian consciousness in the revolutionary moment of February 1848; to (c) their 'rude awakening' in the bloodshed of June; and finally, therefore – since the only workers specified are the street sweepers 'pushing their storms into the silent air' ['pousse un sombre ouragan dans l'air silencieux'] – to (d) the post-1848 clean-up that resulted in a reactionary regime and Paris's 'strategic beautification'. Crossing the 'modern Carrousel' ['le nouveau Carrousel'], a place of intersection, and recalling the stranded swan, the 'I' of the poem can't fully dissociate the optimistic revolution from the abandonment of the workers, the complicities and betrayals of which he too, in the enforced ambiguity of his very language, is an inheritor.

That he associates that situation not only with noise but also with work, and that he associates both noise and work with storm, tempest and thunderous electric discharge – that he understands the modern city, in other words, as a place of energy (Greek *ergon*, work) is no coincidence; and such an association obviously demands further study. Here, though, I want to end on the troubled and tortured image of the swan, haplessly twisting its neck towards the 'ironic sky' ['le ciel ironique'], as much a part of the urban scene as it is out of place in its midst, and part of it *because* it's out of place there. This is Baudelaire's most compelling image of the plight of the modern poet, and of his somersaulting *conscience*, in the modern city.

NOTES

The train of thought represented in this essay owes much to Steve Murphy's remarkable study, *Logiques du dernier Baudelaire*, which I recommend warmly.

1. The compatibility of Baudelaire's primacy with his acknowledgment of Poe as a predecessor exemplifies the paradox of the 'untimeliness' of modernity, which I'll

take up in discussing 'Le Cygne'. (Baudelaire also acknowledged Saint-Beuve as a predecessor.)

2. Baudelaire, 'Exposition universelle 1855', in OC II 579: '*Le beau est toujours bizarre*' (Baudelaire's emphasis).

3. See Gilles Deleuze and Félix Guattari, *A Thousand Plateaus*, trans. Brian Massumi (Minneapolis: University of Minnesota Press, 1987). [*Mille Plateaux* (Paris: Minuit, 1980).]

4. Cf. Gilles Deleuze: 'symptoms are specific signs of a disease but syndromes are units of encounter and crossing that refer to very different causal lineages, variable contexts'. Cited from *Présentation de Sacher-Masoch* (Paris: October 18, 1967) by Steve Murphy, *Logiques du dernier Baudelaire. Lectures du* Spleen de Paris (Paris: Champion, 2003), 494. My translation.

5. Dolf Oehler was the first critic to show convincingly that 'Le Cygne' can be read as an allegory of 1848. See his 'Ein hermetischer Sozialist. Zur Baudelaire-Kontroverse zwischen Walter Benjamin und Bert Brecht', *Diskussion Deutsch*, 26 (December 1975), pp. 569–84, and more generally *Ein Höllensturz der Alten Welt* (Frankfurt: Suhrkamp, 1988), trans. into French by Guy Petitdemange as *Le Spleen contre l'oubli, Juin 1848* (Paris: Payot, 1996).

6. Cf. Deleuze and Guattari, *A Thousand Plateaus*, ch. 14 ('The Striated and the Smooth'), especially pp. 492–9.

7. See OC I 275–6. Since 1869 the letter has been frequently published as a prefatory letter of dedication to the prose poems, although such may or may not have been Baudelaire's intention.

8

E. S. BURT

Baudelaire and intoxicants

Baudelaire devoted one of the two slim volumes he published in his lifetime to the discussion of intoxicants. While references to drugs, alcohol and tobacco were already to be found in *Les Fleurs du Mal* and would continue to dot *Le Spleen de Paris*, it was only with *Les Paradis artificiels* (*The Artificial Paradises*), first published as two articles and then as a volume in 1860, that the poet addressed in a systematic way the question of intoxication and literature. Readers have long puzzled over the rationale for his interest in stimulants. Was Baudelaire's treatise an attempt to justify an indulgence in intoxicants, say by celebrating drugs as enhancing the imagination? Did he aim on the contrary to denounce the use of drugs? These are the motives to which the literature on drugs – already beginning to swell by the mid nineteenth century when Baudelaire wrote – is usually ascribed. But in the case of Baudelaire, neither rationale quite fits.

Let's take the question of Baudelaire's drug use first. To all accounts, Baudelaire appears to have used the stimulants favoured by his century only in moderation. He slightly overstated the case when he boasted in one projected preface to *Les Fleurs du Mal* that his aim was to create a reputation for excess in such matters while remaining strictly sober:

> As chaste as paper, as sober as water, as given to devotion as a communicant, as inoffensive as a victim, I would not be displeased to be taken for a libertine, a drunk, an ungodly man and an assassin.

> [Chaste comme le papier, sobre comme l'eau, porté à la dévotion comme une communiante, inoffensif comme une victime, il ne me déplairait pas de passer pour un débauché, un ivrogne, un impie et un assassin.   (OC I 185)]

However, testimony from his correspondence and contemporaries suggests that he was not far off the mark, and that his use of the drug metaphor has indeed created an unmerited reputation for literal intoxication. Wine he certainly indulged in somewhat, but there is not any evidence of excess.

It is true that Baudelaire worked in a milieu where hashish was used with some regularity. Under the auspices of Joseph Moreau de Tours, a doctor who had written a book on the subject (*Du haschisch et de l'aliénation mentale, études psychologiques*), the Club des Hachischins met and staged its Fantasias, as the drug-séances were called, at the Hotel Pimodan where the poet was in residence. There such writers and artists as Honoré Daumier, Paul Chenavard, Jean Meissonier, Eugène Delacroix, Jean-Jacques Pradier, Gérard de Nerval, Alphonse Karr and Honoré de Balzac partook of the 'green jam', a mixture of extract of cannabis with sugar and spices that was the usual form under which hashish was taken during the middle of the nineteenth century.[1] But according to at least one writer often in attendance, Théophile Gautier, Baudelaire went to the Fantasias rarely and only as a spectator.[2] Gautier may have exaggerated, but scholars are confident that the poet did no more than experiment briefly with hashish.

Baudelaire was more of an adept of opium, and had even a moderate addiction to it at several points. He appears to have begun taking it towards the onset of his losing battle with syphilis, in the late 1840s, to have stopped using it for about five years between 1859 and 1864, and then to have begun again in Belgium, during the final stages of the disease.[3] But opium was for him a medical necessity – at least in the eyes of the doctors of the time. While there were fewer preparations and less of a readiness among doctors to prescribe it in France than in England, opium was the nineteenth-century drug of choice for healing a wide variety of illnesses and conditions. It was prescribed for fretful babies and insomniacs as well as for patients with maladies ranging from the common cold and headache, from gout, rheumatism, stomach cramp, menopause and toothache, to pulmonary infections, cholera, insanity or venereal disease.[4] A few letters and poems testify to Baudelaire's having exploited the psychic effects of the drug, but there is little to suggest that he found those effects sufficiently pleasing to seek them out recreationally. Given the medical reasons for his use, it seems unlikely that Baudelaire wrote the *Paradis artificiels* in an act of self-recrimination for indulgence in what De Quincey called 'The Dark Idol'.

If Baudelaire's point was the praise of a literature inspired by drugs, he went about making it badly. There were writers among the Romantics who celebrated drugs as supplements for the imagination. In France, Senancour and Nodier used opium with the specific purpose of inciting dreams; Gautier made use of his experiences on hashish in several of his tales. In England, the work of writers from De Quincey and Coleridge to Wilkie Collins in one way or another honoured the psychic properties of the drug. But with the exception of a few poems – notably, 'Rêve parisien' and 'Une chambre double' – Baudelaire's work provides little in the way of the splendid visions of an opium-addict or hashish-taker. In a move whose meaning scholars are still debating, he chose to write *against* those artificial paradises produced by the help of intoxicants, most particularly by hashish.

Was Baudelaire's motive then a desire to warn against stimulants? The hypothesis directly contradicts one of his chief aesthetic tenets, namely, that art has no moral purpose and should not be used to teach anything. Why should a poet who was not particularly famous for his rigid morality – six of the *Fleurs du mal* had been censored on moral grounds only a few years before – give up some of the valuable time he might have devoted to writing poetry, to inveigh against drugs? The fact that many readers have found the text too seductive to be persuasive, thinking that his stylish accounts of hashish dreams work against the manifest aim of warning against drug use, is an indication that he might be faithful to his aesthetic principles in the text – a text against drugs that tempts one to take them is not a good teaching text – but it does not help us get any closer to discovering his motive for writing so paradoxically. Why waste time writing about the artificial paradises of the drug-taker if your interest is the artificial paradises of poetry?

The puzzle concerning Baudelaire's motive in writing is reflected in the three textual enigmas of *Les Paradis artificiels*, the first concerning the dedicatee, the second the message, the third the author. Each of these enigmas corresponds to a different section of the work, which in its first appearance, was comprised of three parts (an earlier article, 'Wine and hashish compared as means of multiplying individuality' ['Du vin et du haschisch comparés comme moyens de multiplication de l'individualité'] was added to the volume posthumously by editors).

The first piece, the preface, dedicates the book to a certain, mysterious woman, J. G. F., about whom scholars are divided.[5] They disagree over whether the initials are those of a name (perhaps Juliette Gex-Fagon), or of a woman's attributes, (Jeanne, Gentille Femme or Grande Femme or Grande Féline, Jeune Gentille Femme and so forth) and thus, ultimately over whether the initials belong to a 'real' woman or point in the direction of an ideal, fictional type. Baudelaire did not help matters by desiring the dedication to be 'unintelligible' (OC I 373), and by defiantly stating that 'Besides, it is hardly important that the motive for this dedication be understood' ['Il importe d'ailleurs fort peu que la raison de cette dédicace soit comprise' (OC I 399)]. To understand the enigma of the preface is not to choose between various candidates for a dedicatee, or even to choose between various candidates and a fictional one. It is rather to uncover the stakes for Baudelaire's idea of readers and reading that he should have worked to make the dedication unintelligible and his preferred reader undecidably a real woman or an ideal one.

The second piece, 'The Poem of Hashish', is enigmatic because of the problem already discussed of Baudelaire's message. We can summarise it thus: there is a contradiction between its strategy of argument – eloquent and funny descriptions of experiences on hashish which make the drug seem quite attractive – and its overt message, which is to argue against hashish and possibly opium as perverting the imagination.[6] Baudelaire leaves us uncertain as to whether the text is ultimately to be read as a poetic tract against drugs or an exercise in and theory of poetry as superior intoxicant.

In the third piece of the text, 'An Opium-Eater', the puzzle concerns Baudelaire's strategy in turning over half his book to Thomas De Quincey's *Confessions of an English Opium-eater*. Whatever the point of 'The Poem of Hashish', there is no doubt but that the poet is in a position of authority over his creation. But now his authority is suspect. He is not the author but the translator of the second half of his study on opium. The mystery deepens when we discover that, having decided that the *Confessions* is the definitive work on opium ('The work on opium has been written, and in a manner so dazzling, medical and poetic all at once that I would not dare add anything to it' ['Le travail sur l'opium a été fait, et d'une manière si éclatante, médicale et poétique à la fois, que je n'oserais rien y ajouter' (OC I 403–4)]), Baudelaire then proceeds not only to provide a considerably shortened schematic summary of it, but also to add pieces of his own, acting with far more liberty than was usual even in his century with respect to translations. The reason generally given for the summary – Baudelaire's editor, put off by the bizarreness of De Quincey's digressive text, demanded that Baudelaire shorten it – is not entirely satisfactory, since Baudelaire contradicts himself on his motives, suggesting on the one hand that he shortens against his own desire, and on the other, that De Quincey's text gains by being made less digressive:

> No doubt I will abridge much: De Quincey is essentially digressive . . . In order that the reader may lose nothing of the moving scenes that make up the substance of his volume, the space I dispose of being restricted, I will be obliged, much to my sorrow, to get rid of many highly amusing asides, many exquisite speeches, that have no immediate connection to opium.

> [J'abrégerai sans doute beaucoup: De Quincey est essentiellement digressif . . . Pour que le lecteur ne perde rien des tableaux émouvants qui composent la substance de son volume, l'espace dont je dispose étant restreint, je serai obligé, à mon grand regret, de supprimer bien des hors d'oeuvre très amusants, bien des dissertations exquises, qui n'ont pas directement trait à l'opium.

> (OC I 444]

In the space of two lines, the poet says two different things: I have to abridge because De Quincey is digressive and I have a subject, opium, to present; I have to abridge because my editor won't give me room, and has forced me to cut out juicy details. When Baudelaire adds pieces, he contradicts himself about that strategy too: 'I would not dare add anything' ['je n'oserais rien y ajouter' (OC I 403–4)], 'here and there I have added my personal reflections' ['j'y ai joint, par-ci par-là, mes réflexions personnelles' (OC I 519)]. All of this has led some readers to claim that Baudelaire has not so much translated De Quincey as written a new and brilliant book, whereas others have stated with equal assuredness that the book remains essentially a translation.[7] Again, the question is less to decide whether Baudelaire is the author or the translator of 'An Opium-Eater' than to understand his motive for posing and leaving open the alternative.

It may be that the key to these enigmas lies in the nature of stimulants themselves, as analogies for literature. It is often in terms of mystery or enigma that Baudelaire speaks of them. He calls hashish intoxication 'that mysterious drunkenness' ['cette ivresse mystérieuse' (OC I 407)] and when, in 'La Chambre double,' he tries to summarise the room's aspect under the influence of laudanum, again it is the term 'mystère' that occurs (OC I 281). That mysteriousness is linked to the analogy between drugs and art in the prose poem, 'Mademoiselle Bistouri'. There, the poet describes an encounter with a madwoman who insists against all the poet's protestations that he is a doctor, a dispenser of drugs, and gives him a cigar to smoke and wine to drink while he tries to figure out the 'unhoped for enigma' ['enigme inespérée' (OC I 353)] that her identification of poetry with drugs represents. Baudelaire calls Mlle Bistouri's metaphor for poetry as drug 'enigmatic'. To penetrate further into the enigma, we need to understand what makes the two enterprises analogous enough that one can substitute for the other.

The dominant point they have in common is that both are arts of analogy. Doubling makes the artificial paradises of the one like the artificial paradises of the other.

That the artist must be concerned with analogies is evident enough. Producing a world through the imagination depends on finding an analogy that is at once only an image or substitute, and yet also makes perceptible a hidden wholeness. Because – faced with the fragmentation of everyday life – the analogous world of fiction or poetry can provide us with a totality, the image seems suspect because it is an illusory substitute, and yet beneficial. In drug dreams the freed imagination also substitutes visions for what is. The addict is one for whom the world is impoverished, who is driven to make up for its deficiencies by the drug dream. Such dreams also proceed by analogy, despite their physiological basis. Thus, Baudelaire will insist that the drug dream is 'a magnifying mirror, but only a mirror' ['un miroir grossissant, mais un pur miroir' (OC I 409)], using the familiar notion of the mirror which comes up in discussions of literary representation. Baudelaire is famous for his theory of analogies, set down among other places in the sonnet 'Correspondances', and according to which 'everything, form, movement, number, colour, perfume, in the *spiritual* as well as in the *natural* world is significant, reciprocal, converse, *correspondent*' ['tout, forme, mouvement, nombre, couleur, parfum, dans le *spirituel* comme dans le *naturel* est significatif, réciproque, converse, *correspondant*' (OC II 133)]. It makes sense that Baudelaire would follow up a book of poems, each of which is written according to the thought that everything has an analogy, with a theory of poetry that explores poetry more generally through the analogy of intoxicants. The equivalents give an idea of his poetry, and also make more precise the differences between poetry and drugs.

At first sight, there is nothing particularly new about the analogy between drugs and literature, which is a centuries'-old commonplace reaching back to Plato's *Republic* that sees literature as at once a beneficial, healing drug, and a noxious poison.[8] But Baudelaire has refreshed the parallel, moving away from a presumed likeness between the physical effects of medicine and the spiritual effects of literature on the diseased person to consider the stimulus given the imagination by the psychotropic drug or the poem. Through the 'mysteries of analogy' ['mystères de l'analogie' (OC II 133)], the images of the one will substitute for, and allow us to imagine the images of the other.

Now the analogy between these two arts of analogy is central to the enigmas of the *Paradis artificiels*. A certain intoxicating doubleness of message, dedicatee and author will be mobilised by its means. On the one side, we have said, an analogy substitutes for what is, and as such, is suspect, an illusion or lie with respect to the truth of what is, of nature. But on the other side, the analogy has some advantages over nature in allowing an encompassing view of what otherwise must remain dispersed and fragmentary, present only as confused perceptions. Usually, it is easy enough to distinguish, at least in theory, between something real, the model for an image, and the image itself. We think of a natural flower – rose, hawthorn or tulip – as real, referential, whereas Baudelaire's artificial *Flowers* are images or poems. But in the case of drug-taking and poetry, which is the modelling art of analogy and which the analogous art? The analogy is unstable. According to one pundit, Los Angeles is a city where one has to differentiate between real and false tinsel, and that is more or less what we have here: a Hollywood moment in Baudelaire, where we have to decide whether art is the model of which drug dreams are but an image, or the other way around. Baudelaire suspends us between two equally plausible conceptions of the relation between drugs and art when he makes them analogous. In short, the work's enigmas derive from a problem with the model for the analogy.

One conception works like this. Art is the model for the imagination, and drugs are just the analogue taken from sensuous experience. Art can be viewed as the more fundamental because, unlike drug dreams, which are a function of animal being, it addresses itself to spiritual being. Drugs are a sleazy substitute for art that lead us away from the things of the spirit, while yet giving an idea of what art is all about. Michel Butor, a novelist with interesting things to say about the *Paradis artificiels*, agrees with this notion. He sees it as a text in which Baudelaire teaches us how to read his poetry by means of an analogy with drug dreams. For Butor, Baudelaire's contradictory evaluation of the drug dream makes sense in view of the double evaluation that comes with any analogy: valuable in that it informs us about art, the drug dream dangerously substitutes a sensuously based dream for a spiritually based one.[9]

We can find an example of this conception in 'The Poem of Hashish', where Baudelaire discusses two sorts of dreams, the *natural* dream identified with hashish and perhaps opium, and the *hieroglyphic* dream, in this conception identified with poetry:

> Man's dreams are of two classes. Some, full of his ordinary life, his preoccupations, his desires, his vices, combine more or less bizarrely with the objects glimpsed during the day which have become indiscriminately fixed on to the vast canvas of his memory. Such is the natural dream: it is man himself. But the other sort of dream! The absurd, the unexpected dream, which has no relation to the character, the life and the passions of the sleeper! This hieroglyphic dream, as I will call it, obviously represents the supernatural side of life, and it is precisely because it is absurd that the ancients believed it was divine. Because it cannot be explained by natural causes, they attributed to it a cause exterior to man; and still today . . . there exists a philosophical school that sees in dreams of this sort sometimes a reproach, sometimes advice; in short, a symbolic and moral picture engendered in the very mind of the man who sleeps. It is a dictionary that has to be studied, a language to which only the wise can obtain the key.
>
> In hashish intoxication, there is nothing like that. We do not leave the natural dream.

> [Les rêves de l'homme sont de deux classes. Les uns, pleins de sa vie ordinaire, de ses préoccupations, de ses désirs, de ses vices, se combinent d'une façon plus ou moins bizarre avec les objets entrevus dans la journée, qui se sont indiscrètement fixés sur la vaste toile de sa mémoire. Voilà le rêve naturel; il est l'homme lui-même. Mais l'autre espèce de rêve! Le rêve absurde, imprévu, sans

rapport ni connexion avec le caractère, la vie et les passions du dormeur! Ce rêve, que j'appellerai hiéroglyphique, représente évidemment le côté surnaturel de la vie, et c'est justement parce qu'il est absurde que les anciens l'ont cru divin. Comme il est inexplicable par les causes naturelles, ils lui ont attribué une cause extérieure à l'homme; et encore aujourd'hui . . . il existe une école philosophique qui voit dans les rêves de ce genre tantôt un reproche, tantôt un conseil; en somme, un tableau symbolique et moral, engendré dans l'esprit même de l'homme qui sommeille. C'est un dictionnaire qu'il faut étudier, une langue dont les sages peuvent obtenir la clef.

Dans l'ivresse du hashisch, rien de semblable. Nous ne sortirons pas du rêve naturel. (OC I 408–9)]

If we read this text in conformity with our first conception, it appears that Baudelaire is first criticising the mysteries of the drug dream: they are one drunk's vision arrived at through the combination of experiences by the imagination, and are resolvable by reference to nature, which precedes them. Then the analogue of drugs is set aside, and the differences with poetry allowed to emerge: the latter requires will and discipline, but also accident or inspiration for its production; it is as resistant to, and productive of, explanation as the hieroglyphs of Egypt. Note what Baudelaire's role in finding this analogy would have to be: he would have had to seek the natural, sensuous equivalent (drugs) for a spiritual reality (poetry), constructing his analogy downward, from the idea, which is the reality he wants to get across.

But Baudelaire does not clearly assimilate opium to hashish as productive of natural dreams in the passage, nor equate the hieroglyphic dream with poetry. Indeed, a different construction is possible, in keeping with our revised analogy between drugs and literature, which opposes hashish as the inspiration for natural to opium as the model for hieroglyphic dreams. This time the hypothesis is that the drug dream is the model and art just one in a list of analogous substitutes. Drugs are fundamental to experience because nature is not a plenitude. Man's dissatisfaction with his natural self and his 'filthy dwelling' ['habitacle de fange' (OC I 402)] says that the present lacks something. He has a taste for the infinite that nature does not answer: 'Alas, man's vices contain the proof . . . of his taste for the infinite' ['Hélas! les vices de l'homme contiennent la preuve . . . de son goût de l'infini' (OC I 402)]. If the drug dream is primordial, it is because nature has fallen away, and there are only substitutes.

Here the difference between a recreational drug like hashish, which the user indulges in occasionally, and a medicinal drug like opium, for which the user develops a craving, becomes important, and it is in the light of that difference that the difference between the natural dream associated with the first, and the hieroglyphic dream associated with the second has to be read. Some drugs, hashish among them, point to nature as inadequate because man has a spiritual dimension that is not answered by natural things. Hashish is an additive that stimulates the imagination to recombine what we already know. A means to express humanity's desire for transcendence, the hashish dream sees nature to be lacking with respect to our desire for a spiritual dimension, but it does not negate it entirely. There is a religiosity to hashish which goes along with its ritual aspects and its legendary ability to provide 'an idea of paradise' ['une idée du paradis' (OC I 404)]. It compensates for the failings of nature by a wish for God, who can restore nature to us.

But there are other drugs, like opium, which accept illness, evil, the dropping away of nature itself from under our feet. Its dreams recognise the vacuity of nature and substitute new constructs for nothingness: 'on the breast of darkness, with the imaginary materials of the brain, you build . . . cities and temples that surpass Babylon and Hekatompylos in splendor' ['tu bâtis sur le sein des ténèbres, avec les matériaux imaginaires du cerveau . . . des cités et des temples qui dépassent en splendeur Babylone et Hekatompylos' (OC I 442)]. The cravings of opium are related to a need for substitutes that do not replace what is, but that in succeeding one another repeatedly try to make up for the lack of a Mother Nature, pillowing us instead upon the breast of darkness. The opium addict is an addict of substitutes that substitute for other substitutes. Baudelaire's poem 'Enivrez-vous', which does not just command us to get drunk but also states as a fact that man has always to deal in intoxicants ('one has always to be drunk' ['il faut toujours être ivre']), starts a list of such substitutes: 'with wine, with poetry, with virtue, as you please' (PP 85) ['de vin, de poésie, ou de vertu, à votre guise' (OC I 337)].

A second implication of this conception that makes drugs the universal and poetry the analogue is that the latter will have the character of each drug it imitates. The analogue for hashish is imaginative poetry, which also believes in nature. When Baudelaire criticises the hashish dream, he is also criticising poetry of that sort – including his own. The prose versions of *Les Fleurs du Mal* scattered throughout 'The Poem of Hashish' are cases in point of an attempt on Baudelaire's part to demystify poetry as seductive.[10] The cult of the author, the idolatry of beauty, the temple and religion of art as spiritual exercise give an idea of the transcendent aims of the hashish dream. But imaginative poetry also reinstalls all the values that understanding nature as absence puts into question. Imaginative art believes in the sensuous form as the expression of the idea and in the power of the poet as maker of forms to depict the idea as what is. It claims to show us the supernatural, while actually getting its ideas of the supernatural from nature. Note that to find this analogy, the artist has not started with an idea of poetry that he wants to get across through a physical equivalent; instead, he has a first equivalent of the universal drug experience, hashish, and is now simply looking in another vocabulary for another equivalent. His question is: what is the equivalent in the dictionary of art for hashish in the dictionary of drugs? He exchanges a term not for a referent but for another term.

Opium differs from hashish and will need a different poetry as its analogue. Again, the poet has a term in one realm for which he needs to find an equivalent in another. He looks for a poetry that writes out of the abyss, builds cities over the void, recalls the long list of substitutes man has posited one after another. But what poetry comes to us like the hieroglyphic dreams of opium? The fact that Baudelaire does not cite his own poetry for examples in discussing opium but has recourse to De Quincey's *Confessions* suggests that the poetry analogous to opium comes to him differently, from the outside, not from his own imagination. So here we must look to what De Quincey says about opium to get an idea of the writing that would be its analogue.

De Quincey notes that opium acts on the memory to recover traces of past substitutes. One term he uses to describe those substitutes is palimpsest. A palimpsest is a parchment that has been used, then erased, and used again; on it, texts succeed one another. But sometimes the process can be reversed, the second writing can be effaced and the first can be made to reappear. That is what happens under the influence of opium. The opium dream seeks out the forgotten texts and brings them into consciousness. It makes available substitution on substitution, where there never was a nature for which the first text substitutes. It is concerned with the materiality of those substitutes – the parchment that supports the traces, the traces themselves (OC I 505–6). De Quincey's description tells us what the art must be like. It must operate in a void, moving from analogy to analogy, with each text providing an equivalent of an original scene of the loss of nature or, as Baudelaire makes De Quincey say 'arms of children forever torn from their mothers' necks, lips of children forever separated from their sisters' kisses' ['bras d'enfants arrachés à tout jamais du cou de leurs mères, lèvres d'enfants séparées à jamais des baisers de leurs soeurs' (OC I 507)].

Baudelaire participates in the art he will ultimately name as the equivalent of opium in 'An Opium-Eater': it is the art of translation. A translator does not invent by calling upon the imagination. Instead, he looks for the equivalent in another language of a substitute to be found in a first language. He seeks a substitute for a substitute, and moves from language to language without ever going outside substitution. An art of translation is a demystifying art. Translation is not a divine mystery, an ideal, spiritual exercise, but a lowly exercise in finding material equivalents.[11] It is the linguistic equivalent of the hieroglyphic dreams of opium, for it moves from dictionary to dictionary without ever moving to a referent.

But notice that this second art is called up by a demand in the analogy itself. It is an art that *must* exist because analogy demands that there be an equivalent for everything, that everything be translatable. Baudelaire has to find a poetic equivalent for opium's palimpsestic memory. He does that by a translation that is at once just a search for an equivalent term, and an invention of a new definition of poetry as translation:

> And what is a poet . . . if not a translator, a decipherer? In excellent poets, there is no metaphor, comparison or epithet that is not a mathematically exact adaptation to the current circumstances, because these comparisons, metaphors and epithets are drawn from the inexhaustible well of *universal analogy*, and they cannot be drawn from anywhere else.

> [Or qu'est-ce qu'un poète . . . si ce n'est un traducteur, un déchiffreur? Chez les excellents poètes, il n'y a pas de métaphore, de comparaison ou d'epithète qui ne soit d'une adaptation mathématiquement exacte dans la circonstance actuelle, parce que ces comparaisons, ces métaphores et ces epithètes sont puisées dans l'inépuisable fonds de *l'universelle analogie*, et qu'elles ne peuvent être puisées ailleurs. (OC II 133)]

If, where it is a choice of drugs, Baudelaire opts for poetry and the linguistic artefact rather than opium or hashish, it is because he prefers lucidity about substitutes in his substitutes.

For Baudelaire, analogies always have a double source: a source in nature and a source in language, in forests and in 'forests of symbols' ['forêts de symboles' (OC I 11)]. It thus makes sense that Baudelaire's text on intoxicants be dedicated to a reader undecidably real *and* ideal, and that its message be, undecidably, a celebration of beauty *and* a denunciation of that aesthetics in the name of a poetics valorising translation and the material equivalent.

The poet works with analogies, and it seems safe to say that Baudelaire could have written the whole of the *Paradis artificiels* without ever having tasted any drug but poetry, and still have managed to tell us much about intoxication. With the help of analogy, poetry is always seeing double. And yet, without the development in the nineteenth century of a vocabulary on drugs owed to descriptions of the drug experience like De Quincey's, Baudelaire might not have managed his resounding critique of idealism in poetry, nor, in giving the name of translation to the poet's activity, given us the thorough-going idea of that art that we get from 'An Opium-Eater'. It is by way of his analysis of the intoxicants that are analogies that he recognised within his own poetry a tendency towards sensualist idealism and began to develop a distinctly modern theory of poetry as material substitution.

NOTES

1. Claude Pichois and Robert Kopp, 'Baudelaire et le Haschisch: Expérience et Documentation', *Revue des Sciences Humaines*, 127 (July–September 1967), pp. 467–76.
2. Théophile Gautier, *Baudelaire*, ed. Claude-Marie Senninger (Paris: Klincksieck, 1986), p. 155.
3. Claude Pichois and Robert Kopp. 'Baudelaire et l'opium: Une enquête à reprendre', *Europe*, 45, 456–7 (April–May 1967), pp. 61–78.
4. For an account of opium in England, see Virginia Berridge and Griffith Edwards, *Opium and the People: Opiate Use in Nineteenth-Century England* (New Haven: Yale University Press, 1987). No similarly exhaustive treatment exists for France.
5. See the exchanges in the *Bulletin Baudelairien* between Louis Levionnois ('De la dédicataire des *Paradis artificiels*', 12 (winter 1977), pp. 3–18), Nicolae Babuts ('Baudelaire et J. G. F.', 4 (winter 1979), pp. 3–6) and Christian Moncel ('La dédicataire des *Paradis artificiels* est-elle *Une Femme Imaginaire?*', 14 (winter 1979), pp. 6–9). See also Henri Lecaye, *Le Secret de Baudelaire* (Paris: Jean Michel Place, 1991).
6. Among the texts that discuss this central contradiction: Claire Lyu, '"High" Poetics: Baudelaire's "Le Poème du haschisch"', *Modern Language Notes*, 109 (September 1994), pp. 698–740; Max Milner, *L'Imaginaire des drogues: De Thomas De Quincey à Henri Michaux* (Paris: Gallimard, 2000); Maurice Saillat, 'Baudelaire et l'épreuve des excitants', in *Sur la route de Narcisse* (Paris: Mercure de France, 1958), pp. 97–132; Alexandra K. Wettlaufer, 'Paradise Regained: The Flâneur, the Badaud, and the Aesthetics of Artistic Reception in "Le Poème du hashisch"', *Nineteenth-Century French Studies*, 24, 3–4 (spring–summer 1996), pp. 388–97; Joshua Wilner, *Feeding on Infinity: Readings in the Romantic Rhetoric of Internalization* (Baltimore: Johns Hopkins University Press, 2000).
7. See for instance, Alan Astro, 'Allegory of Translation in Baudelaire's *Un Mangeur d'opium*', *Nineteenth-century French Studies*, 18, 1–2 (fall–winter 1989–90), pp. 165–171; Emily Salines, 'The Opium Landscape in Translation: Baudelaire's *Un Mangeur d'opium* and De Quincey's Autobiographical Writings', *New Comparison*, 21 (spring 1996), pp. 22–39; Michèle Stauble-Lipman Wulf's discussion in *Un Mangeur d'opium*, in *Etudes baudelairiennes*, vols. VI–VII (Neuchâtel: A la Baconnière, 1976).
8. For an analysis of the Platonic use of the analogy between drugs and literature, see Jacques Derrida, 'La Pharmacie de Platon', in *La Dissémination* (Paris: Seuil, 1972), pp. 71–197. See also his 'La Rhétorique de la drogue', in *Points de Suspension* (Paris: Galilée, 1992), pp. 241–68.
9. Michel Butor, 'Les Paradis Artificiels', in *Essais sur les modernes* (Paris: Les Editions de Minuit, 1960), pp. 7–15.
10. For a discussion of Baudelaire's demystification of the aesthetics of *Les Fleurs* in his prose poems see Barbara Johnson, *Défigurations du langage poétique: la seconde révolution baudelairienne* (Paris: Flammarion, 1979). On the question of whether *Les Paradis artificiels* looks backward to the aesthetics of verse poetry,

or forward to the aesthetics of prose poetry, see Robert Guiette, 'Des *Paradis artificiels* aux *Petits poèmes en prose*', in *Etudes baudelairiennes, Hommage à W. T. Bandy*, vol. III (Neuchâtel: A la Baconnière, 1973), pp. 178–84.

11. See Walter Benjamin, 'The Task of the Translator', in *Illuminations* (New York: Schocken Books, 1969), pp. 69–82. For a text that reads the consequences of the art of translation for the Baudelairean symbol in *Les Fleurs du Mal*, see Paul de Man, 'Anthropomorphism and Trope in the Lyric', in *The Rhetoric of Romanticism* (New York: Columbia University Press, 1984), pp. 239–62.

9

J. A. HIDDLESTON

Art and its representation

Baudelaire was the most visual of French nineteenth-century poets. His professed aim was to 'glorify the cult of images (my great, unique and primitive passion)' ['glorifier le culte des images (ma grande, mon unique, ma primitive passion)' (OC I 701)]. Imagery of the most original and disconcerting kind is central to his poetic practice, whether in the verse of *Les Fleurs du Mal* or the prose poetry of *Le Spleen de Paris*. His tendency is to favour the concrete notation as against the abstract, so that the emotions of happiness, grief or longing are expressed not through sentiment or the cold abstractions of an outmoded Romantic rhetoric, but through parallels between the physical and the mental worlds, through what T. S. Eliot was to call 'objective correlatives'. In his view, poetry and indeed all modern art was an 'evocative magic' ['sorcellerie évocatoire' (OC II 118)], 'a suggestive magic containing both object and subject, the world beyond the artist and the artist himself' ['une magie suggestive contenant à la fois l'objet et le sujet, le monde extérieur à l'artiste et l'artiste lui-même' (OC II 598)]. Baudelaire's similes and metaphors are never weak or humdrum; they spring dramatically into life with a physicality so powerful as to give an acute sense of the tactile, and because the gap within the figure, between the tenor and the vehicle, is so great as to produce a creative explosion in the mind of the reader. It was Jules Laforgue who first drew attention to these enormous comparisons,[1] these 'yankee' similes which he thought reminiscent of the *Song of Songs*, such as 'Thy temples are like a piece of pomegranate within thy locks'. It is one thing to state that mankind is wracked by sensual appetite, but quite another to evoke the 'furtive pleasure . . . / A shrivelled orange that we squeeze and press' (FM 5) ['plaisir clandestin / Que nous pressons bien fort comme une vieille orange' (OC I 5)]. Other poems portray a heart 'bruised like a softened peach' (FM 201) ['meurtri comme une pêche' (OC I 99)], a woman's bosom that is 'a fine armoire' (FM 107) ['une belle armoire' (OC I 52)], or eyes 'illuminated like boutiques' (FM 53) ['illuminés ainsi que des boutiques' (OC I 27)].

That a poet with such a powerful and original visual imagination should be profoundly influenced by great painting in his poetry is in no way surprising. Many of the *Fleurs du Mal* are 'transpositions d'art', a kind of sympathetic criticism which exemplifies his view in *Le Salon de 1846* that the best criticism might be a sonnet or an elegy (OC II 418), a suggestive criticism based on 'the sum of ideas or reveries' ['la somme d'idées ou de rêveries' (OC II 579)] that a work has brought into his mind. 'Bohémiens en voyage' 'Duellum', 'Le Masque', 'Une gravure fantastique', 'Le Jeu', 'Sur *Le Tasse en prison*', 'Don Juan aux enfers' all have as their point of departure a painting or drawing, and the titles of many of the prose poems have the immediacy and raciness of the captions of caricatures: 'Un plaisant', 'Chacun sa chimère', 'Enivrez-vous', 'Déjà!', 'Laquelle est la vraie?', 'Perte d'auréole'. The early positioning of 'Les Phares' in *Les Fleurs du Mal* is a clear indication of the importance of the plastic arts in Baudelaire's mental universe. The poem comprises eleven quatrains, eight of which define in a highly condensed vignette the vision expressed by painters considered to be beacons for the rest of mankind: Rubens, da Vinci, Rembrandt, Michelangelo, Puget, Watteau, Goya and Delacroix. There has been much discussion of the choice of artists and the order in which they appear in the poem, but what interests us most is that all of them represent a dualistic view of mankind, torn between its rootedness in time and space and an overpowering aspiration towards an ideal state, the 'aspiration to the infinite' ['aspiration vers l'infini' (OC II 421)] which Baudelaire sees as an essential part of an autumnal or crepuscular Christianity whose most poignant expression lies in Romanticism. It is that 'universal suffering' ['douleur universelle' (OC II 436)], what Laforgue was later to call 'l'universel *lamasabaktani*',[2] that is expressed in the last quatrain of the poem:

> For it is truly, Lord, best witness in the world
> That we might give to you of human dignity,
> This ardent sob that rolls onward from age to age
> And comes to die in meeting your eternity!
>
> (FM 25)

> [Car c'est vraiment, Seigneur, le meilleur témoignage
> Que nous puissions donner de notre dignité
> Que cet ardent sanglot qui roule d'âge en âge
> Et vient mourir au bord de votre éternité!
>
> (OC I 14)]

These artists are beacons because, consciously or unconsciously, their works bear witness to the fundamental truth of Christianity that Baudelaire never relinquished: the doctrine of original sin and the fall of man through his first disobedience in the Garden of Eden. It is this doctrine that explains man's position in society and time. In spite of his acute sense of the relative, and the importance of what he calls the morality of the age (OC II 421), Baudelaire's view of human nature is, in the last analysis, static, and popular notions of progress are dismissed as stemming from a superficial ideology based upon eighteenth-century rationalism and mercantilist politics, incompatible with the dual nature of man and the lived experience of his fallen state.

Delacroix was, of course, the painter of all time whom Baudelaire most admired and whose painterly universe most resembled the one he created in his poetry, so much so that he is at pains to have the painter subscribe to the doctrine of original sin on the flimsiest of evidence. In the obituary essay of 1863 he ascribes to Delacroix the confession that as a child he had been a monster, and from this he is able to conclude that the painter adhered to the Catholic idea (OC II 767), which is Baudelaire's shorthand for original sin. There is little evidence in Delacroix's *Journal* that he held such a belief; indeed, it seems much more likely that he was, if anything, much nearer to the minimal deism of a Voltaire. Baudelaire's sleight of hand is, however, confined to this one instance. He had no need to distort what he found in Delacroix to make it conform to his own preconceptions. As we can with Poe, Flaubert, Laclos and Maturin, we cannot speak of a direct influence; rather he recognised himself in his great contemporary and saw in Delacroix's paintings the counterpart of his own poetry. Mary Magdalene, Medea, Sardanapalus, the Algerian women, the grief-smitten figures in his *Pietà*, Dante and Virgil, even the victorious crusaders entering Constantinople, and indeed the whole cortege of biblical, literary and historical figures who people Delacroix's passion-filled canvases, are all marked by the same poignant and unmistakable yearning that dominates *Les Fleurs du Mal*. Delacroix's figures are eminently Baudelairean, and although he is reported to have been irritated by the poet's insistence on the religious dimension of his works, there is little evidence that any significant distortion took place, except perhaps in *Ovid among the Scythians* in which the exile of the Roman poet amid a barbarous and uncultured race in a remote part of the Roman empire is Christianised by Baudelaire to represent the exile of the soul in the material world.

Baudelaire's interpretation of the enigmatic *Mary Magdalene in the Wilderness* does much to clarify a work that puzzled its contemporaries, who were uncertain if this simple head was that of a woman dreaming, sleeping, or who has just died. Baudelaire goes to the heart of the work and its ambiguities, declaring that this mysterious Magdalene is 'so supernaturally lovely that we do not know if she carries the glory of death or is beautified by the swoon of divine love' ['si surnaturellement belle qu'on ne sait si elle est auréolée par la mort, ou embellie par les pâmoisons de l'amour divin' (OC II 593)]. His interpretation brings out the ambiguities of life, death and divine love, depicted not as abstractions but as an overwhelming physical sensation in which the erotic element is barely concealed. It is entirely compatible with Baudelaire's own mental universe in which the anguish of spleen and the desire for spiritual elevation are presented not as the elegant otherworldliness of the Romantic aesthete, as with Chateaubriand's René or Ary Scheffer's chocolate-box clichés of Saint Augustine and his mother Saint Monica, but as a state of nerves, rooted in the physical being, in the physiology. It is not for nothing that Baudelaire speaks more of 'spleen' than of 'ennui', for what is spleen but a pathological experience of man's fallen condition? So the interpretation fits Baudelaire's world but it is also relevant to Magdalene herself, whose aberrations before becoming a disciple have been well rehearsed and of which Delacroix must have been well aware.

It seems odd that Baudelaire should have had so little to say about Delacroix's most extravagantly Romantic creation, *The Death of Sardanapalus*, which has elements in common with *Magdalene*. His enthusiasm is clear in his exclamation on seeing it again in 1861: 'Seeing the *Sardanapalus* again is like rediscovering youth' ['Le *Sardanapale* revu, c'est la jeunesse retrouvée' (OC II 734)]. Inspired by the account of Diodorus of Sicily and Byron's tragedy, published in 1821, this immense canvas, some four metres by five, depicts the death of the decadent Assyrian ruler Sardanapalus, of which Delacroix gives the following description in the *Salon* of 1827:

> The rebels besieged him in his palace . . . Lying on a superb bed, upon an immense pyre, Sardanapalus gives the order to his eunuchs and palace officials to cut the throats of his wives, his pages, even his horses and his favourite dogs; nothing that had served his pleasures should survive him.

> [Les révoltés l'assiègèrent dans son palais . . . Couché sur un lit superbe, au sommet d'un immense bûcher, Sardanapale donne l'ordre à ses eunuques et aux officiers du palais, d'égorger ses femmes, ses pages, jusqu'à ses chevaux et ses chiens favoris; aucun des objets qui auraient servi à ses plaisirs ne devait lui survivre.][3]

The painting shows the destruction before the funeral pyre is set alight, with the rebels breaking through the walls of the palace. The chaotic scene, structured by colour mass rather than the realistic distribution of objects and bodies in space, comprises the slaughter of a horse, a maidservant who has hanged herself, naked concubines being run through by swords they seem half to embrace, urns spilling forth their treasure of gold and silver, and dominating the whole the recumbent, impassive figure of the decadent king himself, surveying with aristocratic indifference the carnage in which he also is about to be engulfed. Clearly, Baudelaire would have admired the turbulence, the orientalism and the eroticism of some of the postures, which are all features of his own poetry. The ambiguity of love, violence, and death is nowhere more disturbing than in the macabrely sadistic 'Une martyre', which depicts a woman's body on a sumptuous bed and her head resting upon a table like a ranunculus, a literal flower of evil. The implication of the poem is that sadism, like the murderous imagination of Lady Macbeth, that 'soul confirmed in crime' (FM 39) ['âme puissante au crime' (OC I 22)], denotes a powerful and frustrated spirituality which is misdirected downwards into the physical and the sensual. Sardanapalus is profoundly Baudelairean in that he resembles the cruel princes of 'Spleen' and 'Une mort héroïque', and like the poet himself he combines a Hamlet-like sense of futility with the temptation of suicide and the stoical disdain of the dandy.

In both of these paintings there is a strong presence of the bizarre which forms an essential element of Baudelaire's aesthetic. The belief that *beauty is always bizarre* ['*Le beau est toujours bizarre*' (OC II 578)] is central to *Exposition universelle (1855)*. To be convinced of this, says Baudelaire, reverse the proposition and try to think of the beautiful as banal. In *Mary Magdalene in the Wilderness* the bizarre lies in the enigmatic nature of the painting, the suppression of context, situation or locus of the seemingly anonymous head that has something of the simplicity of a study. How do we recognise Magdalene in this sleeping or dying figure, what is she doing, where is she, what significance are we to give to the blue patch of paint, the 'quelque chose de bleu' (OC II 354) that Baudelaire identifies in the top right-hand corner of the canvas and that seems to suggest 'a door opening on infinity' ['une porte ouverte sur l'infini' (OC II 653)]? In *Sardanapalus* the bizarre lies in its unreadability, in the distorted, steeply rising perspective culminating high in the canvas in the head of the king, and in the chaotic pell-mell of the action that fills unnaturalistically every centimetre of the surface.

In his commentaries Baudelaire dwells more on the sense of strangeness than on the narrative of a work. He does not describe or recount, but limits himself to a sensual impression or a physical aspect of the painting that leads to its specificity, to what makes it *sui generis*. In *Jacob Wrestling with the Angel* he confines his comments to the materiality of the mural, and of the *Pietà* in the church of Saint-Denis du Saint-Sacrement, after a brief mention of the Virgin Mary and the 'fantastic simplicity' ['simplicité fantastique' (OC II 435)] of the extraordinary background, he emphasises the colour in this 'cruel and ferocious wretchedness, for which the dark green of hope barely compensates' ['sanglante et farouche désolation, à peine compensée par le vert sombre de l'espérance'], adding that Delacroix's talent is perfectly suited to the Christian religion, that 'religion of universal suffering' ['religion de la douleur universelle' (OC II 436)], which he is able to express in his own manner, independent of the taste and conventions of the time. The implication is that the work would not please the aesthetic conservatives, some of whom indeed thought it unsuitable for a church and even an insult to religion.

The painting to which Baudelaire devotes the most space in 1846 is the luminous and alluring *Women of Algiers in Their Apartment*, born of Delacroix's visit to Morocco in 1832. Many commentators have identified a tranquillity and documentary realism most unlike what we find in his other works. Pierre Daix calls it 'the Realist painting *par excellence*' ['la toile réaliste par excellence'].[4] Typically, Baudelaire's view of Delacroix's 'prettiest and most flowery canvas' ['tableau le plus coquet et le plus fleuri' (OC II 440)] is alert to its melancholy, poetry and suggestive qualities; he identifies 'an indefinable high perfume from a den of iniquity that guides us promptly enough to the bottomless limbo of sadness' ['je ne sais quel haut parfum de mauvais lieu qui nous guide assez vite vers les limbes insondés de la tristesse']. For him the women, whose beauty is inward ['intérieure'], seem smitten less by illness than by moral suffering ['la douleur morale']. Nor does he dwell on the documentary elements in the work, but stresses the sensuality which they connote, which in turn gives on to a quasi-metaphysical yearning, the limbo of Romantic ennui which is the source of their illness and inner beauty. His brief paragraph is a discreet lesson in how to read the painting, a means of setting us, as spectators, on a journey of discovery which we will have to make for ourselves. Responsive to this prompting, we will become aware of the suggestive depth of the mirror, the gleaming silver vessels, the recess behind the curtain, the half-open door, the concealed window which is the source of light and the stealthy gait of the black servant, which serves to emphasise the immobility of the women, with the result that every detail of this so-called Realist work is morally eloquent of the drama it contains.

Baudelaire is particularly sensitive to the dramatic power of gesture in Delacroix: the outstretched arms of the Virgin in *Pietà*, the effortless resilience of the angel in *Jacob Wrestling with the Angel*, the animal-like movement of Juliet's neck, the kneeling woman in the foreground of the *Entry of the Crusaders into Constantinople* and the languor of Sardanapalus and Ovid, to which one could add Dante's arm raised in terror in *The Barque of Dante*, the furtive twist of Medea's body to see if she is observed in the slaughter of her children. All these are part of the theatrical drama of the works, and all escape the clichés and commonplaces of the theatre that Baudelaire mocks in the *Salon de 1846*.

Another quality that Baudelaire admires in his 'lighthouses' is his 'love of what is *large*' ['amour du *grand*' (OC II 646)], which he understands in both a physical and moral sense. He castigates Meissonier for his taste for the small ['goût du petit' (OC II 612)] and for creating fleas ['puces'] rather than full-sized figures. The much-despised Vernet, the greatest, alongside Ary Scheffer, of Baudelaire's 'bêtes noires', is said to create 'world-sized Meissonniers' ['des Meissonier grands comme le monde' (OC II 470)] in spite of the ample dimensions of his battle scenes, for 'grandeur' must go with unity and concentration, and Vernet is guilty of fragmenting his vast tableaux into isolated incidents with diminutive figures whose activity lacks movement and drama. One need only compare his *Battle of Jemappes* with Delacroix's magnificent battles of *Taillebourg* or *Poitiers*, which though considerably smaller in dimension have greater drama and sense of grandeur. So 'le grand' is to be understood above all in a moral sense.

Baudelaire is not interested in an art of circumstance, in genre or landscape painting. He firmly subscribes to the traditional hierarchy of genres with religious, historical and literary subjects at the top. Landscape for its own sake is without interest, and he refuses to 'be moved by sanctified vegetables' ['s'attendrir sur les légumes sanctifiés' (C I 248)], for great art should fundamentally be a statement of what it is to be a human being; it should record the travailing of a soul, a spiritual adventure. Here again, we understand why Delacroix was Baudelaire's ideal painter, since he sought his subject-matter in religion and history, in the myths and literary works of the past and present: in Christianity, Ovid, Dante, Tasso, Shakespeare, Goethe, Scott, Byron; and also in great moments in history: the death of Marcus Aurelius, the crusaders in Constantinople, the battles of Taillebourg or Poitiers, scenes from the Revolution of 1789, Liberty leading the people in the revolution of 1830.

Although he could admire the technical expertise of the school of art for art's sake, he was hostile to their emotional detachment and their obsession with matters of form. In *L'Ecole païenne* (*The Pagan School*) of 1852 he proclaims that 'the immoderate love of form leads to monstrous and unknown disorders' ['le goût immodéré de la forme pousse à des désordres monstrueux et inconnus' (OC II 48)], and elsewhere that 'the puerile utopia of the school of *art for art's sake*, by excluding morality and often passion itself, was necessarily sterile' ['la puérile utopie de l'école de l'*art pour l'art*, en excluant la morale, et souvent même la passion, était nécessairement stérile' (OC II 26)]. Though he mocked their predilection for 'pagan' themes, it was not that the choice of ancient subjects was per se an error, but rather the slavish copying of a form and manner that was not appropriate to the modern period. The famous cry: '*Who will set us free from the Greeks and Romans?*' ['*Qui nous délivrera des Grecs et des Romains?*' (OC II 556)], with which Baudelaire fully sympathised, was aimed at those artists who did not trust their own imagination and were not in tune with the spirit of their own times. After all, Delacroix produced great paintings whose subject-matter was taken from the ancient world and Baudelaire never thought of rejecting them on that ground alone. But this was because Delacroix had certain qualities essential to successful nineteenth-century painting.

The most important quality was *naïveté*, which must be understood in its etymological sense of *nativus*, that which is native or inborn in the artist's temperament. This is no spontaneous outpouring of emotion made fashionable in the flowing style ['*style coulant*' (OC II 105)] of some early Romantics, nor is it to be equated to the rampant individualism of the artistic anarchist. On the contrary, it implies scrupulous self-knowledge and an ability to conquer one's own style and speak with one's own voice. *Naïveté* demands the sincere expression of temperament and the domination of temperament over subject-matter. It requires faith in one's own powers, for great art, like great poetry, 'is essentially *stupid*, it *believes*' ['est essentiellement *bête*, elle *croit*' (OC II 11)]. It is related to strength and will-power, for *naïveté* in a weak temperament would lack direction and drive. In the *Salon de 1859* naivety and temperament are linked to imagination, the queen of faculties, despised by classical thinkers, but given a privileged place by such predecessors of Baudelaire as Rousseau and Madame de Staël. It is imagination that presides over the other faculties: 'imagination arouses them, sending them into combat' ['elle les excite, elle les envoie au combat' (OC II 620)] not just in the arts but in all areas of human activity, in mathematics, science and military strategy. The truly creative faculty, it corresponds, moreover, to the spiritual and religious dimensions: 'it is positively related to the infinite' ['elle est positivement apparentée avec l'infini' (OC II 621)], replacing the mundane observations of analysis by the deeper intimations of supernaturalism ['surnaturalisme']. It is imagination that presides over analogy and metaphor, it teaches the moral implications of colour, it creates a new world ['un monde neuf']. Fantasy is dangerous, like all excessive freedom, and is limited to the individual, whereas, by only the appearance of a paradox, *naïveté* combined with imagination reaches a domain of the mind where individualism and the surface vicissitudes of personal experience are left behind and give access to what is of universal significance, because grounded in the verities of the human condition and the archetypal structures of the human mind.

This focus on the indissolubility of the universal and the particular is at the heart of Baudelaire's commitment to colourists as opposed to draughtsmen, determining his espousal of Rubens, Rembrandt and Delacroix, and his rejection of the tradition of Raphaël that culminates in Ingres. The latter produces geometers and positivists, bent on the exact reproduction of form and outline, whereas the colourist is attentive to the vibrancy of atmosphere and the predominance of colour over contour. The colourist appears to see the world through a magnifying glass, with the result that the *touche* or brush-mark of the artist 'will always eat up the line' ['mangera toujours la ligne' (OC II 426)]. In great colourists there is no vacuum, and rarely a sense of stasis. Contrast the even, monochrome background of Ingres' *Grande Odalisque* with the turbulence of Delacroix's *Pietà* or *Hamlet and Horatio in the Graveyard*. Contrast Ingres' impeccably neat curtains with the flying draperies ['draperies voltigeantes' (OC II 434)] of the *Abduction of Rebecca* or *The Crusaders at Constantinople*. For Baudelaire, colour is not documentary, and certainly not secondary, but a vital part of the drama of the work, its function being primarily expressive. Thus the presence of contrasting green and red that he observes time and again in Delacroix shows his understanding of a characteristic technique of the painter, no doubt arrived at intuitively but which confirms Chevreul's thesis in *De la loi du contraste simultané des couleurs* of 1839 which demonstrates that the juxtaposition of contrasting colours serves to intensify them, making for example the green greener and the red redder, or as Baudelaire has it 'the red sings the glory of the green' ['le rouge chante la gloire du vert' (OC II 422)].

But Baudelaire espouses colourism not just because it is more natural, faithful to empirical observation and dramatic, but because its effect is to universalise the subject-matter. For all his expertise, the draughtsman with his quasi-photographic representation appears to give little beyond what is there; his art is assertive, no doubt, but not suggestive, involving the eye but not the imagination. The colourist paints from memory, suppressing accessory detail. This together with the vagueness of outline has the effect of universalising the subject-matter, so that, although his work may be astoundingly original, it in its turn speaks to the memory of the spectator, who experiences at the same time an intense sense of recognition. The work of the colourist creates a powerful sense of *déjà vu* which causes us as spectators to feel we are participating in the creative process, by gaining access to that region of experience which is the archetypal fund of the imagination. The parallel with Baudelaire's poetry is plain to see; for faced with one of his far-fetched comparisons ['comparaisons énormes'] the reader is astounded at once by the boldness of the figure and by its appositeness which we recognise from our own affective, sensual, memory.

The fundamental ingredients of Romanticism and modern art are then 'intimacy, spirituality, colour, aspiration to the infinite' ['intimité, spiritualité, couleur, aspiration vers l'infini' (OC II 421)]; but in the final paragraphs of the *Salons* of 1845 and 1846, Baudelaire envisages an extension of this modernity to encompass scenes from the contemporary city. He is looking for a painter who will extract the epic side of modern life and show the French how they are 'great and poetic in our ties and polished boots' ['grands et poétiques dans nos cravates et nos bottes vernies' (OC II 407)]. It is the epic quality based on the energy, will-power and heroism he admired in Balzac that Baudelaire wishes to see applied to Parisian life. There is perhaps also a veiled appeal to Delacroix to modernise his subject matter, already modern in the sense of the morality of the age ['la morale du siècle']. If this is indeed a crepuscular epoch as the prevailing preoccupation with real and metaphorical sunsets implies, why do we not show men in the funereal black coat, 'the outer husk of the modern hero' ['la pelure du héros moderne'], expression not just of universal equality, but of the public soul which resembles a procession of undertakers – 'We are all celebrating some burial or other' ['Nous célébrons tous quelque enterrement' (OC II 494)]?

But this heroism of modern life is never realised in any painter. True, in *The Concert in the Tuileries*, Manet, who knew Baudelaire well, did depict people in modern dress, but with no sense of heroism or Balzacian energy. On the contrary, what we find is elegance, leisure, boredom even, in a static and very unDelacroix-like canvas. Baudelaire's failure to recognise the genius of Manet is one of the great enigmas of nineteenth-century culture. In a letter of May 1865 he writes damningly to his friend: *'you are merely the first in the decrepitude of your art'* [*'vous n'êtes que le premier dans la décrépitude de votre art'* (C II 497)]. It is possible that Manet's youth (he was thirty-three at the time and still at the outset of his career with a reputation to make), Baudelaire's failing health and his absence in Brussels kept him distant both physically and morally from Manet's work, which in any case, in spite of certain 'Baudelairean' qualities, was very different from Delacroix's. Crucially, his famous *Déjeuner sur l'herbe* and *Olympia* contained a discordant intertextual irony which Baudelaire may well have thought unbefitting the dignity of the oil on canvas. It is one thing to debunk a great work of the past in a caricature or its generic equivalent in literature, the prose poem as conceived by Baudelaire, but it is quite another to express such stridency in the high art of the oil painting or the verse poem. It is conceivable that the *décrépitude* of Manet's art had much to do with the impression of stasis it conveyed, the presence of the *bizarre* unrelieved by the love of the large ['l'amour du grand'], and the comparative lack of vibrancy, but perhaps more than anything Manet was guilty of confusing the specific qualities of one art form with those of another, of creating a mismatch between medium and content.

The high seriousness of Baudelaire's view of art did not leave him indifferent to the virtues and resources of laughter and caricature. As early as the

1840s he was planning a full-blown study which eventually took the modest form of three essays, one on laughter and two on caricature. The one on laughter takes the traditional view that laughter springs from the pride of the laugher who thinks himself superior to his victim, but gives it an original twist by linking laughter to original sin. Why does the melodrama villain cackle as he lures the unsuspecting innocent into his trap? Out of superiority over his guileless victim no doubt, but also because his convulsions reveal his dual nature, his fallen condition, superior in intellect but irremediably removed from the true and the good. Laughter is the proof of one's fallen condition, displacing the comic from the looked-upon to the looker, from the object to the subject.

Baudelaire distinguishes *le comique significatif*, the laughter that ridicules the foibles of society, from *le comique absolu* or *le grotesque* which appears to transcend duality and exist 'as a *single* species' ['sous une espèce *une*' (OC II 536)]. The grotesque implies a superiority of the individual, not over another person but over nature itself, and it produces an exuberant sense of joy in spite of the side-splitting convulsions it gives rise to. The example he gives is of an English pantomime in which Pierrot is to be guillotined for some unspecified misdemeanour. With much bellowing he is brought to the fatal machine, but when his head falls and rolls across the stage like a piece of sliced meat, Pierrot, moved by his incorrigible propensity to thieve, gets up, stuffs his head into his pocket and walks triumphantly away, which produces shrieks of helpless mirth in the audience. This form of the comic is essentially non-verbal. Pierrot remains mute like the pantomime buffoon in 'Une mort héroïque' who

> excelled above all in those roles which are silent or in which few words are spoken, and which are often the leading parts in those fairy-tale plays whose aim is to represent in symbolic fashion the mystery of life. (PP 70)

> [excellait surtout dans les rôles muets ou peu chargés de paroles, qui sont souvent les principaux dans ces drames féeriques dont l'objet est de représenter symboliquement le mystère de la vie. (OC I 321)]

Here it emerges that the curiously collapsing and telescoping opposites of Baudelaire's universe (ideal/spleen, Heaven/Hell and so on) extend to his notion of the comic and the function of poetry. For the poet is at once the inspired seer and the buffoon or mountebank. What interests us in the context of the comic, however, is the immediacy it gains from the lack of verbal articulation. The *ecstasis* of the poetic ideal, what Baudelaire calls 'the fine days of the spirit' ['beaux jours de l'esprit' (OC II 596)], tails off into silence in its intuition of a timeless dimension, as in 'La Chevelure' or 'Harmonie du soir'. At the opposite pole of irony and realism the derisory illusion of transcendence through the trickery of the grotesque appears also as *ecstasis* beyond words. Such are the extremes in which the modern artist has to operate within a sunset culture, and his emergence as buffoon, at first sight enigmatic and unpredictable, entails a perfectly logical inevitability.

Caricature like comedy is essentially visual and theatrical. It has the exaggeration of expression and gesture associated with pantomime. That is why Baudelaire most admires those caricatures where the words are limited to the caption, as for example Daumier's 'The Last Bath', Hogarth's 'Reward of Cruelty', or Cruikshank's 'A Skaiting Party' [*sic*]. This explains also why he failed to respond to the linguistic deftness of Gavarni, and why he considered Goya such a brilliant creator of the fantastic that on occasion borders on the grotesque. With Goya the caption is often an uncomprehending question at the bizarreness of the vision that has surged into being as inexplicably for its creator, it would seem, as for the spectator. Though in many respects conservative in his view of art and its exalted mission, Baudelaire's range from high art to low, from poetry to prose, from ideal to spleen, from sublime to grotesque is a direct result of his conviction that it should engage with the fundamental issues of the human condition.

His impatience with landscape painting reaches a climax in the *Salon de 1859* where he laments that the predominance of an inferior genre without the essential contribution of imagination is the sign of a 'general debasement' ['abaissement général' (OC II 660)]. There is, however, one painter, Eugène Boudin, whom he had met in July of the same year at Honfleur, whom he favours with a fulsome but paradoxical eulogy. He argues that Boudin would never allow his brilliant pastels improvised *en plein air* before sea and sky to be considered works of art in their own right. They are mere studies to help him complete the painting in his studio, and he would not have the arrogance to claim for them a higher status. Their provisional character is confirmed by details concerning the atmosphere and weather, such as *8 October, noon, wind from the north-west*. However, as he evokes 'these clouds with their fantastic and luminous forms, this chaotic darkness, these green and pink immensities' ['ces nuages aux formes fantastiques et lumineuses, ces ténèbres chaotiques, ces immensités vertes et roses'] which affect the mind 'like a heady drink or like the eloquence of opium' ['comme une boisson capiteuse ou comme l'éloquence de l'opium' (OC II 665–6)], Baudelaire's tone becomes increasingly lyrical. By the end of the paragraph the point of departure has been lost in the intoxication with the fleeting and evanescent, in what appears to be the work of a colourist *à l'état pur*. Baudelaire never again mentions Boudin, who went on to be one of the most successful of nineteenth-century landscape painters. In the evolution of Baudelaire's aesthetic his function is to mark a turning point, at a time when the poet was writing many of the 'Parisian Scenes' in which the emphasis falls increasingly upon the fragmentary and the unstable. It marks a moment of transition from the high art of Delacroix to the minor figure of Constantin Guys, who, strangely, was to become for Baudelaire *the* painter of modern life.

Guys, however, is very different from the painter of modern life called for in the final paragraphs of the *Salons* of 1845 and 1846, not least because there is little heroism or Balzacian grandeur in his drawings. Baudelaire seems deliberately to be seeking modernity in a minor artist and in a minor genre; for Guys avoids the oil on canvas, favouring the less ambitious media of watercolour, wash, and pen and ink drawing, in order to capture street scenes, the vagaries of fashion or the events of the Crimean War. Although, strangely, the high art of Delacroix has much in common technically with the low art of the caricaturist and the painter of modern life – the appeal to memory and recognition, the emphasis on gesture and rapidity of execution, the sense of the incomplete and the oxymoronic 'perfect sketch' ['ébauche parfaite' (OC II 700)] – there is little of Delacroix's Romanticism, and nothing could be further from Taillebourg or Poitiers than Guys' sketches of wounded Turkish soldiers or Lord Raglan's Headquarters at Balaclava. Here is the reality of war, fashionable society and the underworld of the crook and the brothel, with the emphasis falling upon the fleeting and the evanescent. Rarely do we have that sense of the pose characteristic of Ingres; for what he excels in capturing is the aptness of gesture or posture, the movement of the figures caught as it were in flight. In *The Painter of Modern Life* [*Le Peintre de la vie moderne*], Baudelaire identifies the *éternel* and the *transitoire* as the essential ingredients of art. In Delacroix and in *Les Fleurs du Mal* the eternal belongs to the domain of the elevated and the spiritual. With Guys, however, where the fleeting perceptions of the *flâneur* are most in evidence, the eternal resides in the typical, the unchanging truth of gesture and attitude that transcends the ephemeralities of time and location. Furthermore, the sheer accumulation of instances can have a heightening effect as, for example, with the various representations of the soldier ['le militaire'] which provide a composite picture which is more than the sum of its parts, just as the sketches of the Crimea constitute in their totality what Baudelaire calls 'that great epic of the Crimean war' ['cette grande épopée de la guerre de Crimée'], 'that poem made up of a thousand sketches' ['ce poème fait de mille croquis' (OC II 701–2)].

But as always with Baudelaire, no sooner has a value been posited than it is called in question; for the *artiste-flâneur* may espouse the crowd with a selfless erotic intensity, by 'a holy prostitution of the soul' (PP 44) ['une sainte prostitution de l'âme' (OC I 291)], a liberating and joyous flight from the self into the other and the accidents of his *flânerie*, but it is increasingly the ordinary, the ignoble even, that attracts his attention, with the result that his joy gives way to the sense of a vain proliferation, a fall into time and number from which there seems no escape. This is at its most poignant in 'Women and Prostitutes' ['Les Femmes et les filles'] which documents Guys' sick obsession with whorehouses and their grotesque manifestations of the flesh. No sense here of a 'Poem' of modernity. Indeed, the essay on Guys follows a similar curve to that of the prose poems, as the conception of *Le Spleen de Paris* evolves from *Light and Smoke, Prose Poem [La Lueur et la fumée, Poème, en prose* (C II 197)] to *The 6666* (OC I 365), a title based on 666, the apocalyptic number of the beast, to denote a fall into time and endless number, the negative form of the absolute.

The fundamental duality of Baudelaire's universe is of 'Idéal' and 'Spleen', which characterise *Les Fleurs du Mal*; but as the fall into time and number intensified, and as the stridency of the city and the derisory status of the artist became more insistent, a shift in genre became inevitable. Baudelaire felt that 'Parisian Scenes' had transgressed the limits of poetry, and the dissonance of the modern world was increasingly to find an adequate means of expression in the hybrid genre of the prose poem, whose parallel in the visual arts is the caricature and the sketch, the 'realism' of the genre suiting their subject-matter.

Finally, there is a duality in Baudelaire that is not always emphasised, that of presence and absence, plenitude and emptiness, which is relevant to our understanding of his visual imagination. The sense of plenitude is no doubt the major part in Baudelaire's mental world; it is present in the turbulence of Delacroix's explosive canvases which abhor a vacuum, and in the vibrancy of his backgrounds. It takes a different form in the 'explosion in space' ['explosion dans l'espace'] of Guys' figures, which seem to surge out of the drawing and impose themselves on the spectator. But there are other works in which the figures appear threatened or denied by space, as in the painting *Through the Balkans*. That side of Baudelaire that was attracted and repelled by 'the black, the blank, the bare' (FM 151) ['le vide, le noir et le nu' (OC I 75)], that was obsessed with the vanity of all things, could respond readily to such a phenomenon, and the poet who could imagine the world as a theatre stage or the frame for a picture, as in 'L'Irréparable' or 'Le Cadre', could also portray himself as the painter whom a mocking God

'Condemns, alas! to paint darkness itself' (FM 77) (translation modified) ['Condamne à peindre, hélas! sur les ténèbres' (OC 1 38)].

NOTES

1. J. A. Hiddleston, *Essai sur Laforgue et les 'Derniers Vers'* (Lexington, KY: French Forum Publishers, 1980), pp. 97–8, 106–7.
2. Jules Laforgue, *Poésies complètes*, ed. Pascal Pia (Paris: Livre de poche, 1970), p. 31.
3. Lee Johnson, *The Paintings of Eugène Delacroix* (Oxford: Oxford University Press, 1981), vol. 1, p. 114.
4. Pierre Daix, *Delacroix le libérateur* (Paris: Club des amis du livre progressiste, 1963), p. 178.

IO

MARGARET MINER

Music and theatre

What I've always found most beautiful in a theatre . . . is the *chandelier* – a beautiful object, luminous, crystalline, complicated, circular and symmetrical . . . After all, the chandelier has always appeared to me as the principal actor, seen through the large end or the small end of the lorgnette.

[Ce que j'ai toujours trouvé de plus beau dans un théâtre . . . c'est *le lustre* – un bel objet lumineux, cristallin, compliqué, circulaire et symmétrique . . . Après tout, le lustre m'a toujours paru l'acteur principal, vu à travers le gros bout ou le petit bout de la lorgnette.

(OC 1 682)]

Exploring the interaction of music and theatre in Baudelaire's writing is a somewhat delicate and perplexing task, rather like examining the patterns of reflection and refraction from a complicated chandelier. Shining everywhere as a poet, widely recognised as a luminous translator and a brilliant art critic, Baudelaire is rarely counted among notable music critics and figures nowhere as either a theatre critic or a dramatist. Yet if music and theatre play supporting rather than starring roles in Baudelaire's works, they are nevertheless indispensable to the lighting of the whole production.

It seems deceptively simple to glance over Baudelaire's written contributions to the worlds of music and drama, as if scanning them through the wrong end of a telescope. His lone foray into music criticism, an essay entitled 'Richard Wagner et *Tannhäuser* à Paris', first appeared on 1 April 1861 in the *Revue européenne*, and E. Dentu published a slightly expanded version in booklet form on 4 May of the same year. Baudelaire was more active in literary criticism but seldom dealt with the theatre, publishing only such bits and pieces as a couple of short articles on the actor Philibert Rouvière (1855 and 1865) and a brief attack against 'Honest Plays and Novels' ['Les Drames et les romans honnêtes'] (1851). At intervals throughout his writing career, Baudelaire began work on various dramas that he hoped to see staged in Paris: in 1843, he launched a collaboration with Ernest Prarond on *Idéolus*, a play in alexandrine verse; in 1853, he drafted the scenario for an opera, *The End of Don Juan* [*La Fin de Don Juan*]; starting in late 1853, he corresponded with the actor Hippolyte Tisserant about *The Drunkard* [*L'Ivrogne*], a drama to be fleshed out from the poem 'Le Vin de l'assassin';

and between 1859 and 1861, he outlined the five acts of *The Marquis of the First Hussards* [*Le Marquis du 1er housards*], a play to be adapted from a novella by Paul de Molènes. None of these four projects came to fruition, however, and all that remains of them are sketches and fragments.

This overview of course leaves in the dark all the crucial cameo appearances of music and theatre – all the glowing allusions and metaphors and anecdotes, as well as the possibly borrowed or imitated effects of cadence and melody and drama – that permeate the whole of Baudelaire's œuvre, from *La Fanfarlo* to *Les Fleurs du Mal* and from the Salons to *Les Paradis artificiels* to *Le Spleen de Paris*. Roland Barthes has asserted that 'everything happens as if Baudelaire had put his theatre everywhere except precisely in his theatre projects',[1] and one might, with some important qualifications, construct a similar argument concerning music. It would, at least, be counter-productive to limit or isolate the places in which one looks for the workings of music and theatre in Baudelaire's writing. And although it would not be unfruitful to search for the two separately, it may be particularly valuable to hunt for them together. What follows is an attempt to see music and theatre from the right end of an opera glass, discovering how they may share more than just their paradoxically marginal centrality in Baudelaire's work and what some of their principal points of convergence may reveal.

Mind play

Baudelaire died in 1861, nine years before Wagner's specially designed Festival Theatre was finished in Bayreuth. He therefore never attended any of Wagner's music dramas under the conditions that the composer considered ideal and that have continued to impress his critics ever since. Here, for example, is James Treadwell's recent meditation on the opening moments of a Bayreuth performance:

> What happens is simply that the lights go down; but because the orchestra pit is hooded from the audience . . . there is a moment of total darkness before your pupils dilate enough to take in the dim glow being cast by those hidden lights on the silvery-grey curtain. Briefly but startlingly, the whole environment disappears. You feel yourself to be suspended in emptiness, your attention totally absorbed by the faint glimmer in the space where Wagner's world will shortly appear.
>
> Then the sound begins . . . In the first few seconds, the actual music being played isn't really relevant. You are riveted instead by the way you are hearing it, the scene music has placed itself in. Sound arises with no visible sign and from no apparent source, conspiring with the near-total darkness to make you believe that it is some kind of purely spiritual emanation . . . A blend

of simple technologies creates for you a moment which distils everything most fundamental to [Wagner's] art: its intensification of aesthetic experience, its almost physical engagement with the audience, its desire to captivate the attention.[2]

Baudelaire, in contrast, neither heard nor saw any of Wagner's works thus performed to their optimal effect. His defining encounter with them came early in 1860 at the Théâtre-Italien in Paris, where Wagner conducted three concerts featuring a few choral and instrumental excerpts from *Tannhäuser* and *Lohengrin*, plus the overtures from *Der Fliegende Holländer* and *Tristan und Isolde*. These concerts were followed in March 1861 by a controversial production of *Tannhäuser* at the Paris Opéra, after which Baudelaire was reduced, as he claimed, to straining for snatches of Wagner from friends' pianos and casino orchestras (OC II 786). Even so, he evoked these encounters in ways that both foreshadowed and helped shape the reaction of later writers who witnessed the full collaboration between Wagner's music and his Festival Theatre. In an enthusiastic letter of 17 February 1860 to Wagner about the three Paris concerts, Baudelaire described something close to the blind, weightless astonishment in which Bayreuth pilgrims such as Treadwell would one day find themselves theatrically plunged and musically overpowered:

> I often experienced a feeling of a strange nature, pride and sensuous pleasure in understanding, in letting myself be penetrated, invaded, a truly sensual voluptuousness, which resembles that of rising in the air or rolling on the sea.
>
> [j'ai éprouvé souvent un sentiment d'une nature assez bizarre, c'est l'orgueil et la jouissance de comprendre, de me laisser pénétrer, envahir, volupté vraiment sensuelle, et qui ressemble à celle de monter dans l'air ou de rouler sur la mer.
> (C I 673)]

By the time he wrote 'Richard Wagner et *Tannhäuser* à Paris' in March 1861, however, his unknowing prefiguration of the Bayreuth adventure had taken on the air of

> a spiritual operation, a revelation. My voluptuous pleasure had been so strong and so terrible that I could not stop myself from wanting to return to it constantly. Into what I had felt, there entered . . . something new that I was powerless to define, and that powerlessness caused me anger and curiosity mixed with a strange delight.
>
> [une opération spirituelle, une révélation. Ma volupté avait été si forte et si terrible, que je ne pouvais m'empêcher d'y vouloir retourner sans cesse. Dans ce que j'avais éprouvé, il entrait . . . quelque chose de nouveau que j'étais

impuissant à définir, et cette impuissance me causait une colère et une curiosité mêlées d'un bizarre délice. (OC II 785)]

As before, Baudelaire insists here on the strange, soul-conflicting fascination that overcame him and that would similarly come to overmaster Bayreuth audiences. But the pronounced shift in tone calls attention to itself. From the voluptuous comprehension expressed in his letter ('sensuous pleasure in understanding'), Baudelaire sinks in his essay towards abstract bafflement ('something new that I was powerless to define'). The letter-writer's happy, passive openness ('pride . . . in letting myself be penetrated') turns into the essayist's intractable, analytical frustration ('that powerlessness caused me anger and curiosity mixed with . . . delight'). One might account for these changes partly by recalling that the letter resulted from Baudelaire's wonderment after the concerts whereas the essay took its impetus from his disappointment at the failure of *Tannhäuser* in Paris: joining a trajectory represented over and over in Baudelaire's works, the drama realised in the theatre had not matched the music dramatised in the mind.

One should also remember, though, that during the interval separating his 1860 Wagner letter from his 1861 Wagner essay, Baudelaire completed *Les Paradis artificiels*. A preliminary version of *Un Mangeur d'opium*. Baudelaire's free adaptation of Thomas De Quincey's *Confessions of an English Opium Eater* appeared in the *Revue européenne* in late January 1860; one can imagine Baudelaire returning from the first Wagner concert to correct some of the proof sheets. In the chapter on 'Voluptés de l'opium', Baudelaire notes that De Quincey long restricted himself to taking the drug mainly on evenings he spent at the opera. This was, Baudelaire explains, because music 'interpreted and illuminated by opium' ['la musique interprétée et illuminée par l'opium' (OC I 467)] affected the author of *Confessions* in a particular way:

His whole past came to life in him, he said, not by an effort of memory, but as if present and incarnated in the music . . . all the triviality and the coarseness inherent in human affairs were excluded from that mysterious resurrection, or melted and drowned in an ideal mist, and his former passions found themselves exalted, ennobled, spiritualised.

[Toute sa vive passée vivait, dit-il, en lui, non pas par un effort de la mémoire, mais comme présente et incarnée dans la musique . . . toute la trivialité et la crudité inhérentes aux choses humaines étaient exclues de cette mystérieuse résurrection, ou fondues et noyées dans une brume idéale, et ses anciennes passions se trouvaient exaltées, ennoblies, spiritualisées. (OC I 467)]

As later passages from the chapter on 'Tortures de l'opium' emphasise, not all the memories crowding the theatre of dreams (OC 1 504) that came to be almost continually 'lighted in the opium eaters' brain' ['allum [és] dans leur cerveau] (OC 1 506)] as if for a sort of theatre rehearsal (OC 1 482) were so ideally uplifting; when there appeared 'the most vulgar events from his childhood' – apparently forgotten – 'he *recognised* them immediately' ['les plus vulgaires événements de l'enfance, des scènes depuis longtemps oubliées', 'il les *reconnaissait* immédiatement' (OC 1 481; Baudelaire's emphasis)]. But as Baudelaire tells it, the specific virtue of this second theatre, illuminated in De Quincey's mind by opium and music while he sat in the opera house, was to stage dramas of his past that were not to be recognised so much as relived with improvements: provided it was musical, the inner theatre could make the creative present dance beautifully with the remembered past.

The theatre as a metaphor for the mind is also fundamental to *Le Poème du haschisch*, which Baudelaire first published in 1858 but which reappeared as part of *Les Paradis artificiels* in June 1860. As Claire Lyu has shown, the central section of this text presents itself as a stage where a sober poetic voice organises a play involving a variety of intoxicated voices that gradually undermine our assumed distinctions between sobriety and intoxication.[3] Beyond this, though, the narrator-impresario is concerned to unveil the drama that plays in the mind of each solitary hashish user, a mind both like and unlike that of the uninitiated. The section's title, 'Le Theatre de Séraphin', seems to place this drama under the sign of a real theatre that attracted the children of nineteenth-century Paris with marionettes and magic lanterns, thus prolonging the magic of the lantern shows with which Joseph Séraphin entertained pre-Revolutionary audiences. But in *Le Poème du haschisch*, this title is a somewhat ironic concession to a supposedly ignorant public that imagines drug intoxication as a vast theatre of conjuring tricks and sleight of hand (OC 1 408). If hashish puts on extraordinary performances in the user's brain, insists the narrator, it is only by a heightened staging of elements from 'his ordinary life, his preoccupations, his desires, his vices' ['de sa vie ordinaire, de ses préoccupations, de ses désirs, de ses vices' (OC 1 408)] so that the ensuing drama 'will always preserve the tonality of the individual' ['gardera toujours la tonalité particulière de l'individu' (OC 1 409)]. In the case of a poet, for example, hashish would intensify the synesthetic 'analogies' that normally perform within the 'poetic brain' until they penetrate, they invade, they overwhelm the mind with their despotic character. Musical notes become numbers, and if your mind is gifted with any mathematical aptitude, the melody or the harmony you listen to is transformed, while

keeping its voluptuous and sensual character, into a vast arithmetical operation (OC 1 419). And when pushed in this way to its extremity, pursues the
narrator, so highly dramatised an analogy will exceed the mind's theatre to
such an extent that the personality disappears (OC 1 419), with the whole
mental stage collapsing into an absence of subjective awareness: you forget
your own existence (OC 1 419) as music ultimately 'incorporates itself into
you, and you melt into it' ['s'incorpore à vous, et vous vous fondez en elle'
(OC 1 431)].

The narrator-impresario of *Le Poème du haschisch* has by this point joined
the adaptor of *Un Mangeur d'opium* and the dramatiser of 'Richard Wagner'
to produce an intertextual show of echoes and reflections; one is not surprised
to find Baudelaire mentioning both his Wagner study and his *Paradis artificiels* within a few lines of each other in a letter addressed to his mother
in April 1860. The capitulation of the concert-going poet ('letting myself
be penetrated, invaded') responds to the capture of the hashish-using poet
('they penetrate, they invade'), and the profoundly sensual, strenuously cerebral 'operation' imposed on the opera-goer answers the 'voluptuous' intensification of musical into mathematical abstraction visited on the addict.
The opium-eater also comes to partner the Wagner enthusiast in a play of
memories and identities: rehearsing De Quincey's operatic mixture of self-
recognition and self-alienation, Baudelaire writes in his letter to Wagner
that

> at first it seemed to me that I knew this music, and later . . . I understood
> where this mirage came from; it seemed to me that this music was *mine* and I
> recognised it as every man recognises the things he is destined to love.
>
> [D'abord il m'a semblé que je connaissais cette musique et plus tard . . . j'ai
> compris d'où venait ce mirage; il me semblait que cette musique était *la mienne*,
> et je la reconnaissais comme tout homme reconnaît les choses qu'il est destiné
> à aimer.   (OC 1 672–3)]

Taken as a whole, this dialogue among Baudelaire's writings suggests that
when music displays the propensity of drugs to invade and saturate – to
enhance subjective sensation until subjectivity vanishes into its own excess –
it does so with particularly theatrical timing and dramatic flair. As if Wagner's
music were staging a recognition scene, for example, the listener moves from
a pointed perception ('il m'a semblé') of familiarity to a pervasive sense ('il
me semblait') of identification, amplified by the counterpoint of remembered
possession ('*mine*') and anticipated emotion ('destined to love'). What comes
back from Baudelaire's venture into Wagner's artificial paradise looks something like notes and sketches towards a dramatics of the mind.

The mental operation most fundamentally implicated in this venture is not, I think, the interaction of memory with anticipation or of familiarity with estrangement, although these play indispensable parts in the Wagner writings and in Baudelaire's work generally. It is first of all the elusive, liminal move between self-absence and self-awareness, between consciousness and oblivion, that Baudelaire finds dramatised in Wagner's music. Presciently figuring once again the Bayreuth experience, with its music imponderably, imperatively emerging from blank disorientation, Baudelaire claims in 'Richard Wagner' that 'it seems sometimes, in listening to this ardent and despotic music, that one rediscovers, painted on a background of shadows, torn by reverie, the vertiginous conceptions of opium' ['Il semble parfois, en écoutant cette musique ardente et despotique, qu'on retrouve peintes sur le fond des ténèbres, déchiré par la rêverie, les vertigineuses conceptions de l'opium' (OC ii 785)]. Unsurprisingly, this assertion echoes a sentence from *Un Mangeur d'opium*, which in turn recalls a phrase from Baudelaire's 1853 essay, 'Morale du joujou'. In both the latter, Baudelaire attributes to children the innately dramaturgic ability 'to perceive or rather to create on the fertile canvas of shadows a whole world of strange visions' ['d'apercevoir, ou plutôt de créer, sur la toile féconde des ténèbres tout un monde de visions bizarres' (OC i 480)] and to make their toys 'actors in the great drama of life, reduced by the dark room of their little brains' ['acteurs dans le grand drame de la vie, réduit par la chambre noire de leur petit cerveau' (OC i 582)]. Thanks to the overtones from these two remarks, the assertion from 'Richard Wagner' implies the involvement of music in a theatrical process of subject formation, a process during which music stars opposite the listening subject in a scene of suspenseful self-construction and self-complication. But more vividly than Baudelaire's letter to the composer, his Wagner essay insists that whatever music stages in the mind is inevitably a drama of seeming, of intermittent semblances ('it seems sometimes') flickering out of darkness. It is not even clear whether such 'vertiginous conceptions' most resemble the painted backdrop against which the listening subject will pass from inert scenery into self-conscious action, or whether they are more like the theatre curtain that must be 'torn' open for the subject to pass from unconscious dream into waking reverie and appear to itself on stage. Impossible to figure fully, this passage is at once the 'despotic' focus and the 'ardent,' overexposed blind spot of the dramaturgy imposed on the mind by Wagner's music, so that the listening Baudelairean spectator remains stubbornly curious, fascinated and frustrated by 'something new that I was powerless to define'.

Historically, Baudelaire's music-dramatics of the mind – his proto-Bayreuth theatre of subjectivity – is situated somewhere between the smoke-and-mirrors stage of phantasmagoria spectacles from the early nineteenth century and the drama of motion pictures illuminated in early twentieth-century cinema. When Baudelaire describes the opium-eater's play of mental images as 'that whole phantasmagoria' ['toute cette fantasmagorie'] it is in order to emphasise how fragile the boundaries are between his unconscious dreams of sleep and his acutely conscious dreams of waking (OC I 480). Likewise, the Wagner listener's precarious choreography of self-loss and self-awareness, or of oblivious permeation and active curiosity, mimics the strange dance of involuntarily imagined ghosts and eagerly scrutinised magic lantern projections that first attracted Parisians to phantasmagoria shows in 1798. Terry Castle has argued that these sound-and-light spectacles, gradually interpreted over the next century as a model for certain operations of the psyche, became 'the figure of the inward spectre-show',[4] according to which ideas and memories were (and are) commonly understood to haunt the mind. I want to suggest that Baudelaire's theatre of the mind similarly participates in the nineteenth century's evolving complex of representations for the psyche and its workings. Partially separated from spectral associations and invaded by musical energies, Baudelaire's mind stage figured enigmatic passages into and within consciousness in ways that anticipate not only Wagner's Festival Theatre, but also – among others – the public movie theatre and the intimate theatre of psychoanalysis. In cinema's rapt audiences, or in the psychoanalytic claim that 'fantasy unfailingly calls up an entire scene complete with protagonists – dramatis personae – and plot',[5] or in a recent meditation on neuropsychology that uses the light dawning on the sets of an otherwise dark theatre as 'a powerful metaphor for . . . the simple and yet momentous coming of the sense of self into the world of the mental',[6] one recognises Baudelairean listeners absorbed in a kind of music that plays them on stage from the inside out.

Feeling melo

As 1860 gave way to 1861 and his Paris production of *Tannhäuser* approached, Wagner published a *Lettre sur la musique* that prefaced a French translation of the librettos for *Der Fliegende Holländer, Tannhäuser, Lohengrin* and *Tristan und Isolde*. Baudelaire, who did not know much German, relied heavily on both the translations and the prefatory *Lettre* when preparing his Wagner essay, and he did not fail to seize on the autobiographical passage in which Wagner describes his theatrical upbringing: even as a child, reports Baudelaire, he lived in the midst of the theatre, was familiar with the wings and composed some comedies (OC II 787). Since Baudelaire had previously singled out toy theatres in his 'Morale du joujou' as a good example of playthings apt to affect the formation of a child's identity (OC I 585), it's not surprising that Wagner's childhood should strike him as especially exemplary in this respect. But Baudelaire acknowledges that the young Wagner was devoted as much to music as to theatre – the *Lettre* in fact specifies that he wanted to compose music for a tragedy he had written – and concludes that because of the way in which Wagner's mind came to be fashioned, 'it was impossible for him not to think in a double manner, poetically and musically' ['il lui fut impossible de ne pas penser d'une manière double, poétiquement et musicalement' (OC II 787)].

Baudelaire's own perennial preoccupation with multifarious forms of human doubleness is too well known to need much emphasis. As Ross Chambers puts it, Baudelaire was 'a strongly dualistic thinker, for whom . . . dichotomizations . . . seemed both inevitable and exhaustive'.[7] Among the permutations of doubleness most visible in his work around the time of his Wagner encounters is 'La Chambre double', a prose poem first published in 1862 that juxtaposes the ideal, atemporal chamber of a dreaming opium eater with the repulsively time-bound bedroom of the awakened addict. Transposed into moral and emotional abstraction, such doubleness – involving both the emphatic division and the presupposed wholeness of the human subject – also marks a number of fragments from *Mon cœur mis à nu*, the uncompleted autobiographical project Baudelaire began around 1859–60. In the most celebrated of these fragments, Baudelaire claims that

> there is in every man, at every hour, two simultaneous postulations, one towards God, the other towards Satan. The invocation to God, or spirituality, is a desire to rise in rank; the one to Satan, or animality, is a joy in descending.

> [Il y a dans tout homme, a toute heure, deux postulations simultanées, l'une vers Dieu, l'autre vers Satan. L'invocation à Dieu, ou spiritualité, est un désir de monter en grade; celle de Satan, ou animalité, est une joie de descendre.
>
> (OC I 682–3)]

This aphoristic claim is amplified, as Rosemary Lloyd notes,[7] throughout the second half of 'Richard Wagner', where Tannhaüser's alternating beatitude of redemption and joy in damnation are said to exemplify the beleaguering doubleness of general, universal man (OC II 785–7):

> *Tannhaüser* represents the fight between the two principles that have chosen the human heart for their primary battleground, that is to say, between the flesh and the spirit, Hell and Heaven, Satan and God.

> [*Tannhäuser* représente la lutte des deux principes qui ont choisi le cœur humain pour principal champ de bataille, c'est-à-dire de la chair avec l'esprit, de l'enfer avec le ciel, de Satan avec Dieu. (OC II 794)]

Similarly, Baudelaire dwells at length on the Manichean conflict that he finds at the centre of both *Lohengrin* and *Der Fliegender Holländer*. The latter, as Baudelaire understands it, opposes the salvation offered by an angel of God to the terrible sentence of damnation imposed by Satan (OC II 803–4), thus dividing between Senta and the Dutchman the double postulation that Wagner would later concentrate within *Tannhäuser*. Baudelaire shows some inclination to magnify this postulation even further by juxtaposing *Tannhäuser*'s unusually striking portrayal of voluptuous and orgiastic temptation with *Lohengrin*'s exceptionally vivid painting of mysticism (OC II 806). But he also underlines the particular form of inward doubleness that he finds responsible for Elsa's tragedy in *Lohengrin*, declaring that like antiquity's Psyche – the mythological figure whose inquisitiveness threatened her marriage with Cupid in disguise – Elsa embodies the scene of a struggle fuelled by curiosity, a conflict between a secretive divinity and a suspicious human wife in which doubt has killed faith (OC II 799).

For Baudelaire, then, these operas exteriorise and concretise a drama that never finishes playing itself out in the human psyche, where doubleness is at once inescapable and destabilising. What the creative duality of Wagner's thinking – poetic and musical – ultimately ignites into consciousness is an apparently interminable inner conflict: the glimmering stage of the mind becomes a glaring theatre of operations, riven by the profound shock of awe-inspiring forces in repeated confrontation. Wagnerian opera is not alone, moreover, in intensifying Baudelaire's awareness of this towering clash; it is in similarly martial and histrionic terms, for example, that he describes the psychology of laughter in 'De l'essence du rire et généralement du comique dans les arts plastiques'. Probably begun as early as 1846 but not published in final form until a few months after *Les Fleurs du Mal* came out in 1857, this essay argues that laughter arises from 'a double or contradictory sentiment' ['un sentiment double, ou contradictoire' (OC II 534)], the human being's mindfulness of both 'infinite wretchedness in relation to the absolute Being' and 'infinite grandeur in relation to animals' ['misère infinie relativement à l'Etre absolu', 'grandeur infinie relativement aux animaux' (OC II 532)]. Baudelaire thus suggests that the sound of laughter, like the music of *Tannhäuser*, makes especially audible the perpetual colliding of these two infinites (OC II 532), the endlessly fascinating smash of spleen with ideal or of fallenness with superiority. This is the fatal crash that echoes, notably, through 'Une mort héroïque', the late (1863) prose poem that plays out a version of Baudelaire's double postulation against the layered backdrop of 'De l'essence du rire' and 'Richard Wagner et *Tannhäuser* à Paris'. Double-featuring Fanfioulle, an unsurpassable comic mime whose Italianate name (from *fanciullo*: boy) suggests a psyche shaped from childhood by the stage, and the Prince, a brilliant despot who never had a theatre vast enough for his genius, the prose poem uses the deadly noise of a whistle followed by stifled giggles to amplify the psychological battle between opposing powers that are joined by their equally unsatisfiable ambition (OC 1 72).

'Une mort héroïque' might serve as a coda – a trailing effort that prolongs as much as it closes – for Baudelaire's own stillborn theatre projects. Although these were conceived in varying circumstances and show differing degrees of ambition, they all nonetheless aspire to a heightened representation of the mind's doubleness and its escalating consequences. This is most blatant in the first and last of the projects. Towards the beginning of his career (1843), Baudelaire and his friend Ernest Prarond set out to collaborate on *Idéolus*, a five-act comedy of manners with neo-classical trimmings and Romantic flavouring; they got only to the middle of Act 2, with Prarond drafting scenes in alexandrine verse that Baudelaire then slightly revised. Named after its principal protagonist, the play was to spotlight a sculptor assailed by an ascending series of doublings. Divided between desire for the courtesan Forniquette and devotion to the virtuous Nubilis, he is also pinned between marble blocks and completed statues, which embody his inner split between daunted inertia and delighted inspiration:

> Always to feel within oneself, inner struggles,
> Two men ceaselessly vying with each other for every hour:
> The first, a counterweight to the fervent artist,
> But, too heavy, dragging him along too often;
> The second filled with fire, but jostled by the other,
> Keeping the faith with *the virtue* of an apostle.
>
> [Sentir toujours en soi, luttes intérieures,
> Deux hommes sans repos se disputant les heures:
> Le premier, contrepoids de l'artiste fervent,
> Mais trop lourd avec lui l'entraînant trop souvent;
> Le second plein de feu, mais coudoyé par l'autre,
> Gardant avec la foi *la vertu* d'un apôtre.
>
> (OC 1 606)]

Baudelaire apparently recognised the conventional crudeness of this predicament, since a few lines later he laughingly substituted 'banality' for Prarond's 'immortality' (OC 1 1448, n. 3). Almost twenty years later, however, he was still occupied with the theatrical possibilities of comparably stark and traditional doublings. Proposing in the fall of 1860 to adapt a novella by his friend Paul de Molènes for the Théâtre du Cirque, Baudelaire opened his outline of the play – to be entitled *Le Marquis du 1er housards* – with lines that might have served as a rehearsal for his 1861 discussion of *Tannhaüser*:

The work's goal is to show the fight between two principles, within the same brain. The son of an émigré serves the Emperor with enthusiasm but around him several people . . . appeal unceasingly to his childhood memories, to the pride of his race, in order to draw him back toward Louis XVIII and the Count of Artois. As in the old compositions, we rediscover here the *good* and the *evil* angel.

[L'ouvrage a pour but de montrer la lutte entre deux principes, dans le même cerveau. Un fils d'émigré sert l'Empereur avec enthousiasme; mais autour de lui plusieurs personnes . . . font sans cesse appel à ses souvenirs d'enfance, à l'orgueil de la race, pour le ramener vers Louis XVIII et le comte d'Artois. Comme dans les vieilles compositions, nous retrouvons ici le *bon* et le *mauvais* ange. (OC 1 635; Baudelaire's emphasis)]

In Baudelaire's other two theatre sketches, both from the early 1850s, the doubling brought about by inner conflict is metaphorically structured into relations between protagonists rather than concentrated in a single but divided mind. Suggestively, both these projects were intended not just for the theatre, but for the musical stage, as if their enlarged scale of doubleness required more intense means of representation. In the surviving snippet of *La Fin de Don Juan*, which Baudelaire thought briefly of developing into a libretto for the Paris Opera, one glimpses a dizzying succession of doubles that split and multiply the central figure of Don Juan: his mercenary servant ('the future bourgeoisie' ['la future bourgeoisie'] juxtaposed with 'the falling nobility' ['la noblesse tombante']); his corrupt son ('a precocious second *version* of his father' ['une seconde *épreuve* précoce de son père']); the vengeful statue vis-à-vis a watchful angel; the ghost of Catalina, another failed rebel whose charisma mirrors the Don's (OC 1 627–8). More extensive and more provocative is the outline for a five-act drama that Baudelaire drafted with the encouragement of the actor Jean-Hippolyte Tisserant. Tentatively enti-tled *L'Ivrogne* (*The Drunkard*) the play was to have elaborated Baudelaire's verse poem, 'Le Vin de l'assassin', in which a drunken worker murders his wife by throwing her into a well. On stage, the material juxtaposition of an alcoholic sawyer's violence with his wife's gentleness would have corre-sponded to mental postulations that divided the worker, first between baffled admiration and jealous resentment of his wife's patient virtue, then between triumph and guilt for her murder. Significantly, though, Baudelaire's sketch also hints at an analogous division of mind for the wife, who finds herself doubled by religious resignation and persistent restlessness. Driven by this split, she seeks out her tipsy husband at a cabaret, thus initiating the series of events that lead to her death: eerily anticipating Baudelaire's response to Elsa and her anxious curiosity in *Lohengrin*, she cannot survive the confrontation in which 'doubt has killed faith'.

Had *L'Ivrogne* ever been published, it would probably have fallen under the general heading of melodrama; the various theatres for which Baudelaire envisioned it – the Gaîté, the Porte Saint-Martin or the Odéon, where Tisserant performed – all featured variants of that popular genre through the mid nineteenth century. That Baudelaire planned to write a 'rabble-pleaser' ['drame populacier'] (OC I 630) has roused the curiosity of critics: in Claude Pichois' view, Baudelaire must have grasped 'the necessity, for those who were looking for living forms of theatre, of resorting to melodrama' (OC I 1461, n. 1); for Richard D. E. Burton, *L'Ivrogne* signals a moment of hesitation between 'Baudelaire's republican sympathy with workers in the late 1840s and his conservative elitism in the late 1850s';[9] Roland Barthes sees the 'atrocious Passion for vulgarity' in Baudelaire's theatre projects as part of the 'vast background of negativity' against which *Les Fleurs du Mal* may be appreciated.[10] Yet while all these interpretations are plausible, it is also worth emphasising that strong elements of what Peter Brooks has called the melodramatic imagination are at work throughout Baudelaire's writing, from the early 1840s to the late 1860s. Focused since its eighteenth-century beginnings on the intensely polarised playing out of moral division and confrontation, nineteenth-century melodrama made tangible theatre out of exaggerated doubleness; it placed the materialising forces of stagecraft in the service of 'fundamental bipolar contrast and clash'[11] that might otherwise stay obscured behind, say, the predictable indecision of an émigré officer in Napoleon's army or the sordid disintegration of a working-class marriage. Melodrama was consequently well suited to embodying variations on Baudelaire's double postulation and mounting them on stage. But melodrama was equally well configured to serve as a metaphor for dramatic action in the Baudelairean theatre of the mind: if none of the melodramatic projects Baudelaire drafted ever reached the boards of Paris theatres, it may have been partly because projecting them on to the inner stage of consciousness was enough.

Whether directed inwards to the reflective mind or outwards to the sensationalist theatres of Paris's Boulevard of Crime, *L'Ivrogne* is a particularly concentrated example of Baudelaire's melodramatic imagination, not only because of the lurid antagonism played out in it but also because of the prominence it gives to music. An obligatory accompaniment to melodrama since the genre's evolution out of pantomime spectacles in the late 1700s, music would have played an essential, structuring role in the elaboration of *L'Ivrogne*: Baudelaire insists that the specifics of the play's characters

and situations must derive from 'The Sawyer' ['Le Scieur de long'], a sin-
gularly harsh folk song 'whose melody is horribly melancholy' ['dont l'air
est horriblement mélancolique' (OC I 630)]. Once again eerily foreshadow-
ing his admiration for Wagner, Baudelaire expresses his 'immense desire'
to showcase 'The Sawyer' by making the third of L'Ivrogne's five acts into
a *song-joust* in which the murderous sawyer would compete (OC I 630;
Baudelaire's emphasis), just as the middle act of *Tannhäuser* stages a song
contest involving Wagner's protagonist; in both cases, the contest precipi-
tates the events that lead to the heroine's death. Although faint and unexpected to the point of uncanniness, such a parallel between *Tannhaüser* and
the sawyer – like the analogy between *Lohengrin's* Elsa and the sawyer's
wife – is sufficiently compelling to remind one of how much Wagner's earlier works owed to his 'fondness for melodrama and bombast', a fondness
evident in his characters' 'conventionally melodramatic style of presentation' and in his operas' 'musical representation of opposing worlds'.[12] As
Elizabeth Paley has noted, nineteenth-century melodrama evolved somewhat differently in France than in Germany, where its provocative mix of
music and declamation attracted serious composers and where its music was
often saved for representing the visionary and the supernatural.[13] But the
uncanny wisps of resemblance that draw *L'Ivrogne* (abortively outlined in
1854) towards *Tannhäuser* and *Lohengrin* (fragmentarily heard in 1860–
1) help to explain further why Baudelaire's discovery of Wagner produced
both the feeling that 'I knew this music' (1860 letter) and the impression
of 'something new that I was powerless to define' ('Richard Wagner'). With
its double pull towards both a shadowy recognition of the repressed and
a spotlighted inner conflict of the soul, what music acts out once it has
lighted the Baudelairean mental stage is an especially ardent 'melodrama of
consciousness'.[14]

Flowers of music drama

On New Year's Day, 1860, two weeks before the first publication of *Un
Mangeur d'opium* and three weeks before the first of Wagner's Théâtre-
Italien concerts, Baudelaire signed a contract for the second, expanded edition of *Les Fleurs du Mal*. A little more than a year later, shortly before the
failure of *Tannhäuser* in Paris goaded Baudelaire into publishing his Wagner
essay, the new edition of *Les Fleurs* appeared. Of the two poems in it that
most explicitly picture the theatre, 'L'Irréparable' and 'Le Rêve d'un curieux',
the former is retained from the 1857 edition. Baudelaire likely wrote it in
late 1853 or early 1854, around the time he was also sketching plans for
L'Ivrogne, although the poem's final lines may look back towards 1847–8,

when he was attracted to the actress Marie Daubrun. They evoke a stage on the Boulevard du Crime:

> – I've seen, within a tawdry theatre
> Warmed by a brazen band,
>
> . . .
>
> A Being made of light, and gold, and gauze
> Lay the great Satan low;
> But in my heart, no home to ecstasy,
> Sad playhouse, one awaits
> Always in vain, the fine and filmy wings!
>
> (FM 115)

> [– J'ai vu parfois, au fond d'un théâtre banal
> Qu'enflammait l'orchestre sonore,
>
> . . .
>
> Un être, qui n'était que lumière, or et gaze,
> Terrasser l'énorme Satan;
> Mais mon cœur, que jamais ne visite l'extase,
> Est un théâtre ou l'on attend
> Toujours, toujours en vain, l'Être aux ailes de gaze!
>
> (OC I 55)]

The melodramatic play in question here is characteristically filled with the clash of cosmically opposed forces and warmed by music that amplifies otherworldly interventions in human affairs. Yet the double postulation being represented is somehow hindered or weakened: even though it is literally and exaggeratedly acted out, it never turns a moral division of the psyche into spectacle. Unbalanced, the mind's theatre is plunged into gloom and silence, like some satanic Bayreuth scene in which both performers and audience endlessly wait for godlike glimmers of music drama.

Something similarly alarming happens in 'Le Rêve d'un curieux', a sonnet first published in May 1860 and then added to the 1861 edition of *Les Fleurs du Mal*. After starting in the quatrains to recount a dream in which he was on the brink of dying, the wakened subject continues in the tercets:

> I was a child, eager to see a play,
> Hating the curtain standing in the way . . .
> At last the chilling verity came on:
>
> Yes, I was dead, and in the dreadful dawn
> Was wrapped. – And what! That's all there is to tell?
> The screen was raised, and I was waiting still.
>
> (FM 281)

[J'étais comme l'enfant avide du spectacle,
Haïssant le rideau comme on hait un obstacle . . .
Enfin la vérité froide se révéla:

J'étais mort sans surprise, et la terrible aurore
M'enveloppait. – Eh, quoi! n'est-ce donc que cela?
La toile était levée et j'attendais encore.

(OC I 128)]

Provocatively, the poem is dedicated to Baudelaire's friend F[élix] N[adar], of whom a fragment in *Mon cœur mis à nu* says that his vitality is such that he must have 'all his viscera in duplicate' ['tous les viscères en double'], a diminished kind of doubleness that only helps him succeed 'in everything that is not abstract' ['dans tout ce qui n'est pas l'abstrait' (OC I 695)]. The same may be unnervingly true of the sonnet's narrator: troubled, perhaps, by an over duplication of bodily organs, he faces in his dream an infinite multiplication of sameness: the curtain rising on his death divides neither audience from stage, nor boredom from drama, nor liberated mind from inert body. As a consequence, it is difficult to trust the differentiating power of the poem's title, since by the first line there may be nothing to separate dream from consciousness or death (un)dramatised in the mind from death played out in reality. 'Le Rêve d'un curieux' thus participates in the movement from sensuous pleasure to powerless curiosity that marks Baudelaire's reaction to Wagner between his 1860 letter and his 1861 essay. In Baudelaire's poem as in the experience of music evoked in his Wagner essay, it is as if *Lohengrin*'s Elsa (whom Baudelaire sees as a descendant of Psyche) were unable to distinguish between her death from curiosity and an opium dream of her death from curiosity.

The nightmare that 'L'Irréparable' and 'Le Rêve d'un curieux' thus evoke is a spreading failure of melodramatic doubleness: once the inner conflict of the soul disappears from the mental stage, as in 'L'Irréparable', there follows an effacement of the divide between inner spectacle and outer spectator, and this collapse of subjective awareness leads to deadly indifferentiation between waking and dream, as in 'Le Rêve d'un curieux'. Baudelaire offers a graphic illustration of such psychic catastrophe near the beginning of 'Richard Wagner', implicitly warning readers of what might happen should they resist Wagner's (and Baudelaire's) melodramatics of the mind. At a dress rehearsal for *Tannhäuser*, explains Baudelaire, a prominent anti-Wagnerian music critic planted himself obstructively near the ticket booth, 'trying hard to laugh like a maniac, like one of those unfortunates who, in asylums, are said to be *agitated*' ['s'exerçant à rire comme un maniaque, comme un de ces infortunés qui, dans les maisons de santé, sont appelés des *agités*'

(OC II 781)]. This excitable listener had lost, according to Baudelaire, all self-awareness, all possibility of either shaping or critiquing the musical drama playing in the theatre of his mind. Incapable of appreciating *Tannhäuser*'s double realisation – musical and poetic – of the double postulation, the critic also lacked what Baudelaire calls in 'De l'essence du rire' the 'power to double oneself rapidly and to witness, as a disinterested spectator, the phenomena of one's *self*' ['la force de se dédoubler rapidement et d'assister comme spectateur désintéressé aux phénomènes de son *moi*' (OC II 532; Baudelaire's emphasis)]. Baudelaire admits in the same essay, however, that this capacity for self-doubling is rare, to be found only in the occasional philosopher; the mere illumination of consciousness on the mind's stage does not in itself ensure a successful play of doubleness. As Leo Bersani argues, Baudelaire's two postulations may effect only a false doubling. The mind apparently divided between them may in fact remain threatened by paralysing homogeneity, by the impossibility of staging its own indifferentiation: 'Implicitly, the entire dualistic position – God versus Satan, spirit versus flesh – is exposed as . . . an illusory protection against the dangers of sameness.'[15]

It is partly, I believe, as an anticipatory response to such an argument that one should read 'La Musique', a poem that appears in all editions of *Les Fleurs du Mal*;

> Music will often take me like the sea!
>   When clouds are low
> Or in clear ether, I, towards my pale star
>   Set sail and go;
>
> With chest thrust forward and with lungs puffed out
>   My sails are tight;
> I climb the backs of all the heaped-up waves
>   As day turns night;
>
> Throbbing within me are the passions of
>   A suffering ship;
> The mild breeze, or the tempest and its throes
>
>   On the abyss
> Rock me. At other times, dead calm, the glass
>   Of hopelessness.
>
>   (FM 139)

> [La musique souvent me prend comme une mer!
>   Vers ma pale étoile,
> Sous un plafond de brume ou dans un vaste éther,
>   Je mets à la voile;

La poitrine en avant et les poumons gonflés
Comme de la toile,
J'escalade le dos des flots amoncelés
Que la nuit me voile;

Je sens vibrer en moi toutes les passions
D'un vaisseau qui souffre;
Le bon vent, la tempête et ses convulsions

Sur l'immense gouffre
Me bercent. D'autres fois, calme plat, grand miroir
De mon désespoir!

(OC I 68)]

Frequently interpreted as either the obvious starting point or the definitive summation of Baudelaire's writing on music, 'La Musique' is not often associated with his thinking about the theatre. Yet the curtain raised ['toile levée'], sail-like ['Comme de la toile'] that closes – or rather, does not close – 'Le Rêve d'un curieux' suggests that Baudelairean theatre does not lie far away from 'La Musique'. Recent criticism has renewed the traditional preoccupation with the poem's doubleness: for Rosemary Lloyd, the dualism of its rhythm is ultimately crippling since the sonnet is 'condemned to end on that bleakly abrupt five-syllable line';[16] for Gretchen Schultz, in contrast, the poem 'creates the possibility of a lyric practice free of confining oppositions'.[17] Without attempting here to join this debate at full volume, I would like to suggest that 'La Musique' should be at least partially understood as a protective affirmation of doubleness, the melodramatic doubleness that allows movement and meaning in Baudelaire's theatre of consciousness. One might usefully remember that storms at sea lavishly punctuated opera as well as melodrama in the nineteenth century, and Baudelaire's Wagner essay emphasises the alternation of tranquillity and tempest that drives both drama and music in *Der Fliegende Holländer* (OC II 803–5). Could one therefore interpret 'La Musique' as the emergence of self-conscious subjectivity out of the looming antagonism between storm and calm that divisively doubles the seascape of the melodramatic mind? Such a reading would have to place the poem at just the right distance, exaggerating its suspenseful, preconscious darkness while intensifying the glimmering awareness of its 'pale star'. This is perhaps the kind of reading Baudelaire had in mind when he wrote in *Mon Cœur mis à nu* that 'after all, the chandelier has always appeared to me as the principal actor, seen through the large end or the small end of the lorgnette' ['après tout, le lustre m'a toujours paru l'acteur principal, vu à travers le gros bout ou le petit bout de la lorgnette' (OC I 682)]. By lighting up stages from the Boulevard of Crime to the Bayreuth Festival Theatre, Baudelaire's writing doubles and redoubles our chances to see how music and drama illuminate each other, inside and outside the mind.

NOTES

1. Roland Barthes, 'Le Théâtre de Baudelaire', in *Essais critiques* (Paris: Seuil, 1964), p. 43.
2. James Treadwell, *Interpreting Wagner* (New Haven: Yale University Press, 2003), p. 4.
3. Claire Lyu, ' "High Poetics": Baudelaire's *Le Poème du haschich*', MLN 109, 4 (1994), pp. 701–22.
4. Terry Castle, 'Phantasmagoria: Spectral Technology and the Metaphorics of Modern Reverie', *Critical Inquiry* 15, 1 (1988), p. 49.
5. Mikkel Borch-Jacobsen, *The Freudian Subject*, trans. Catherine Porter (Stanford, CA: Stanford University Press, 1982), p. 17.
6. Antonio Damasio, *The Feeling of What Happens* (San Diego: Harcourt, 1999), p. 3.
7. Ross Chambers, *Loiterature* (Lincoln: University of Nebraska Press, 1999), p. 221.
8. Rosemary Lloyd, *Baudelaire's World* (Ithaca, NY: Cornell University Press, 2002), p. 208.
9. Richard E. Burton, *Baudelaire and the Second Republic: Writing and Revolution* (Oxford: Clarendon Press, 1991), p. 273.
10. Barthes, 'Le Théâtre de Baudelaire', p. 47.
11. Peter Brooks, *The Melodramatic Imagination: Balzac, Henry James, Melodrama and the Mode of Excess* (New York: Columbia University Press, 1985), p. 36.
12. Treadwell, *Interpreting Wagner*, pp. 34–5.
13. Elizabeth Paley, ' "The voice which was my Music": Narrative and Nonnarrative Musical Discourse in Schumann's *Manfred*', *19th-century Music*, 24, 1 (2000), pp. 3–4.
14. Brooks, *The Melodramatic Imagination*, pp. 153–97.
15. Leo Bersani, *Baudelaire and Freud* (Berkeley: University of California Press, 1977), p. 95.
16. Lloyd, *Baudelaire's World*, p. 205.
17. Gretchen Schultz, 'Baudelaire's Frontiers', in *The Gendered Lyric: Subjectivity and Difference in Nineteenth-Century French Poetry* (West Lafayette, IN: Purdue University Press, 1999), p. 205.

11

ROSEMARY LLOYD

Baudelaire's literary criticism

Criticism, for Baudelaire, whether of art, music or literature, was at its best when it was amusing, poetic and impassioned, and when it was driven by an urgent intellectual desire to deduce the reasons that justify the emotion these arts aroused (OC II 127). That emotion was at times so intense as to provoke a physical reaction: thus, recalling the first time he read the works of the poet, novelist and critic Théophile Gautier, Baudelaire asserts that his admiration for Gautier's skill was strong enough to create in him a kind of nervous convulsion (OC II 118). Finding a way of understanding that reaction, and conveying it in writing, dominates much of his criticism, giving it its particular savour and edge.

Indeed, to understand those reactions and to represent a work well, Baudelaire asserts in an article published in 1851, you need to *get inside its skin*. This expression, which he puts in italics to signify its novelty, had recently been created by an actor explaining his technique for conveying characters (OC II 1094). It is typical of Baudelaire's interest in the modern and his ability to transfer concepts created for one genre to another different genre that he seizes with such energy and acumen on this term from the theatre. In his literary criticism, Baudelaire constantly attempts to get inside the skin of the work he is reviewing, devoting considerable intellectual energy to analysing the writings of his contemporaries, not merely the well known, like Victor Hugo, Gustave Flaubert and Théophile Gautier, but also lesser-known figures such as the worker poet, Pierre Dupont, and Marceline Desbordes-Valmore, whose *Elégies* (1819) was the first volume of Romantic poetry published in France.

While his literary criticism is often overlooked, it offers not just an impassioned view of the contemporary publishing scene, but also a series of rare insights into his own techniques, an oblique but revealing glimpse of the strings and pulleys that set his creative writing in motion. It includes, moreover, some sharp advice to those of his contemporaries who shared his own ambitions as a writer: 'These days it is essential to produce a great deal, which means moving fast, which means hurrying slowly, so that every blow strikes home and every single touch is useful' ['Aujourd'hui il faut produire beaucoup; – il faut donc aller vite; – il faut donc se hâter lentement; il faut donc que tous les coups portent, et que pas une touche ne soit inutile' (OC II 17)]. This is the young Baudelaire, dashing off his 'Advice to Young Writers' ['Conseils aux jeunes écrivains'] in 1846, and insisting already on what would become, through the influence of Edgar Allan Poe, an even more powerfully expressed artistic credo, according to which every element of creative work must contribute to the overall effect. As is so often the case, it is a tenet he extends to his critical writing, for in analysing the work and reception of his contemporaries Baudelaire is always also analysing, exercising and extending his own writing skills, always making sure that every single element pulls its weight.

Baudelaire began publishing articles of literary criticism in November 1845 and continued until 1864. While some of these articles review individual works, others attempt to provide a more sweeping assessment of a writer or a movement, and others still, notably those devoted to Edgar Allan Poe and Thomas de Quincey, intertwine criticism, translation and paraphrase. Most of the early articles were written, at least in the first instance, for publication in newspapers and periodicals, imposing on him the inevitable restrictions and conventions of such vehicles. Later on, he produced a group of articles for Eugène Crépet's anthology devoted to contemporary writers, a work in which samples of the writers' work were introduced by critical essays. In reading them, we need to bear this fact in mind, since they are shaped in large measure by the choice of the poems that accompanied them, which Baudelaire played a role in choosing.[1] The early articles offer a striking variety of techniques and styles, and although in the later essays he was constrained to follow the format, and sometimes the judgments, that Crépet set down, he continues to reveal the desire to experiment either with contemporary themes or with the genre of criticism itself. Although for many readers his critical insight is at its sharpest in his writing on art, the literary criticism projects a particularly vivid light not just on his contemporaries and on the period in which he was writing, but also on the ways in which Baudelaire explored the potential of images, techniques and convictions that would later find their way into his creative writing.

Reading these pieces, we have a sense of a writer testing beliefs, trying out stylistic devices, exploring problems and trying to form an image of an ideal reading public, one that would create the atmosphere favourable to his more daring creative experiments. But he is also, of course, providing intensely personal responses to the literature of his time, reacting to works like Gustave Flaubert's *Madame Bovary* and Victor Hugo's *La Légende des siècles* as they were published, and attempting to situate his friends, rivals and enemies within a constantly changing hierarchy. We may feel on reading him that he is strangely reluctant to express praise for some writers or that he barely acknowledges the flaws of others, but this is to ignore the context in which he wrote, the hurly-burly of the moment, the political and pragmatic realities with which he was contending, the demands of editors and the strategies and conventions associated with anthologies. As he himself puts it in his advice to young writers, there is no point in attacking someone who is strong: and anyway, even if you have areas of disagreement with that person, you will always be together on certain issues (OC II 16).

Throughout the articles there is a sense of Baudelaire exploring the limits and possibilities of critical writing and in doing so pursuing ideas and techniques that recur in other aspects of his work. We can, for example, discover variants on the prose poems, as happen for instance in his response to the Pagan School,[2] where he briefly explores the actions of 'a prankster artist who had been given a false coin' ['un artiste farceur qui avait reçu une pièce de monnaie fausse' (OC II 49)], a theme developed much further in the prose poem called 'La Fausse Monnaie'. We find him testing out arresting ways of opening his articles, that art of the *entrée en matière* that he deploys with such mastery in some of the verse and prose poems. In the literary criticism, this skill appears in such striking formulations as

> In the year just passed a considerable event took place. I won't say it is the most important, but it is one of the most important, or rather one of the most symptomatic . . .
>
> [Il s'est passé dans l'année qui vient de s'écouler un fait considérable. Je ne dis pas qu'il soit le plus important, mais il est l'un des plus important, ou plutôt l'un des plus symptomatiques . . .   (OC II 44)]

or, in more pithy fashion, 'I know no sentiment more embarrassing than admiration' ['Je ne connais pas de sentiment plus embarrassant que l'admiration' (OC II 103)]. Elsewhere he explores the possibilities of personal reminiscence as a way of leading into the work under discussion: in this way, he gives us a showy pen-portrait of his first meeting with Gautier, in which the older poet quizzes the younger one on his familiarity with dictionaries. This not only brings the writer's personality sharply alive for the reader but also prepares the ground for the assertion attributed to Gautier that anyone who is found wanting by any idea, however subtle and unexpected, is no writer: 'the inexpressible does not exist' ['l'inexprimable n'existe pas' (OC II 118)], Baudelaire has him affirm, implacably.

Baudelaire's criticism is a testing ground not just for the skills of individual writers but also more generally for criticism itself. He raises questions concerning the nature and limits of criticism, especially concerning its links with biography (an area given particular prominence by the most eminent literary critic of the day, Sainte-Beuve). In this regard he asserts that the general public likes to know what kind of education a poet has received (OC II 28), or argues that whereas some lives are full of heroic or public events others take place almost exclusively 'under the cupola of the poet's skull' ['sous la coupole de son cerveau' (OC II 104)] and demand a quite different approach from the critic re-creating their biography. In other passages treating the same area, we can find him testing his gift for metaphor in finding a parallel between the external world and the life of the person under scrutiny. Of the actor Philibert Rouvière, for example, he affirms with virtuoso skill:

> Here is an agitated and twisted life, like those trees – the pomegranate for instance, – that are knotted, baffled in their growth, giving fruit that are complex and tasty, and whose proud red flowers appear to tell their own story through a sap long compressed.

> [Voilà une vie agitée et tordue, comme ces arbres – le grenadier, par exemple, – noueux, perplexes dans leur croissance, qui donnent des fruits compliqués et savoureux, et dont les orgueilleuses et rouges floraisons ont l'air de raconter l'histoire par une sève longtemps comprimée.   (OC II 60)]

Part of this discussion on biography concerns the nature of criticism itself, but part is clearly connected to another preoccupation that threads its way through the articles and is of more personal import: that of the unpredictable nature of literary fame. While in his very early advice to young writers, Baudelaire can boldly deny the very existence of 'le guignon' or bad luck, his later articles confront the question with a deeper and more poignant sense of the arbitrary nature of popularity, the shakiness of fame and the dubious nature of public opinion. Why is it, he asks at one point, that one person's name is in everyone's mouth, while that of someone else still crawls in the darkness of library stacks or sleeps in manuscript form in the files of some review or other (OC II 33)? And when, in 1856, he comes to write his study devoted to the life and works of Edgar Poe, he acknowledges that there are in literary history cases of writers who 'bear the words "ill-fated" written in mysterious letters in the sinuous wrinkles of their brows' ['des hommes qui portent le mot *guignon* écrit en caractères mystérieux dans les plis sinueux de leur front' (OC II 296)]. More bitterly still, he contrasts the unhappy fates of Poe and Gérard de Nerval with that of Hégésippe Moreau, a minor poet whom he describes as a spoilt child who did not deserve his good fortune (OC II 157).

Some of the pleasure of reading the literary criticism stems from the way in which ideas and techniques reappear across time and genres, their transformations reflecting Baudelaire's own experiences and his intellectual evolution. Even in the advice to young writers, a piece that might seem to have more to do with braggadocio than with literature, Baudelaire tries out metaphors that will later resurface elsewhere. The image of the poet as vanquished sword fighter, better known for its role in the prose poem 'Le Confiteor de l'artiste', makes an early appearance here, where the fencing poet attempts to drive off a creditor but realises that he has not only failed in his attempt and wasted his energy, but earned the scorn of the fencing master. More generally, the section entitled 'Methods of Composition' shows him playing, as he had in his account of the art salon of the same year (1846), with the interrelationship of word and image: covering a canvas, he asserts, is not loading it with colours, but sketching out the main parts of your picture with a thin layer of paint. The canvas, he asserts, must be filled – in the mind – at the moment when the writer takes up his or her pen to write the title (OC II 17).

The more mature criticism is often remarkable for its striking metaphors. In his article on Léon Cladel, for instance, he draws on science to refute the need for a work of literature to point an obvious and laboured moral: 'as for the morality of the book, it bursts from it quite naturally as heat does from certain chemical mixtures' ['quant à la moralité du livre, elle en jaillit naturellement comme la chaleur de certains mélanges chimiques' (OC II 1870)], he asserts. Balzac, to give another example of an unexpected but striking metaphor, appears as a prodigious meteor 'that will cover France with a cloud of glory, like a strange and exceptional sunrise, or a polar dawn inundating the frozen desert with its enchanting lights' ['ce prodigieux météore qui couvrira notre pays d'un nuage de gloire, comme un orient bizarre et exceptionnel, comme une aurore polaire inondant le désert glacé de ses lumières féeriques' (OC II 78)]. In a study devoted to Théophile Gautier, to whom Baudelaire dedicated Les Fleurs du Mal, the poet's muse puts in an unexpected appearance as Queen of Sheba:

Thus she advances, in her various guises, this bizarre muse with her multiple outfits, a cosmopolitan muse gifted with the suppleness of the Athenian general, Alcibiades; sometimes she appears great and sacred, her brow bound with the oriental mitre, her clothes flowing in the wind while at others she struts along like a tipsy Queen of Sheba, her little copper parasol in her hand, on the porcelain elephant that decorated the mantle-pieces in the age of gallantry.

[Ainsi va, dans son allure variée, cette muse bizarre, aux toilettes multiples, muse cosmopolite douée de la souplesse d'Alcibiade; quelquefois le front ceint de la mitre orientale, l'air grand et sacré, les bandelettes au vent; d'autres fois, se pavanant comme une reine de Saba en goguette, son petit parasol de cuivre à la main, sur l'éléphant de porcelaine qui décore les cheminées du siècle galant.

(OC II 122)]

One of the delights of reading Baudelaire's early literary criticism derives from a sense of sweeping confidence and an energetic openness to new possibilities. Each of these youthful pieces deploys a different critical technique in a virtuoso display of approaches which in itself points to the extent to which these pieces are also a flexing of the writerly muscles. Thus, the very brief account of *Les Contes normands*, a collection written by the Normandy author Philippe de Chennevières under the pen name Jean de Falaise, manages, for all its apparent conventionality, to include a pithy statement of aesthetic principle:

Whereas all writers today aim to create for themselves a borrowed temperament and soul, Jean de Falaise has given his own soul, his true soul, in all honesty, and has quietly created an original work.

[Pendant que tous les auteurs s'attachent aujourd'hui à se faire un tempérament et une âme d'emprunt, Jean de Falaise a donné la sienne, la sienne vraie, la sienne pour de bon, et il a fait tout doucement un ouvrage original.

(OC II 3)]

His lively little piece of November 1845, entitled 'How to pay your debts when you have genius' ['Comment on paie ses dettes quand on a du génie' (OC II 6)], is a seductively witty pastiche of Honoré de Balzac's style and themes, twining some of the novelist's most memorable titles into a story in which Balzac is seen as the hero of a tale as ingenious as any of those in his novels.

What made him look so grim, the great man? Why was he walking like that, chin hanging down to his belly? Why was he wrinkling his brow to the point of making it a *Wild Ass's Skin*? Was he dreaming of pineapples at a penny a dozen, of a hanging bridge made of lianas, a villa with no staircase, its bedrooms hung with muslin? Had some princess on the verge of turning forty sent him one of those deep glances that beauty owes to genius? Was his brain, pregnant with some industrial machine, tortured by all the *Sufferings of an Inventor*?

[Qu'avait-il donc à être si noir, le grand homme! pour marcher ainsi, le menton sur la bedaine, et contraindre son front plissé à se faire *Peau de chagrin*? Rêvait-il ananas à quatre sous, pont suspendu en fil de liane, villa sans escalier avec des boudoirs tendus en mousseline? Quelque princesse, approchant de la quarantaine, lui avait-elle jeté une de ces œillades profondes que la beauté doit

au génie? ou son cerveau, gros de quelque machine industrielle, était-il tenaillé
par toutes les *Souffrances d'un inventeur?* (OC II 6–7)]

This is pastiche at its most creative, at once flattering and exploratory, and
it reveals a skill Baudelaire will return to, frequently if more soberly, in his
later critical writing.

Another technique Baudelaire delights in employing appears first in the
review of Louis Ménard's *Prométhée délivré* (1846). This article opens with
a lively conversation between critic and reader, in which, predictably, the
reader plays the role of stooge, forced to ask the questions that let the critic
show off his paces. But even when he is poking somewhat sarcastic fun both
at his naive reader and at Ménard's blend of the pagan and the modern,
Baudelaire still finds space to include some of those pithy and powerful
comments that illuminate not just his own aesthetics but literature more
generally. Here, for example, he chides Ménard for the vague and misty
form of his poetry, an accusation he clarifies with this arresting assertion that
casts considerable light on his poetic creativity: 'He knows nothing about
powerfully coloured rhymes, those lanterns that illuminate the path of the
idea' ['il ignore les rimes puissamment colorées, ces lanternes qui éclairent la
route de l'idée' (OC II 11)]. Thinking of rhyme not as an ornament having
little to do with the intellectual demands of a poem, but as a light that guides
both poet and reader along the path of the idea is both a demanding and a
liberating approach.

Baudelaire will return to something like this conversational style when
he represents Flaubert working out his novelistic method in preparation for
writing *Madame Bovary*. What, he has the novelist pondering, is the most
fertile region for stupidity and imbecility? The provinces, comes the swift
and inevitable reply. What is the most worn-out subject, the tune that's been
played so often that all its possibilities have been exhausted? Adultery. And
Baudelaire goes on to depict Flaubert not only accepting the challenge of
choosing precisely those areas but also assuring himself that, given his great
stylistic and descriptive gifts, he can concentrate on analysis and logic to
show that all subjects are indifferently good or bad, according to the way
in which they are treated. This is Baudelaire getting inside the skin of the
work in ways that shed light not just on the novel itself but also on his own
creative methods.

By 1848, that traumatic year of revolution that put an end to France's
monarchy only to have it replaced by an empire, Baudelaire's style had
become more sober and his criticism less flamboyant, but his review of his
friend Champfleury's short stories establishes several central tenets in his
critical methodology and, perhaps because it is less determinedly virtuosic,

allows several revealing glimpses into his own literary situation. Running through this review are two dominant threads: the search for a personal artistic method and the importance of relying on 'nature', by which Baudelaire means both the observation of reality and an acknowledgment and exploitation of the writer's temperament, the refusal to don what he terms elsewhere a borrowed soul. Baudelaire had already given cogent expression to this latter conviction in his account of the art salon of 1846 where he emphasised the value of 'technical knowledge combined with self-knowledge, but with the knowledge of the techniques modestly leaving the major role to the artist's nature' ['la science du métier combinée avec le *gnôti séauton*, mais la science modeste laissant le beau rôle au tempérament' (OC II 431)]. Champfleury's acknowledgment of Balzac in the last volume of the tales under review allows Baudelaire to take up the vital theme of artistic method, arguing that Balzac is the only writer whose method is worth studying (OC II 22), before he moves on to concede that in attempting to sum up Champfleury's technique he may be expressing himself poorly, but he will be understood by all who have felt the need to create for themselves a personal aesthetic. This sense of speaking directly to those who share his fascination not just with what is being written but more vitally with the writing process itself dominates much of his later criticism, giving it its particular energy and edge.

In many of these later articles, Baudelaire seizes on the opportunity to paint with a broader brush, establishing the writer in question within the framework of contemporary schools or practice. The art for art's sake school comes in for some rough treatment for its apparent exclusion of passion and rationality. 'To dismiss passion and reason is to kill literature' ['Congédier la passion et la raison, c'est tuer la littérature' (OC II 47)], he will announce vehemently. Just as criticism has to be impassioned and personal, revealing the work of art through the critic's own temperament, a foregrounding of the role of the viewer that makes Baudelaire seem much closer to late twentieth-century criticism than the *ex cathedra* judgments of his contemporary Sainte-Beuve, so the work of art itself, if it is not to contradict human nature, should reflect the intense individuality of the writer rather than offering a skilful display of technical brilliance. An immoderate taste for form, he asserts in 1852, leads to monstrous and unknown disorders. Notions of what is exact and true disappear, he argues, if the form of the work takes over from its content (OC II 48).

If art for art's sake is dubbed puerile (OC II 26), so also are certain exaggerated tendencies of Romanticism, notably the cynicism and diabolic tendencies associated with Byron and with the minor French Romantics who followed in his wake. Equally, Baudelaire excoriates what he perceives as the growing materialism of the age, a materialism that has distorted the

appreciation of what is best in literature. Romanticism is waning, as Baudelaire acknowledges in the sonnet entitled 'The Setting of The Romantic Sun'
['Le Coucher du soleil romantique'] and in the first of the two articles he
devotes to Théophile Gautier. There are attempts to create a Realist school,
but Baudelaire protests that poetry is by its very nature at once what is most
real in this world and what is only completely true in another world, a second
reality created by the magic of the muse (OC II 121). Writers as depoliticised
as Baudelaire claimed to be by the failure of the 1848 revolution sought
escape by turning to art for art's sake, focusing on formal beauty and imper-
sonality, denying the possibility that morality could enter into any aesthetic
criterion, while others turned away from the modern world in an attempt
to reinvigorate the pagan culture of the Greeks. Looking back to an earlier
age, Baudelaire seems convinced, at least for the purposes of his argument,
that enthusiasm for works of imagination has waned dramatically since the
early 1840s, in the eyes of a public increasingly concerned with material
possessions.

This desire for setting the individual works he reviews within a wider
historical context can also be seen when, in his 1857 review of Flaubert's
Madame Bovary, he seizes on the opportunity to explore the situation of
the contemporary novel, reaching the sardonic conclusion that seven years
after the death of Balzac, only one novelist, Paul de Kock (on whom James
Joyce would confer immortality through his reference to this minor novelist
in *Ulysses*) has succeeded in forcing open the shaky door of popularity.
Similarly, Baudelaire provides a brilliant, concise review of the early days
of Romanticism (OC II 110–11) or a more sketchy picture of the situation
of poetry in the years leading up to 1848 (OC II 169).

Baudelaire's concerns are not of course just with specific works or with
tracing the literary developments of the day. He also uses the critical articles
to raise much wider questions. Is there such a thing as pernicious literature,
he asks rhetorically at one point, replying immediately that any art that
disturbs the conditions of life, depicting vice as other than both seductive
and destructive, is pernicious. But he adds belligerently, and as if already
preparing his own trial for offences to public morals in 1857, that he defies
anyone to find a single work of imagination that unites all the conditions of
beauty and yet are pernicious (OC II 41). What is the relationship between
truth and beauty? What is it that most defines particular writers? If for
Gautier it is the 'exclusive love of Beauty, with all its subdivisions, expressed
in the most appropriate language' ['l'amour exclusif du Beau, avec toutes ses
subdivisions, exprimé dans le langage le mieux approprié' (OC II 117)], for
Banville, on the other hand, it is lyricism, the ability to create impressions
that are so intense that the reader feels as if he or she has been launched

towards a higher region (OC II 164). Baudelaire's study of Poe allows him to take further his thinking on imagination, that queen of faculties as he calls it (OC II 328), and on the importance of totality of effect, that 'vital condition of every work of art' ['condition vitale de tout œuvre d'art' (OC II 332)]. For Victor Hugo he is able to set aside the corrosive envy he reveals in his letters and conclude admiringly that Hugo's natural domain is the excessive and immense ['l'excessif, l'immense sont le domaine naturel de Victor Hugo' (OC II 137)], and to acknowledge the ways in which the poet's exile in the Channel Islands colours his writing:

> he talks with the waves and the wind; in days gone by, he wandered alone in places seething with human life; today he walks in solitudes populated by his thought. He may well be all the greater and more exceptional for that. The colours of his reveries are tinged with solemnity, and his voice has grown deeper in rivalry with that of the Ocean.

> [il converse avec les flots et le vent; autrefois, il rôdait solitaire dans des lieux bouillonnant de vie humaine; aujourd'hui, il marche dans des solitudes peuplées par sa pensée. Ainsi est-il peut-être encore plus grand et plus singulier. Les couleurs de ses rêveries se sont teintées en solennité, et sa voix s'est approfondie en rivalisant avec celle de l'Océan.   (OC II 130)]

As this last quotation suggests, one of the areas in which Baudelaire's literary criticism is at its most arresting is in its use of pastiche (signalled in the passage quoted above by the words 'autrefois/aujourd'hui' ['in days gone by/today'] which recall the subdivisions of Hugo's collection *Les Contemplations*). Through such devices Baudelaire sometimes includes in his articles passages that go beyond standard analysis to offer creative and active explorations of his subject's techniques. The closing paragraph of his review of the Romantic poet Marceline Desbordes-Valmore draws, for example, on her frequent use of flower imagery and the overwhelming sense of melancholy that dominates so much of her poetry to create a pastiche that is above all a tribute to her writing. And in evoking the range of topics in Hugo's poetry, for example, Baudelaire clearly relishes the opportunity to speculate on the cosmos in ways that will demonstrate the great poet's skill through its echoes not just of his themes and images but also his rhythms, his lexicon, his word plays and his passionate questioning:

> Germinations, blossomings, flowerings, eruptions, whether successive, simultaneous, slow or sudden, progressive or complete, of stars, planets, suns, constellations, are you simple forms of God's existence or are you dwelling places prepared by his goodness or his justice for souls he seeks to educate and bring progressively closer to himself? Worlds eternally studied, never perhaps to be

known, oh tell us! is your destination that of Heaven or Hell, purgatory or prison, villas or palaces etc. . . .

[Germinations, éclosions, floraisons, éruptions successives, simultanées, lents ou soudaines, progressives ou complètes, d'astres, d'étoiles, de soleils, de constellations, êtes-vous simplement les formes de la vie de Dieu, ou des habitations préparées par sa bonté ou sa justice à des âmes qu'il veut éduquer et rapprocher progressivement de lui-même? Mondes éternellement étudiés, à jamais inconnus peut-être, oh! dites, avez-vous des destinations de paradis, d'enfers, de purgatoires, de cachots, de villas, de palais etc . . .]   (OC II 138)

It is difficult to imagine any passage of standard analysis bringing so suddenly alive the themes and devices that run through much of Hugo's mature poetry.

Impassioned and experimental, enlivened with pastiche and studded with aphorisms, Baudelaire's literary criticism holds up a mirror to his creative writing. It affords us glimpses into the mid nineteenth-century literary world, shows us reputations being made or unmade, reflects the precarious nature of journalistic publication at a time of unpredictable government censorship and above all allows us to get inside the skin not just of the works under discussion but much more importantly of Baudelaire's own methodology. The best response to a great work of art, he remarks in his art criticism, might be a sonnet or an elegy: his own responses to works of literature offer us a fascinating hybrid of analysis and creativity, forging in their own unique way a new genre.

NOTES

1. On this see my *Baudelaire's Literary Criticism* (Cambridge: Cambridge University Press, 1981).
2. Writers who drew their inspiration from Greek and Roman mythology.

12

BERYL SCHLOSSMAN

Baudelaire's place in literary a cultural history

Among Baudelaire's French contemporaries, only the novelist Gustave Flaubert has had a comparable impact on literature and culture. Beginning with Realism, Symbolism and Naturalism in the second half of the nineteenth century, Baudelaire's influence is international and interdisciplinary. The legacy of his poetry, prose, criticism and translations can be discerned throughout the verbal and visual arts, and in the disciplines devoted to the study of literature and culture.

The poet's interpretations of the arts and of modern life have shaped the understanding of modernity as a trajectory that leads from Baudelaire's times and places to our own, and from Paris as the capital of the nineteenth century to the modern world of the twenty-first century. Throughout the twentieth century, literature and culture were rich with Baudelairean influence; his works continue to speak to his readers with an unparalleled immediacy.

Like a magician, Baudelaire conjures up a set of figures and images that come to life in his literary works: poetry, prose poetry and stories; in his critical works on literature and art; and in French translations and critical adaptations of works written in English. These figures and images inform Baudelaire's world – as well as his modernity as an artist, a critic and a translator. He explores the experience of the self and the other through a singular vision of poetry: time, memory, pleasure, love, suffering and evil are the major elements of this exploration. Throughout Baudelaire's works, the separation of mind and body informs his perspective on original sin, laughter, comedy and the human condition. He formulates the intensity of imaginative vision in literature and in the connections among the arts.

Through the use of simile, correspondence and allegory as poetic techniques, Baudelaire emphasises the power of images to evoke time and place. In poetry and in prose, his vision allows the reader access to scenes and atmospheres; sentiments and relationships; city streets and supernatural landscapes; the vividness of the present, the longing for the past and the adventures of the unknown. Baudelaire's writing is innately interdisciplinary:

ne translates visual images into their verbal counterparts, and uses words to portray pictures, sculpture, music and architecture. Baudelaire underscores the unity of form and content, and he elaborates the fusion of poetry and prose in verbal art.

Baudelaire's impact on literary and cultural history is illustrated by the figures, images and poetic techniques that inform his writing. Baudelaire combines aspects of the old and the new to create a Modernist poetics. Modernism is literally transromantic: early Modernism emerges from Baudelaire's transformation of French Romanticism, and this transformation continues to influence writers, artists and critics. In essays, translations, verse and prose poetry, from the early poetics of *Spleen et Idéal* to the final sections of *Les Fleurs du Mal* and *Les Petits Poèmes en prose*, Baudelaire's transromantic aesthetics goes beyond the boundaries of genre to surprise and entrance the reader.

Narrator and reader

The introductory poem of *Les Fleurs du Mal* takes evil and violence out of the streets and into the reader's life. The power of this poem and many others originates in the new relationship between the theatrical and poetic voice of the speaker or narrator, and the familiar but anonymous 'you', the poem's presumed reader. For Baudelaire, evil is everywhere: the Catholic dogma of original sin pervades the human condition. With a tone that is disturbingly bitter and intimate, the narrator accuses the reader of every human failing. Evocations of prostitution, hypocrisy and acts of criminal violence lead to the narrator's final dramatic example.

The last figure of human weakness presented in the speaker's identification with the reader leads to a strangely anti-climactic ending. The poem paints a final portrait of someone suffering from *ennui*, a French name for the Romantic concept of Spleen. The victim of Spleen is subject to a state of boredom and a disconcerting lack of will-power. After a detailed list of humanity's crimes, the personified vice of *ennui* is proclaimed to be the most horrible of all sins.

Is the narrator's denunciation of the figure of *ennui*, passively smoking the water pipe, an ironic dismissal of the poor reader? If the narrator is ironic here, then it is only at his own expense: he dramatically reveals the reader to be his own likeness and his brother. The resemblance between self and other defines Baudelaire's term of likeness, my semblance or 'mon semblable'. Baudelaire's aesthetic of resemblance leads from Shakespeare's Hamlet to the Modernism of Arthur Rimbaud, Stéphane Mallarmé, Guillaume Apollinaire, Virginia Woolf, James Joyce, Marcel Proust, Nathalie Sarraute, Marguerite

Duras and Samuel Beckett. Baudelaire transforms Hamlet's vision of his murdered father mirrored in himself into the image of modern humankind, set loose in an urban wilderness of violence and desire.

Baudelaire's theatre of violence features criminal acts of murder and suicide, verbal threats and accusations and the solitary melancholy of illness, marginalisation and generalised suffering. In his portrayals of the artist, the lover and the criminal, a sense of intimacy connects these fictional characters with the reader.

In the poems and prose poetry, the identity of the speaker or narrator – frequently masculine, but sometimes neutral – is not known. Accompanied by this mysterious speaker, the reader plunges into Baudelaire's cityscapes, deserted spaces, cemeteries and boudoir scenes. It may seem paradoxical, but the violence that permeates *Les Fleurs du Mal* has not prevented readers from viewing Baudelaire as one of the greatest poets of desire, love and memory.

Correspondence: sensuality and art

In one of Baudelaire's most celebrated poems, 'Correspondances', the poet evokes Emanuel Swedenborg's doctrine of the correspondences to illustrate the human connection to the natural world as a 'forest of symbols'. With his vision of correspondence, Baudelaire takes up the question of meaning in a secular context that contrasts 'the spirit' with 'the senses' but gives the last word of the poem to sensuality. The poem links sensual experience and the vocabulary of art within an aesthetics of suggestion. Baudelaire reshapes the Romantic concept of synaesthesia (the transformation of one form of sensory perception into another, for example seeing music or hearing a work of visual art) as a form of voluptuous sensual experience and as the translation of that experience into art. Many of Baudelaire's poems and prose poems achieve the effects of correspondence: like Balzac and Gautier before him, Baudelaire was fascinated by E. T. A. Hoffmann's literary experimentation with synaesthesia. In the sonnet 'Correspondences', voluptuous experience dominates the second quatrain, and the translation into art of sensual exchanges of sounds, colours and sensory qualities occurs in the sestet. The poem accomplishes the art of correspondence that it thematises.

The plenitude of correspondence connects the power of involuntary memory – the most sensually oriented form of memory – with the evocative powers of art. In his novel, *A la recherche du temps perdu*, Marcel Proust places the programme of Baudelaire's 'Correspondences' at the centre of his character's experience of time rendered visible, and the ambition to capture that experience in writing. In the poem, Baudelaire articulates an aesthetic approach to experience that will allow the senses, the arts and thought or spirituality to connect across time and space, within the exquisite and eternal moment of a sonnet. Baudelaire's readers continue to be intrigued by the promise of this mysterious poem.

In Proust's novel, the approach unfolds across time within the span of a life. The magical awakening that takes place across the arts and the senses in Baudelaire's poem turns into a scene of resurrection in Proust's novel: the sensual and spiritual experience of memory magically overturns the passage of time. The final figure of this resurrection appears as a young woman, the daughter and granddaughter of several major characters, introduced to the narrator in the matinée scene that ends the novel. Art and love, carefully paired in Baudelaire's poems, receive a decisive echo in Proust's novel of vocation, and the figure of the young woman appears precisely when the narrator thinks his life is over.

Baudelaire's women and men

Like other nineteenth-century writers influenced by the culture of Christianity and moved by its offshoot of Satanism, Baudelaire is fond of attributing the responsibility for evil to women. But evil in Baudelaire is inseparable from suffering and subjectivity: the lyric voices in Baudelaire's love poems indicate a tenderness for women that contradicts the poet's famous misogyny. Other writings, including the private journals, underline the importance of Baudelaire's identification with women rather than with men throughout his life.

Like the sketches and paintings by Constantin Guys, Baudelaire's 'painter of modern life', Baudelaire's written portraits of women include magnificent ladies and weary prostitutes at the opposite poles of society, as well as a range of social roles in between them. Baudelaire places a special emphasis on women at the margins: street singers, a young widow holding a child by the hand and elderly ladies alone in public gardens.

Compared to Baudelaire's portraits of men as philistines and hated figures of authority, his portraits of women receive a homage of sympathy and identification. Men appear in a more favourable light in Baudelaire's works as poets, *flâneurs* and artists, or criminals, poor workers, rag-pickers and gypsies in exile, whereas women are generally conceived as figures expressive of tenderness, beauty and the feminine. As ladies and prostitutes, actresses, dancers, widows, elderly women and young girls are vectors of the poet's confidence. Among women, only hard-hearted coquettes and *femmes fatales* receive the bitter treatment that Baudelaire's poems reserve for threatening masculine figures of authority. One exception is the mother of the poet in 'Bénédiction', an early figure who never reappears in Baudelaire's writing.

After the early poems of the 1840s, Baudelaire evokes more nuanced figures of women. His maternal portraits culminate in one of the great long poems of the 'Parisian Pictures', 'Les Petites Vieilles' ('The Little Old Women'), with its palette of tones and its tender depiction of anonymous women in the streets of Paris.

Beyond realism: melancholia

Baudelaire's depiction of the human condition returns to the sensibility familiar to readers of French classical and baroque literature, with a difference: Baudelaire brings this sensibility into a modern framework. Poems like 'Une charogne' introduce the figure of a woman to personalise the encounters between the subject and her/his perceptions of mortality. Baudelaire elaborates a range of tones – from elegiac tenderness to biting sarcasm and satire – within a melancholic atmosphere charged with mourning. Baudelaire's emphasis on the materiality and corruption inherent in *le mal* contrasts with the values of spirituality and humankind's higher nature.

Baudelaire explores this duality throughout his writings: from the poetics of correspondence to the nature of laughter, human nature is afflicted with a double perspective, a duality of high and low. While the origin of this duality is a commonplace of Christianity, the development it takes in Baudelaire's writing has had an extraordinary impact on the writers and artists of modernity. Baudelaire's twofold nature inspires important developments in Modernism that include the art of Manet and Cezanne, who frequently recited 'Une charogne', and the German poetry of Rainer Maria Rilke, in addition to the French canon of poetry and prose, from Arthur Rimbaud, Lautréamont and Stéphane Mallarmé to Apollinaire, André Gide and Marcel Proust. In theatre, Baudelaire's influence can be perceived in the innovative works of Antonin Artaud, Bertold Brecht, Jean Genet and Samuel Beckett. Although it was deeply suspicious of all canonical cultural values, the Surrealist movement saw the modernity of Baudelaire as one of its major points of origin.

Baudelaire's impact extends to French cinema, beginning with Germaine Dulac's silent film, *La Souriante Madame Beudet*. Dulac's protagonist, the unhappily married Madame Beudet, sees the tragedy of her double life reflected in *Les Fleurs du Mal*. The tone of Truffaut's New Wave classic, *Jules et Jim*, and especially the character of Catherine, played by Jeanne Moreau, recalls many of Baudelaire's poems and prose poems. Baudelaire's emphasis on the vocations of art and love is thematised in the film; Truffaut's emphasis on the triangle of love and friendship is Baudelairean in tone and sensibility. The devoted friends are eager to experience literature, passion and pleasure;

friendship and passionate love become inextricable. Catherine incarnates the best and the worst of Baudelaire's women. She is by turns tender and cruel, destructive and sensual, capricious and charming. In recent cinema, Agnès Varda in particular explores the Baudelairean resonances of love and loss in her film entitled *Jacquot de Nantes*. In philosophy and criticism, the impact of Baudelaire is visible throughout the work of Georges Bataille, including his writings on literature, eroticism and religion. Especially in the essay entitled 'La Littérature et le mal', a major aspect of modern and contemporary French literature finds its source in the writing of Baudelaire.

Floating through the crowd

As a figure for the poet, Baudelaire's speaker has stepped down from the role of the romantic bard, played by Alfred de Musset, Victor Hugo and Alfred de Vigny – famous French Romantic poets who saw themselves as leaders of men in politics and authorities on spiritual matters as well as literature. Unlike them, Baudelaire's speaker mingles with the crowd of anonymous women and men. This crowd includes artists, acrobats, widows, *flâneurs*, dandies, revolutionaries, beggars, street-singers and prostitutes. Elbowed by the crowd, anonymous as these Parisians are anonymous, Baudelaire's speaker sees himself in their images.

Baudelaire's speaker addresses himself to one of these Parisian characters, to a woman as an object of love or a figure of memory, or to an unknown anonymous reader. In each relationship, the explicit or implicit 'you' of the poem becomes someone who embodies the modernity of time and place, as well as someone who understands the roles that Baudelaire's speaker plays because he or she also plays roles.

'Le Cygne' uses the direct address (apostrophe) to present several characters in a poem about exile and dedicated to the exiled French writer, Victor Hugo. In this famous poem from the 'Tableaux parisiens', the narrator takes the reader back into Roman antiquity through a personalised allusion to Virgil's *Aeneid*. Baudelaire uses simile, metaphor and allegory to create a set of four intertwined figures, including the narrator, a man walking through the upheaval of modern Paris. The swan is an anthropomorphic animal who speaks in a Parisian scene from the narrator's memory: at the same time, the swan allegorically represents the exiled poet, Ovid. The narrator evokes the swan and Andromache as he walks along the streets of Paris. The figure of an African woman completes this set of four characters. In this poem, Baudelaire uses a set of analogies connecting ancient Rome to Paris in the 1850s to explore the interrelated themes of the city, political exile and the suffering of loss.

The poem begins with an apostrophe that connects the narrator to the Trojan heroine, and nineteenth-century Paris with Roman antiquity: 'Andromache, I think of you!' A second use of apostrophe in the poem occurs in the supernatural voice of the swan, related to the exiled Latin poet Ovid. Speech is denied the Trojan Andromache, Hector's widow who survived the Trojan War, and an unnamed African woman dying in Paris, but the narrator, who emphasises their state of silence, speaks for them, and presents them to the reader. The poem evokes the contrast between the old and the new, between disappearance and mourning as a form of preservation of the past, in an elegiac account of poets and heroines, ancient and modern. The city becomes a kind of palimpsest: texts and memories are written in a set of layers. They connect at points of correspondence – moments of transport, in time and in poetic images. The poem is in two parts, or two layers, as if to illustrate the mirror effect or the reflection of the present and the past in each other. At the end of this long poem, the trickling rivulet of Andromache's theatre of mourning in the first stanza is transformed into an ocean of exile. The mirroring effect of the narrator meditating on the fate of Andromache opens out as a vast panorama that sweeps away all personal identities. The narrator's voice eloquently fades away at the end.

The faces in Baudelaire's Parisian crowd search for work, pleasure or a role to play; they are actors, street entertainers, gamblers, prostitutes looking for men or solitary men following women, idle smokers, bohemians, homeless rag-pickers, gypsies and artists. The poetic narrator takes the poem's theatre of violent experience over the threshold separating the reader from the text: the poem becomes a mirror that Baudelaire holds up to the reader.

The artist in the city

The crowd, an indicator of modernity, is frequently the backdrop of Baudelaire's stage; the crowd permeates his writings. From the poet in the streets to the art critic taking in the latest salon or gallery exhibit, the experiences that form the subjects of Baudelaire's poems and prose writings take the speaker or narrator into the crowd. Many of Baudelaire's innovations in style are rooted in his vision of the city dweller's experience. What differentiates Baudelaire's approach to city life from similar attempts by Romantic and post-Romantic French authors is that the poet's narrators (first-person speakers) are hard to place: sometimes they are identified as men, or as poets, but often they are as unidentifiable as the anonymous figures that fill the crowd. This stroke of originality allows Baudelaire's speakers to circulate in the crowd. According to Baudelaire's views of the art of 'bathing in the multitude', his narrators absorb the being of strangers – including all the characters dwelling heroically at the edges of society. A pioneer writer and critic of his time, Baudelaire found many of his human subjects at the margins of society: in the poor workers drinking inexpensive wine at the city limits, in the counter-culture of artists, musicians, actors, writers and circus performers viewed as unconventional and even dangerous 'bohemians' by the middle and upper classes; among the poor, especially those who tried to make a living from the streets – petty criminals, as well as the prostitutes, rag-pickers, vendors and street-performers who fascinate the poet with their artful means of survival and the forms of theatricality inherent in their activities. As subjects of the crowd, Baudelaire's narrators portray a range of emotions, social situations and fates, and they share the ambiguity of voice that is a trademark of modernity.

Another example of stylistic innovation that Baudelaire explicitly anchors in the experience of the modern city dweller is the erasure of generic lines separating poetry from prose, or more specifically, traditional verse forms from prose fiction. In *Les Fleurs du Mal*, Baudelaire combines tradition and innovation within a poetics that is revolutionary in voice, theme, tone, vocabulary and in some instances, verse form. The prose poems continue the pursuit of a new poetics within the contexts of the 'Tableaux parisiens', written in the years before and after 1857. In this year, the first edition of *Les Fleurs du Mal* appeared and came under attack from the French government. It can be argued that the poet's innovations (rather than the scabrous or obscene content of a handful of poems) were to blame for the censure that Baudelaire received.

In the dedication of *Le Spleen de Paris* (*Petits poèmes en prose*) to Arsène Houssaye, Baudelaire constructs a distinctive formulation of prose poetry that remains as modern today as it was in the mid nineteenth century. His definition combines the freedom of prose to be musical without the formal constraints of prosody (meter and rhyme) with the poetics of *Les Fleurs du Mal*. In Baudelaire's writing, correspondence and allegory shape a verbal art of suggestion that includes the evocation of the fine arts in language, the moral landscape of modern life, the portrayal of beauty and a devastating irony that undercuts the illusions created by beautiful representation. In the preface to *Le Spleen de Paris*, Baudelaire does not mention the secret architecture – the structure of a book, with a beginning, middle and an end – that he described to defend *Les Fleurs du Mal* under attack in 1857. Instead, Baudelaire recalls the aesthetic of the fragment; he presents the prose poems as fragments of a whole, to be taken in any order desired. The notion of the work as a quasi-organic entity, a whole, might indicate that Baudelaire's thought about the book of prose poems is not radically different from his conception of the book of verse.

As the dedication promises, Baudelaire's versatile prose poems capture the movements of sensibility and conscience for a range of anonymous narrators. He seeks out the adventurous possibilities offered to the anonymous city dweller in Paris, the capital of modernity. The flexibility of prose forms ranges from short parables, lyrical mood poems, prose echoes of verse poems, to ironic fables and myths adapted to Parisian life. Baudelaire pursues the aesthetic impulse that he developed in *Les Fleurs du Mal*: a moment of lyrical illusion is posited and dramatically dispelled in the final lines.

Modern beauty and modern art

Baudelaire's concept of beauty is heterogeneous, and linked to time. It is a combination of qualities that he names 'eternal' (unaffected by the course of time and shifts in taste and fashion) and 'transitory' – dependent on the particulars of time, place and fashion. Beauty must contain an element of the bizarre as well as plastic or sculptural qualities, and a form of exaggeration that appears in rhetoric as hyperbole. Baudelaire evokes layers of meaning or the image of a spiral, a palette of suggestive qualities, and the interaction of light and dark. These traits are typical of Renaissance and baroque allegory, reshaped in a modern vein in Baudelaire's writing.

In his writings on art, important examples of Baudelaire's revival of allegory are the work of Alfred Rethel and Charles Meryon, championed by Baudelaire alone. Baudelaire's impact on art history goes beyond the work of these artists to appreciate the contributions of many artists of his time, including the work of Delacroix, his primary mentor in art, Honoré Daumier, honoured for his caricatures and a great painter not recognised in his own time, and Constantin Guys, an illustrator who was considered a minor artist. Baudelaire rehabilitates the reputation of Guys, his 'painter of modern life' destined for literary glory, and comparable in the scope and ambition of his work to Manet. Baudelaire sees Guys as a master of the quick sketch that is essential to his vision of an art of modernity. Through his sketches, drawings and paintings, as well as his work as an illustrator in the age before photo-journalism, Constantin Guys produces a rich and unique evocation of modern life in the nineteenth century.

In his studies of the work of nineteenth-century artists, Baudelaire emphasises the role of the imagination. He is impressed by the imaginative vision that enables Delacroix to adapt (or 'translate') complex works of literature (including Shakespeare's *Hamlet*, Goethe's *Faust* and episodes from Lord

Byron's *Don Juan*) into serial works of visual art and to capture a wide range of dramatic scenes, animal studies, landscapes, seascapes, religious subjects and scenes of everyday life in form and colour.

Baudelaire's art criticism influences critical tastes and painterly style – beginning with Baudelaire's contemporaries, especially Manet – in part through the aesthetics of modern beauty, the role of the inventive imagination and the expressive use of colour and texture that Baudelaire explores in his studies on Delacroix. Baudelaire's conception of the painting of modern life demonstrates his independence from Delacroix and shapes the aesthetics of Impressionism and post-Impressionism. The work of Morisot, Manet, Cézanne and Van Gogh reveals the impact of Baudelaire's poetry and criticism.

Translation and imagination

Baudelaire's valorisation of the role of imagination is confirmed in the work of two major nineteenth-century writers, Thomas de Quincy and Edgar Allan Poe. Baudelaire's adaptation of Thomas de Quincy's writings on drug addiction and his early youth in the streets of London emphasises the allegorical qualities of imagination. Through dreams and reveries, the past returns to de Quincy, each time in a new appearance, with mysterious indications that the writer struggles to understand. Imagination reshapes experience into beautiful or terrifying memories, and infuses them with the passage of time.

Some of Baudelaire's most remarkable writing occurs in his extensive translations of the fiction of Edgar Allan Poe. Like Thomas de Quincy, Poe was familiar with life in the streets, and vulnerable to artificial paradises. At Poe's death, Baudelaire wrote a moving tribute that indicates his affinities with the American writer. Baudelaire translates his adventure stories, tales of shipwreck, detective stories, mystical ghost stories, horror stories based on character study and psycho-pathology and stories that explore modern city life. Poe is acknowledged as the inventor of the detective story, and Baudelaire draws attention to his poetics of composition. Following Baudelaire, Mallarmé translates Poe's verse, and Valéry explores some other aspects of Poe's impact on French literature. Baudelaire's translations of Poe's fiction continue to play a role in confirming Poe's reputation as a great modern writer.

Like De Quincy, Poe was a subject of modern life who depicted the fascination and the solitude of the modern city. Baudelaire recognised that both of these writers were engaged, as he was, with 'the painting of modern life'. In poems like 'Le Vin des chiffoniers' or 'A une passante', Baudelaire portrays the theatre of urban experience from the perspective of a man in the crowd; in other works, he portrays the writer wandering through the streets in search of rhymes. He uses techniques drawn from the ideas of 'translation', allegory and correspondence. In his art of suggestion, the traces of involuntary memory enter the poetic imagination. Beyond the nineteenth century, Baudelaire offers an art of modernity.

13

MARY ANN CAWS

A woman reading Baudelaire

> Mind the gap
>> (Announcement on the London Underground)

Making a binary move: all too easy with Baudelaire. On every level, in every genre. Political and social and moral: men against women; or perhaps the dark muse Jeanne Duval, available, and the white marble Madonna Mme Sabatier, available or not. These two women are both grandly illustrated in the poems in prose and verse, too clear to bear pointing out, especially, for Jeanne, the prose poems of sadistic clarity, and, for Mme Sabatier, the highly visual details in 'A une madone', as opposed to the woman in the prose poem 'La Belle Dorothée', in which the blazing sun and the complexion work in opposition against and for each other: 'Her red sunshade, filtering the light, projects on to her dark face the blood-red rouge of its reflections' (PP 66) ['Son ombrelle rouge, tamisant la lumière, projette sur son visage sombre le fard sanglant de ses reflets' (OC I 316)]. (See the specific details in 'A une madone', 'Les Bijoux', 'Le Serpent qui danse', and the concrete visuality of the 'sea of ebony' ['mer d'ébène'], 'blue head of hair' ['cheveux bleus'], 'your heavy mane' ['ta crinière lourde'], 'mingled scents / Essence of cooa-oil, pitch and musk' ['des senteurs confondues / De l'huile de coco, du musc, et du goudron'], in 'La Chevelure', as opposed to the unspecific canals, cities, vessels ['canaux', 'villes', 'vaisseaux'] of 'L'Invitation au voyage'). You think: there is a split everywhere: between rich child and poor ('Le Joujou du pauvre') or then between the noble impoverished lady in black walking outside the amusement park, holding her child by the hand – the price of the entrance would of course mean one less comfort or pleasure for the child – as opposed to the gaiety and bright dresses within ('Les Veuves'). Or on the concrete level, just the double room, 'La Chambre double', with its so clear division. On the psychological level: 'Laquelle est la vraie?' when the lovely girl dies and the little person appears: 'I am the real Benedicta!' (PP 90) ['C'est moi, la vraie Bénédicta!' (OC I 342)]. The male narrator stomps his refusal and sinks into the grave of the dead. VERY Poe-like. But, *pace* the Poe-lovers, this is Baudelaire, and his sensitivities are different, his nuances differently nuanced. It is not about creepiness, it is about reality and falsity, or what we take the mind or poem as doing for the present and future of our representations as they enhance our imaginations. And, of course, vice versa.

What is of overwhelming interest to me, reading as a woman and trying to unthink the so prevalent binary appearances, is exactly how the poems struggle against that too simple scheme of things. I find this: that the Baudelairean role reversals help undo those black and white, life and death binary structures, particularly in the prose poems, on which I will concentrate. Take, on the practical level: the pragmatic woman and dreaming man staring at the clouds in 'La Soupe et les nuages', which undoes the cliché about strong men and weak women, given this insistent female cook person against the gloriously romantic and impenetrable X: the soft man and hazy male. Take the creepy tale of 'Mademoiselle Bistouri' – her strong stick has phallic under-, over- and side-tones. The reversals go some way towards rethinking the mental prefiguration of the elements. Now this makes a certain kind of programmatic sense, that the genre of the prose poem should lend itself to flexibility.

Apart even from the fact that a great panoply of examples against the too-simple binary offers itself up here, the prose poem already bears within itself, like the detailed image of the thyrsus, its doubling. Barbara Johnson speaks of the 'code struggle' between prose and poetry[1] and that struggle intensifies the complication of the reading. See the following notes about the thyrsus, in relation to De Quincey's thought:

> the *thyrsus* of which he has so jokingly spoken, with the candour of a vagabond who knows himself well. The subject has no value other than that of a dry, bare stick; but the ribbons, the vines, and the flowers can, through their mad intermingling, provide a precious richness for the eyes. De Quincey's thought is not only sinuous, the word is not strong enough; it is naturally spiral.
>
> (PP 124–5)

> [le *thyrse* dont il a si plaisamment parlé, avec la candeur d'un vagabond qui se connaît bien. Le sujet n'a pas d'autre valeur que celle d'un bâton sec et nu; mais les rubans, les pampres et les fleurs peuvent être, par leurs entrelacements folâtres, une richesse précieuse pour les yeux. La pensée de De Quincey n'est pas seulement sinueuse; le mot n'est pas assez fort: elle est naturellement spirale   (OC I 515)]

Here's to the ribbons, of course, would say any feminist, here's to the spiral.

What wraps around, therefore, carries the aesthetic value, mad though it be in its attachment to and wandering about the stick. Together, they work. Rather like any couple, as in man and woman, man and man, woman and woman – too bad Baudelaire had to cut his lesbian poems out of his publication the first time round, after the trial of 1857. Good that Baudelaire appreciates 'the beauty of very mature women' (PP 108) ['la beauté des femmes très mûres' (OC I 363)]. But here we are, and in this examination of coupling and the binary, I shall be reading as what I just said: a woman.

What sort of difference might that make? Well, here is Barbara Johnson – whose favourite term is difference – reading the genre.

> Neither poetry's 'other' nor its 'same,' the prose poem thus constitutes nothing less than poet's double, is double space as the space of its own division, as its 'other stage,' where what has been repressed by poetry interminably returns in the uncanny figures of its strange familiarity, where poetry, the linguistic fetish, the 'dream of stone' – whether a Commendatore's statue or an implacable Venus with marble eyes – suddenly begins to speak from out of the Other, from out of what is constituted by its very inability to determine its own limits.[2]

It has seemed to me, in these years of reading Baudelaire no longer as a young person, but as a woman of a certain age, that indeed the prose poem might turn out to be what, in the 'L'Invitation au voyage' is presented as, in Johnson's terms, 'the truly unreachable utopian place . . . the very place where one is'.[3] When we were children, we were warned about the moral of believing that the grass was always greener on the other side. And now it appears that we are already on the other side, that, as female readers, our binary obsessions have themselves become other. We are ourselves the other side from something and if we can figure out what exactly that other something is, we will see where it is we are.

Now whatever theory we might adduce for our present reading, it will be certain to fall short of the text. Of course. And yet, even as I gladly heed Edward Kaplan's warning: that Baudelaire's practice easily surpasses our theories,[4] I want to take up two men critics reading Baudelaire: Kaplan and Paul de Man, and one woman beside myself, Johnson again, and see how this difference in reading works. The time frame goes like this: Johnson is reading De Man and is read by Kaplan whereas I am looking back at and sideways at all three.

One of Johnson's main points is to challenge De Man, in his championing of teaching as an impersonal phenomenon, instead of an interpersonal one. For him, she says, 'self and other are only tangentially and contiguously involved'.[5] Now if this is so, there would seem to be no chance of overcoming the binary, for the distance inscribed in the pedagogy would rule out intermingling even of genre. That is, of course, if we push the analogy far enough: would not the genre of teaching in that fashion undo the undoing of the gulf between self and other, or of the opposed elements occasioning the 'code struggle' in the prose poem? What to do about the undoing of undoing, particularly in the case of a notable deconstructionist critic, or, rather two of them? Is this again a binary opposition, male and female?

On the very opposite side is Kaplan, with his firm belief in empathy, in the working out of the binary, where the distance becomes penetrable, say, by beauty or by compassion. Martin Buber's famous formulation about an intimate relation between persons and their God or the idea of God – 'all real living is meeting' – is pertinent here, for we are no longer separate, but now in possible communication. And in the long run, each scene with the poet shows how, in a crowd and in solitary reverie, the active and fertile poet has a certain femaleness to his character, thus the figure of the fertile dreamer: 'Multitude, solitude: equal and interchangeable terms for the active and fertile poet'.[6] Kaplan addresses the question to Barbara Johnson, whose reply is characteristically subtle. I had been writing about my optimism, says Kaplan, and about the scepticism of Paul de Man:

> My initial article, 'Baudelaire's Portrait of the Poet as Widow' (1980) had defended an implicit ethic against the view that allegory proves ultimately incapable of reflecting personal presence or the Absolute. Barbara Johnson's response placed my denial of de Man's 'negativity' into a balanced perspective: 'The existence of poetic energy, which you take as compensation for the loss of immediacy or possession, can be read positively (as you do, as creative maternity) or negatively (as the confirmation of inescapable loss by the very language that seeks to overcome it, as I think Paul de Man does). De Man's apparent belief in the fallacies of identification and your apparent belief in the saving action of empathy are probably irreducibly divided.'[7]

That's it then. Now what might be the consequences of this argument – Kaplan and de Man on opposed sides, and Johnson summing up their argument WITHOUT BRIDGING THE GAP? Mind the gap again, as in the London Underground. Mind not just in the sense of: pay attention to, but perhaps also about the mind itself. Where the gap is.

Let's relook at the gap. Take 'Les Yeux des pauvres'. The violently unfriendly beginning announcement: 'Oh! so you want to know why I hate you today' (PP 67) ['Ah! vous voulez savoir pourquoi je vous hais aujourd'hui' (OC I 316)] is explained, of course, by the terrible reaction of the beloved woman, in all her 'feminine impenetrability' ['imperméabilité féminine'] to the triple confrontation between her eyes and the eyes of the poor in all their terribleness. But the set-up is intensely dramatic: the lovers have been together, have been happy: what a banal but delightful joy:

> We had just spent in each other's company a long day which to me had appeared short. We had indeed promised each other that we would share all our thoughts and that henceforth our two souls would be as one . . . a dream which has

nothing original in it, after all, save that, although all men have dreamt it, none has realized it. (PP 68)

[Nous avions passé ensemble une longue journée qui m'avait paru courte. Nous nous étions bien promis que toutes nos pensées nous seraient communes à l'un et à l'autre, et que nos deux âmes désormais n'en seraient plus qu'une; – un rêve qui n'a rien d'original, après tout, si ce n'est que, rêvé par tous les hommes, il n'a été réalisé par aucune. (OC I 318)]

Then they meet up with a forty-year-old and weary man, with two little boys, each with his different reaction to the new café with its gilt and its laughing company and its statues, all 'in the service of gluttony' (PP 68) ['au service de la goinfrerie' (OC I 318)]. Looking at them, and contemplating the vessels out of which they were drinking, he and his companion, 'I felt a trifle ashamed of our glasses and our jugs which were bigger than our thirst' (PP 68) ['je me sentais un peu honteux de nos verres et nos carafes, plus grands que notre soif' (OC I 319)]. The narrator turns to his beloved, sure that he will read his thoughts in her eyes, until she says they should be chased away, those terrible poor people with their large eyes. End of the communication, end of the scene, unresolved. Misogynistic, you might say, for the compassionate man is clearly ill-matched with the uncompassionate cold female.

But is there not something self-congratulatory and even a bit smug about his telling us the story? No chance of his not being on the right side. The terrible and well-known Baudelairean irony is in play. The play is what makes the poem work. And it makes us work, too.

The second example is much like the first. In 'La Corde', the narrator expresses his horror (clearly, in the French, and for Baudelaire's reading, thinking and moment, the narrator's gender was bound to be male). The rope left dangling from a nail on the roof beam after a hanging turns out to be the cause of great excitement, first, to the mother of the hanged child, and then, to the public at large: more women than men write to him to beg for a piece of the rope – which can be sold, for good luck. Here is the creepy part: the narrator, after explaining ('I must confess' (PP 80) ['je dois le dire' (OC I 331)]) that there were more women writers than men, and that not all belong to the lower classes – 'take my word for it' (PP 80) ['croyez-le bien' (OC I 331)] – saves the letters. Nothing like gloating over the scene, as if the narrator were hanging on – hanging on – to a sex differential. Or some differential or other. Proudly. This isn't quite what we would expect.

Finally, 'Les Fenêtres', based on the famous image of the imagination, is a very peculiar prose poem indeed. So it has to be, as it is about life and the reading of it. As complicated as a Jamesian story, it goes where you don't expect it to at the outset:

> There is no object more profound, more mysterious, more fertile, more shadowy, more dazzling than a window lit by a candle. What one can see in sunlight is always less interesting than what happens behind a pane of glass. In that dark or glowing hole life lives, dreams, suffers. (PP 87)

> [Il n'est pas d'objet plus profond, plus mystérieux, plus fécond, plus ténébreux, plus éblouissant qu'une fenêtre éclairée d'une chandelle. Ce qu'on peut voir au soleil est toujours moins intéressant que ce qui se passe derrière une vitre. Dans ce trou noir ou lumineux vit la vie, rêve la vie, souffre la vie. (OC 1 339)]

High Romanticism. And, whatever story is told about the inhabitant of the room could be told as easily about someone else – fine and well, gender does not matter. 'Had it been a poor old man, I would have reforged his story just as easily' ['Si c'eût été un pauvre vieux homme, j'aurais refait la sienne tout aussi aisément'.] Oh, congratulations, wow. But the smugness is unbearable, as the narrator trundles off with a high opinion of himself: (presumably himself): 'And I go to bed, proud that I have lived and suffered in characters other than my own' (PP 87) ['Et je me couche, fier d'avoir vécu et souffert dans d'autres que moi-même' (OC 1 339)]. Well, one might be tempted to say, good for you!

Here is the clincher, and it includes us, the readers. So that is where the rub is and the interest is, like the 'mon semblable, mon frère' (OC 1 6) ['fellowman, my twin' (FM 7)] phrase: 'Perhaps you will say to me: "Are you sure that that legend is the right one?" What does external reality matter, if it has helped me to live, to feel that I am and what I am?' (PP 87) ['Peut-être me direz-vous: «Es-tu sûr que cette légende soit la vraie?» Qu'importe ce que peut être la réalité placée hors de moi, si elle m'a aidé à vivre, à sentir que je suis et ce que je suis?' (OC 1 339)]. The solipsism is nothing short of extraordinary. What matters is not, at all then, related to binary difference, but to the narrator's distinction from others. Feeling, but for the self. The binary has no place here, in this closed-off environment. There is just, finally, the self.

As Kaplan says, towards the end of his book, about the children's question: 'Mais où est l'âme?' Where indeed is the soul in all of this? And that is the point, for me as a reader at least, of the prose poems. We do not know exactly, precisely, even vaguely, where we stand or where the speaker stands, in what has at first seemed a simple binary plot. On the other hand, is that not where the soul would always have had its being and standing and caring, that is, behind the text?

I cannot pretend to try to think about resolving the issues or even locating them anywhere but in this sketching out of them, and yet – having thought it over – this is where my reading does indeed take itself, to somewhere behind, like a voyage made of necessity without invitation. Whatever invitation Baudelaire might have wanted us to think he was issuing, I could not do other than to lose it. Because, in any case, it wasn't the real one, but one constructed out of a collage of suppositions. Maybe Baudelaire was doing a Cubist act before his time. Always he was before his time, whatever that expression could possibly mean.

The subtlety of a Baudelaire prose poem is that the meaning(s) – no, the meanings – always recede. Like his in-some-sense successor Mallarmé's 'White Water Lily' ('Le Nénuphar blanc') the communicating vessel has drawn up its oars from the water and just the faintest rustle of the person who might have come down to bridge some gap remains. We have to stay with the rustle.

NOTES

1. Barbara Johnson, *The Critical Difference: Essays in the Contemporary Rhetoric of Reading* (Baltimore, MD: Johns Hopkins, 1980), p. 25.
2. *Ibid.*, p. 48.
3. *Ibid.*, p. 41.
4. Edward Kaplan, *Baudelaire's Prose Poems: The Esthetic, the Ethical, and the Religious in 'The Parisian Prowler'* (Athens and London: University of Georgia Press, 1990), p. 73.
5. Johnson, *The Critical Difference*, p. 43.
6. Kaplan, *Baudelaire's Prose Poems*, p. 61.
7. *Ibid.*, p. 73.

14

CLIVE SCOTT

Translating Baudelaire

If we set out to write a history of English-language translations of Baudelaire, in the belief that all translations, in neat chronological sequence, face
the same problems and solve them in different ways, as the presiding *Zeit-
geist* dictates, then we would be sorely deluded. Deluded, principally because
a history of 'formal' translations of Baudelaire[1] is not a history of the translation of Baudelaire; the history of Baudelairean translation has unimaginably
ramified, is unimaginably frayed, is irrecoverable. To investigate this condition and to reflect on the issues at stake for any translator of *Les Fleurs du
Mal*, I would like to take my cue from Baudelaire's first English champion,
Swinburne.

The question which is critical to translation and likely to undermine any
attempt to develop a prescriptive poetics of translation is, quite simply, 'What
does the translator seek to translate?' Our preoccupation should be not only
to decide what translation is, but what is being acted out in translation.
For Baudelaire himself, translation seems to have been a process of self-
discovery, or self-recognition; in a letter to Théophile Thoré of June 20 (?)
1864 Baudelaire refers to his Poe translations in these terms:

> Do you know why I so patiently translated Poe? Because he resembled me.
> The first time I opened a book of his, I saw, with horror and delight, not
> only subjects I had already dreamed, but *actual* PHRASES thought by me and
> written by him twenty years earlier.

> [Savez-vous pourquoi j'ai si patiemment traduit Poe? Parce qu'il me ressem-
> blait. La première fois que j'ai ouvert un livre de lui, j'ai vu, avec épouvante
> et ravissement, non seulement des sujets rêvés par moi, mais *des* PHRASES
> pensées par moi, et écrites par lui vingt ans auparavant.   (C II 386)][2]

For Arthur Symons, translation, particularly of Baudelaire, was more like
the licence for an addiction. In the Preface to his 1925 translations, he puts
it thus: 'Why did I translate *Les Fleurs du Mal*? Because, for one thing, that
book of his, in regard to my earliest verses, was at once a fascination and

an influence, and because from that time onward his fascination has been like a spell to me . . .'³ For Robert Lowell, Baudelaire, among others, acted as a mediator, through whose agency he might provoke himself to poetry, and test his own poetic capacities: 'This book was written from time to time when I was unable to do anything of my own . . . My Baudelaires were begun as exercises in couplets and quatrains . . .'⁴

Swinburne, who introduced Baudelaire to the Victorians, is, for many, responsible for the creation of that decadent, 'hothouse', satanic Baudelaire, who has monopolised the English-speaking world at the expense of the urban, Modernist Baudelaire. Swinburne's summary of the 1861 *Les Fleurs du Mal* in his *Spectator* review (6 September 1862)⁵ not only accounts for Arthur Symons' decision, made in 1925, to use the style of the 1890s in his translations, but continues to haunt the most recent versions. Norman Shapiro, who cut his translating teeth on Georges Feydeau, author of *vaudevilles* in the time of the *belle époque*, and the seventeenth-century writer of fables, Jean de La Fontaine, asks himself 'What is a translator of French farce and fable . . . doing amid the miasmic depths and pervasive demonic gloom of Baudelairean passions?'⁶ But the decadent version of Baudelaire is important precisely because of what it authorises, and particularly because of what it authorises as an undermining of Victorian literary traditions. As Patricia Clements points out: 'Swinburne intended his Baudelaire to be subversive: he proposed him as an antithesis to a confining English tradition, and, from the beginning, for English poets, the identification of Baudelaire entailed some remarkable exclusions . . . Making a "brother" of him, Swinburne turned away from "Tennyson & Cⁱᵉ". . .'⁷

What exactly might this subversiveness consist of? Swinburne's Baudelaire affirms a cosmopolitan brotherhood of poets designed, it seems, to undo national poetic establishments; Swinburne's Baudelaire insinuates that form should serve neither rhetoric nor aesthetic enhancement, but an alternative order of experience, and that it might demonstrate its power to transform by taking, as its raw materials, subjects of the most sordid kind: 'Thus, even of the loathsomest bodily putrescence and decay [Baudelaire] can make some noble use; pluck out its meaning and secret, even its beauty, in a certain way, from actual carrion.'⁸ Through Swinburne's agency, Baudelaire weaves himself into the very fabric of British literature. Swinburne does not translate Baudelaire, that is, does not seal him off in a textual space of his own, a space in which the translator pleads innocence and the reader feels free to identify a target for praise or blame, in a public relations exercise which is tantamount to a referendum. Instead, as we shall see, he incorporates Baudelaire by linguistic stealth. This is already translation as treachery, foreign infiltration, poison fed into the veins of the native language, whereby the native language is an unwitting instrument of its own contamination.

In Swinburne's premature elegy to Baudelaire, 'Ave atque vale', triggered by the false news of Baudelaire's death in April 1867, we find, for example, manifold assimilations of Baudelairean images, but we find, too, an abbreviated paraphrase of 'La Géante' (OC I 22–3):

> Hast thou found place at the great knees and feet
> Of some pale Titan-woman like a lover,
> Such as thy vision here solicited,
> Under the shadow of her fair vast head,
> The deep division of prodigious breasts,
> The solemn slope of mighty limbs asleep,
> The weight of awful tresses that still keep
> The savour and shade of old-world pine-forests
> Where the wet hill-winds weep?[9]
>
> (lines 58–66)

But this is not so much a paraphrase as a gravitational synthesis of fragments of Baudelaire heard, half-heard, mis-heard, imagined and re-combined. Lines 58 and 63 seem to amalgamate Baudelaire's 'J'eusse aimé vivre auprès d'une jeune géante, / Comme aux pieds d'une reine un chat voluptueux' (lines 3–4) and 'Ramper sur le versant de ses genoux énormes' (line 10). Baudelaire's line 13: 'Dormir nonchalamment à l'ombre de ses seins' is picked up in Swinburne's 'asleep' (line 63) (but here the sleep belongs to the Titan-woman rather than the poet), 'Under the shadow' (line 61) and 'prodigious breasts' (line 62). Line 59 refers, it seems, to lines in 'L'Idéal', the poem which precedes 'La Géante' (OC I 22): 'Ce qu'il faut à ce cœur profond comme un abîme . . . . Tes appas façonnés aux bouches des Titans!' (lines 9, 14). The references to hair and 'old-world pine-forests' in lines 64–5 do not relate to 'La Géante', but are, perhaps, reminiscences of 'La Chevelure' (OC I 26–7): 'Tout un monde lointain, absent, presque défunt, / Vit dans tes profondeurs, forêt aromatique!' (lines 7–8). And while, in line 66, I hear a faint echo of line 8 of 'La Géante' – 'Aux humides brouillards qui nagent dans ses yeux' – I might easily be falling prey to a self-deceiving ear.

Pierre Brunel investigates other sites of probable or potential Baudelairean presence in Swinburne.[10] In 'Dolores' for example, which clearly draws significantly on 'A une Madone', Brunel finds possible paraphrases, or reminiscences, of lines from 'J'aime le souvenir de ces époques nues', 'Avec ses vêtements ondoyants et nacrés' and 'Le Voyage'. But, equally, when I read the second stanza of 'At the Empire' by Theodore Wratislaw, author of two volumes of verse and a contributor to *The Yellow Book* and *The Savoy* –

The calm and brilliant Circes who retard
Your passage with the skirts and rouge that spice
The changeless programme of insipid vice,
And stun you with a languid strange regard;[11]

– I wonder whether the third line is a 'translation' of line 88 of 'Le Voyage' (with transposition of adjectives): 'Le spectacle ennuyeux de l'immortel péché' and the fourth line a 'translation' of line 8 of 'Parfum exotique': 'Et des femmes dont l'œil par sa franchise étonne?' Or are these merely allusions, or citations? If the truth be told, I do not know exactly what the linguo-literary status of these lines is. These modes of covert assimilation serve only to emphasise that translation should be as inclusive in their purview as Gérard Genette's rather more desirable – because non-prejudicial – term 'transtextuality',[12] or should at least be considered a special case of intertextuality.

Intertextuality makes possible the view that each text belongs to the total network of texts which is constantly being added to, and in which every text acts on and modifies every other text. No text is the simple *result* of a previous text; no translation is an uncomplicated consequence of a foreign-language original. Intertextuality destroys both the notion of causality and the linearity of time (literary history), inasmuch as it makes all texts available achronologically. Intertextuality, at a stroke, undermines that belief in the ordered sequence and autonomy of individual texts implicit in the traditional practice of translation, and spells the death of authorial control. The author is no longer the repository of the meaning of his/her own text, since meaning circulates freely from one text to another. In short, texts themselves are the authors of their own productivity, tirelessly taking each other up and/or rewriting each other.

It is not by accident that I earlier used the word 'referendum' to describe what 'formal' translations wish to elicit. This is the term that Barthes uses to describe the 'readerly' text, which it is only possible to consume passively, where 'reading is nothing more than a *referendum*',[13] offering only options of acceptance or rejection. The readerly text is the text that resists the multiplication of its meanings, which makes a virtue of self-confirming whole-ness, which institutionalises itself, in the sense of coming to exist beyond interferences from the present. The writerly text, on the other hand, never loses its engagement with passing time, because it always differs from itself, in a perpetual present 'upon which no *consequent* language (which would inevitably make it past) can be superimposed; the writerly text is *ourselves writing*, before the infinite play of the world . . . is traversed, intersected, stopped, plasticized by some singular system (Ideology, Genus, Criticism) which reduces the plurality of entrances, the opening of networks, the infinity of languages'.[14] The direction of my argument will be clear. Too much translation attempts to singularise the source text by making it more intelligible; too much translation operates with the myth of a retrievable consistency of voice and with consistency as a primary aesthetic desideratum; too much translation seeks to sink the presentness of an orally performed text into the pastness of a written text. If these things are true, then the object of a new translation is clear: to translate a Work into a Text, to translate the readerly into the writerly, to translate the culturally institutionalised into the culturally undefined, re-inventable, open-ended.[15]

What might we have in mind when we speak of a writerly translation, a translation that treats the source text as writerly? We might think of that process whereby the fluidity of the original text in the translator's mind produces a re-ordering of material in a fluid translation: Lerner's translation (1990) of 'Parfum exotique' has 'Of the heavy smell that drifts from the tamarinds' as its third, rather than twelfth, line, and 'Feeling your breathing while my soul is winging / Its way above strange shores and distant hills' in its second tercet rather than in its first quatrain; and his version of 'Remords posthume' opens with lines 9–10 of the source text.[16] Ulick O'Connor's version (1995) of 'Les Petites Vieilles' consists only of its third part.[17] Nicholas Moore's thirty-one versions of 'Spleen' ('Je suis comme le roi . . .') (1973) are writerly in at least two senses: they implicitly accept that translation is pastiche and will usually involve the interventions of third parties (here, among others, Wallace Stevens, Auden, H. D., Betjeman); they imply that multiple translations are an inevitable concomitant of our each possessing language in different ways, at different times.[18] In my turn, I have attempted translations of Baudelairean poems which involve transformations of poetic form, or which engineer shifts in point of view or 'speaker', or which introduce montage techniques (the intercutting of related texts or new verse).[19]

Ironically, paradoxically, what lies at the centre of the writerly is the oral, the unique eventfulness of the individual reader's voice. Put in prosodic terms, Baudelaire's poems, through their linguistic and metrical features, *expressly* attract the paralinguistic, that is, all those features of oral performance that lie outside the printed text, all the contingencies and relativities of tone, accentuation, tempo, pausing, pitch, that a particular reader might bring to them. Take the final stanza of 'Hymne à la beauté', for instance (OC I 24–5):

> De Satan ou de Dieu, qu'importe? Ange ou Sirène,
> Qu'importe, si tu rends, – fée aux yeux de velours,
> Rythme, parfum, lueur, ô mon unique reine! –
> L'univers moins hideux et les instants moins lourds?

Here, in the first line, the interruption of the question by the caesura (fixed metrical juncture at the sixth syllable) – 'De Satan ou de Dieu,// qu'importe? Ange ou Sirène' – lifts 'qu'importe' into a space of its own, expressing either a careless nihilism or the sense of liberation from moral responsibility (depending on the voice-tone adopted). A question which responds to a moral choice begins to propose the unreality, or non-necessity, of moral choice, a proposition intensified by the repetition of this structural dislocation, over the line-ending between the first and second lines. But in the second line, the initial 'Qu'importe' is affected by another ambiguity which relates to its mute 'e': read 'Qu'importe, / si tu rends', it would mean 'What does it matter, as long as you . . .'; read 'Qu'impor/te, si tu rends', it would veer towards 'What does it matter if you . . .'. The first half of the third line allows five different rhythmic configurations, depending again on the treatment of the mute 'e', on grouping and on whether the half-line is read with a 'classical' two accents or with an eccentric, but justifiable, three accents. Thus:

$$\begin{array}{l} \quad / \qquad / \quad / \\ \text{Rythme,/parfum,/lueur,} \\ \quad / \qquad\quad / \quad / \\ \text{Ry/thme, parfum,/lueur,} \\ \quad / \qquad\qquad\quad / \\ \text{Ry/thme, parfum, lueur,} \\ \quad / \qquad\qquad / \\ \text{Rythme,/parfum, lueur,} \\ \qquad\qquad / \quad / \\ \text{Rythme, parfum,/lueur,} \end{array}$$

In the second half of the same line, the fact that the adjective 'unique' comes before the noun, and the protraction of its second, accentuated syllable by the mute 'e' ('ô mon uni/que reine!'), colours the many facets of the word – single, exclusive, singular, exceptional, irreplaceable, incomparable – with either a bitter irony or a self-surrendering commitment.

This brief analysis is designed to show that Baudelaire's prosody constantly challenges the voice to make decisions about expression. His verse is haunted by all the potentialities of tonal shift, variable grouping, pausing, speed of delivery, which invite the reader to make contingent and unreliable choices, to catch at fugitive modalities, to undo and problematise classical proportions. This may be a teasing pleasure for the reader, but it is a problem for the translator who wishes to situate the poem in the real time of its performance by the voice, who wishes to inject into the written the 'essential quality of presentness' ['qualité essentielle de présent'] (OC II 684). When I translate these lines, therefore, I seek to translate not so much the meaning of the words as their susceptibility to different kinds of oral projection; and the variations in font and typographical disposition that I introduce, are designed not only to record my own voice's acting out of the text, its insistence on certain sounds, certain pauses, certain relationships between words and phrases, but also to incite, or invite, readers of the translation to imagine their own vocal explorations and variations:

> From the DeVil
> > or from God
> > does it . . . matter?
> > > > Angel? . . . Siren?
> – It *doesn't* matter
> > > IF -
> **Fay** with the VelVet look
> > **RHYTHM, PERFUME . . .**
> Yes, and LIGHT
> > my *ONLY* queen –
> You make the world
> > lesshideoustothe eye
> > and clock-ticks
> less like
>
> > **leaden**
> > **weights.**

Many of the constraints that translation imposes on itself derive from flawed assumptions. I felt free to let rhyme go from my translation, partly because sense required it, but also because to suppose that English rhyme is comparable with French rhyme is itself dangerously misleading: rhymes in French are more abundant and choices are, therefore, more significant; French rhyming practice distinguishes between the 'genders' of rhyme-words (feminine = final (tonic) rhyme-syllable followed by mute 'e'; masculine = final (tonic) rhyme-syllable not followed by mute 'e'), and, in regular verse, prescribes the alternation of masculine and feminine rhyme-pairs; French rhyme capitalises, for expressive purposes, on the reader's awareness of different degrees of rhyme (*rime pauvre, rime suffisante, rime riche*). In these circumstances, to imply that English rhyme is equivalent to French rhyme is to dupe the reader.

Conversely, the denigration of the use of free verse by translators perpetuates a prejudice which dates from free verse's inception. For Walter Martin, a relatively recent translator of Baudelaire (1997), free verse has become constitutionally incapable of anything but 'floppiness';[20] Shapiro, reviewing the varied results of translators who have 'accosted' *Les Fleurs du Mal*, identifies one group as 'intentional attempts to turn Baudelaire into a formless twentieth-century free-versifier';[21] Clark and Sykes assume, too automatically perhaps, that 'free verse in particular inevitably discards the nuances and rhetorical emphases of Baudelaire's balanced and subtly patterned prosody'.[22] There have been rare counter-voices, Lowell's perhaps the best-known;[23] but Yves Bonnefoy, too, places the modern translator in the existential space of free verse:

> Free verse is poetry, in its necessary freedom of expression and research. And one of the consequences of this, which I must now emphasize, is that it is as such the only place where the contemporary poet can define and solve the problems he meets in his existential or cultural condition: for instance, in his relationship with the poets of the past and his task of translating them.[24]

And, indeed, translation itself makes it difficult not to flirt with freedom, as the Baudelairean translators of the 1890s did,[25] and as, say, James Liddy, F. W. Leakey and Anthony Ryle have done since.

What are the translational advantages of free verse? First, free verse is, as Bonnefoy insists, the writing of the modern sensibility. Second, it is just as disciplined as regular verse and its variations just as expressively subtle. Third, it more easily allows the incorporation of paralinguistic features. Fourth, it provides no convenient excuses for lexical and syntactic infelicities. Fifth, free lineation makes available the language of margins and allows the poet to negotiate difficult rhythmic sequences.[26] Sixth, free verse is peculiarly appropriate to the language of translation in that it foregrounds the improvised, improvising, tentative openness of the text and thus promotes the writerly, multi-dimensional nature of the translational act. Seventh, all these things together help to ensure that the reader is more engaged in the construction of the text. Because the text is more eventful, more challenging, more equivocating, so the reader, even if lacking knowledge of the source language, is drawn into processes of creative decision-making.

Even if we accept that the text is shifting, that it refuses stability and closure, can we nonetheless identify what in it is peculiar to the poet being translated, what, in our case, is 'Baudelairean'? Some translators believe that the poet needs to be identified beforehand, from the total œuvre, so that his characteristic 'voice' can be safeguarded, whenever a text of his is newly translated. Some believe that translation is itself a pursuit of the poet, or a construction of the poet. Some believe that the act of translation inevitably erases the poet: he cannot speak in a language foreign to him. If the latter is the view, then either Baudelaire becomes a meaningful absence, who putatively exists at the intersection of all translations of his work – Lerner invites the reader to put his version of the opening lines of 'Spleen I' alongside those of Shanks, Campbell and Lowell, because 'what the four versions have in common must, surely, be from Baudelaire';[27] or he simply disappears, in order that another self, born of the effect that his work has had on another imagination, in another language, place, age, may come into existence. It is the identifiable presence of Baudelaire which justifies the intentionalism by which translation is sustained – the decisions of the translator are based on assumptions about the poet's intentions – and which justifies, too, those 'would/might have' arguments that we find, for example, in Lowell[28] and in Vernon Watkins.[29] But Lowell has to concede that the tone for which he is prepared to sacrifice literal meaning is *a* tone, 'for *the* tone is something that will always more or less escape transference to another language and cultural moment'.[30]

In rather parallel fashion, the translator, too, sacrifices authorship in the interests of the text's susceptibility to change, possession in the interests of participation. If we look to a translational practice in which a translation spurs readers to essay their own versions, then we should equally expect the readers of translations to wish to modify the translation they have in front of them. A translation, made up as it usually is of rational choices that *any other knowledgeable person* could make, expressly offers itself to judgment in a way that creative writing does not. Furthermore, translation is deeply implicated in legitimate plagiarism. In these circumstances, one might argue that the language a translator puts before the reader does not belong to that translator in any definitive way. If I read the first two stanzas of Allen Tate's translation of 'Correspondances' –

> All nature is a temple where the alive
> Pillars breathe often a tremor of mixed words;
> Man wanders in a forest of accords
> That peer familiarly from each ogive.
>
> Like thinning echoes tumbling to sleep beyond
> In a unity umbrageous and infinite,
> Vast as the night stupendously moonlit,
> All smells and colors and sounds correspond.[31]

– I am urged to modifications which, nonetheless, leave many of these lines intact, and urged, too, to a variation of fonts as a way of indicating what acoustic design I hear in the text, what sounds press on my consciousness:

> Nature is a tempLe where, aLive,
> PiLLars often **breathe** a tremor
>   of mixed words;
> Man wanders in a forest of **accords**
> That peer

famiLiarLy
　　from each ogive.

Like thinning echoes tumbLing
　　　to sLeep *sLeep*
　　　　beyond
In a shadow-fiLLed,
　　　　　unending
　　　　　unity
Vast as the night, and vast as moonLight,
SmeLLs and colours . . . sounds . . . aLL corres*pond*.

There are certain sequences in Tate whose rhythm I would like to change, certain words I do not feel at home with, certain phrasings I want to emphasise, certain pauses I want to insert, certain phonetic elements which randomly catch my ear with greater or lesser relief. My consequent recourse to a variable typography, as in my version of the final stanza of 'L'Hymne à la beauté' above, has, too, a more general significance, relating to textual sexuality.

Baudelaire's decadence or obscenity, like Swinburne's, lies not so much in a sexuality depicted in his writing as in the sexuality *of* his writing, in a constant, sado-masochistic reversal of values.[32] The sexuality of Baudelaire's writing, as of Swinburne's, also entails, as we have seen, the text's hopeless textual promiscuity. But most especially, perhaps, this sexuality means poetry's maximisation of the materiality of language; the text is a body whose solicitations we cannot control or dissociate ourselves from, since we read the poem with our own bodies. When we accuse translation of making the original text more intelligible, of being over-preoccupied with meaning, when we speak of translation as the promotion of a linguistic consensus, of the linguistically normal or average, we are condemning moves which seem designed to clear the original text of potential charges of irrationality and inadvertent depravity, and we are using translation to save our bodies from the (unwanted?) embrace of the textual body. Robert Buchanan's attack on Dante Gabriel Rossetti and, by explicit association, on Swinburne, in 'The Fleshly School of Poetry' (*Contemporary Review*, October 1871) reveals where 'straight' translation, even of subversive texts, is itself likely to promote establishment values. Buchanan taxes the 'fleshly gentlemen' with committing themselves 'to aver that poetic expression is greater than poetic thought, and by inference that the body is greater than the soul, and sound superior to sense; and that the poet, properly to develop his poetic faculty, must be an intellectual hermaphrodite, to whom the very facts of day and night are lost in a whirl of aesthetic terminology'.[33] Poetry's inevitable tendency to let sound compete with sense, to let the signifier exceed the signified, means that poetry is constantly releasing in the reader a psycho-physiological surplus, psychic impulsions, which are as irresistible as they are haphazard. In Swinburne's case we may say that sound patterns activate that state of possession, of self-dissemination, closely related to Baudelaire's 'vaporisation du *Moi*', and below or beyond ordinary consciousness, which Jerome McGann identifies as the trance state.[34] What versions of the Baudelairean text does the unconscious or semi-conscious mind read? How can we communicate the possibilities of this psycho-phonetic activity other than by variations in font and font-size? Translation can work to make subtexts more visible, may feel that its principal task is to translate the materiality of language and thus bring the textual unconscious to the surface.

When we meet James Robertson's Scottish versions of Baudelaire (2001), e.g.:

> Big wuids, ye fleg me like kirks that are ower muckle.
> Ye howl like a kist o whistles, an the dule chaumers
> O ma cursed hert, dinnlin wi the deid-ruckle,
> Echo back yer deep wae's rumours.[35]

we are salutarily reminded of certain inbuilt translational prejudices: we find it difficult to imagine that an official language does not necessitate an official language, that a written language does not necessitate a written language (Robertson's version is a transcription of a spoken language). And while we allow that an original text may be experimental and that a translation may imitate that experimentality, we do not expect a 'regular' original text to be the pretext for an experimental translation. Translating Baudelaire should teach us to translate ourselves out of certain translational assumptions, and thus, in a sense, to be truer to the spirit and nature of Baudelairean textuality. Faced with four possible uses of Baudelairean translations – to teach Baudelaire in translation, to teach 'the translated Baudelaire', to teach creative writing by translating Baudelaire, to teach translation through the translation of Baudelaire – we might conclude, and perhaps with horror, that it is the first of these which is the least defensible. There is no Baudelaire in translation. There are Baudelairean texts which have incited writers to translation, and will continue, naggingly, to do so.

NOTES

1. For a succinct and very helpful history of this kind, see Carol Clark and Robert Sykes, eds., *Baudelaire in English* (Harmondsworth: Penguin Books, 1997). My lines of argument in this chapter frequently run against the tradition of formal translation. This tradition is full of wonderful achievements and continues to be an indispensable mediator of Baudelairean texts for the English-speaking reader.

I want here to present an alternative approach, not as a replacement of the tradition, but as a complementary accompaniment.

2. For a full assessment of Baudelaire as translator, see Emily Salines, *Alchemy and Amalgam: Translation in the Works of Charles Baudelaire* (Amsterdam: Rodopi, 2004).

3. Arthur Symons, *Charles Baudelaire: 'Les Fleurs du Mal', 'Petits Poèmes en prose', 'Les Paradis artificiels'* (London: The Casanova Society, 1925), n.p.

4. Robert Lowell, *Imitations* (London: Faber and Faber, 1971), pp. xii–xiii.

5. Throughout the chief part of this book, he has chosen to dwell mainly upon sad and strange things – the weariness of pain and the bitterness of pleasure – the perverse happiness and wayward sorrows of exceptional people. It has the languid lurid beauty of close and threatening weather – a heavy heated temperature, with dangerous hothouse scents in it; thick shadow of cloud about it, and fire of molten light.

   (Clyde Kenneth Hyder, ed., *Swinburne as Critic*
   (London: Routledge and Kegan Paul, 1972), pp. 29–9)

6. Norman R. Shapiro, ed. and trans., *Charles Baudelaire: Selected Poems from 'Les Fleurs du Mal'*, foreword by Willis Barnstone, engravings by David Schorr (Chicago: University of Chicago Press, 1998), p. xxix.

7. Patricia Clements, *Baudelaire and the English Tradition* (Princeton: Princeton University Press, 1985), p. 8.

8. Hyder, *Swinburne as Critic*, p. 30.

9. Algernon Charles Swinburne, *Selected Poems*, ed. L. M. Findlay (Manchester: Fyfield Books, 1987), pp. 161–2.

10. Pierre Brunel, 'Baudelaire et Swinburne', *Bérénice*, 7 (1983), pp. 113–25.

11. Theodore Wratislaw, *'Caprices'* (1893) *with 'Orchids'* (1896), ed. R. K. R. Thornton and Ian Small (Oxford: Woodstock, 1994), p. 20.

12. Gérard Genette, *Palimpsests: Literature in the Second Degree*, trans. Channa Newman and Claude Doubinsky (Lincoln: University of Nebraska Press, 1997), p. 1.

13. Roland Barthes, *S/Z*, trans. Richard Miller (New York: Hill and Wang, 1974), p. 4.

14. *Ibid.*, p. 5.

15. Roland Barthes, 'From Work to Text', in *Image–Music–Text*, ed. and trans. Stephen Heath (London: Fontana/Collins, 1977), pp. 155–64.

16. Laurence Lerner, ed. and trans., *Baudelaire* (London: J. M. Dent, 1999), pp. 15, 20.

17. Ulick O'Connor, *Poems of the Damned: Charles Baudelaire's 'Les Fleurs du Mal – The Flowers of Evil'* (Dublin: Wolfhound Press, 1995), p. 18.

18. Nicholas Moore, ed. and trans., *Spleen* (London: The Menard Press, 1990). Rosemary Lloyd has very suggestive things to say about Baudelaire's multi-vocalism and his exploitation of plagiarism, parody and pastiche in *Baudelaire's World* (Ithaca, NY: Cornell University Press, 2002), pp. 63–7.

19. Clive Scott, *Translating Baudelaire* (Exeter: University of Exeter Press, 2000).

20. Walter Martin, ed. and trans., *Charles Baudelaire: Complete Poems* (Manchester: Carcanet, 1997), p. 441.

21. Shapiro, *Charles Baudelaire: Selected Poems from Les Fleurs du Mal*, p. xxx.

22. Clark and Sykes, *Baudelaire in English*, pp. xlix–l.

23. 'Strict metrical translators still exist. They seem to live in a pure world untouched by contemporary poetry. Their difficulties are bold and honest, but they are taxidermists, not poets, and their poems are likely to be stuffed birds. A better strategy would seem to be the now fashionable translations into free or irregular verse' (Lowell, *Imitations*, p. xi).

24. Yves Bonnefoy, 'On the Translation of Form in Poetry', *World Literature Today*, 53 (1979), p. 378.

25. See Clive Scott, 'The Liberated Verse of the English Translators of French Symbolism', in *The Symbolist Movement in the Literature of the European Languages*, ed. Anna Balakian (Budapest: Akadémiai Kiadó, 1982), pp. 127–43.

26. Scott, *Translating Baudelaire*, pp. 234–5.

27. Lerner, *Baudelaire*, p. xxiv.

28. 'I have tried to write live English and to do what my authors might have done if they were writing their poems now and in America' (Lowell, *Imitations*, p. xi).

29. Watkins comments that the addition of material to the source text by the translator does not matter 'if it is something essential to the fulfilment of the translated poem, something [the poet] himself would have chosen', were he in the translator's shoes ('The Translation of Poetry', in *Selected Verse Translations, with an Essay on the Translation of Poetry*, intro. by Michael Hamburger (London: Enitharmon Press, 1977), p. 20).

30. Lowell, *Imitations*, p. xi.

31. Clark and Sykes, *Baudelaire in English*, p. 17.

32. See Richard Sieburth, 'Poetry and Obscenity: Baudelaire and Swinburne', *Comparative Literature*, 36 (1984), pp. 343–53.

33. Quoted in Carolyn Hares-Stryker, ed., *An Anthology of Pre-Raphaelite Writings* (Sheffield: Sheffield Academic Press, 1997), p. 238.

34. Jerome McGann, *Swinburne: An Experiment in Criticism* (Chicago: University of Chicago Press, 1972), pp. 164–5.

35. James Robertson, 'Obsession', in *Fae the Flouers o Evil: Baudelaire in Scots* (Kingskettle: Kettillonia, 2001), p. 7.

15

JUDITH VOLLMER

The stroll and preparation for departure

The surroundings, the atmospheres in which the whole narrative must be steeped.[1]

[Les milieux, les atmosphères, dont tout un récit doit être trempé.

(OC I 655)]

I turn a corner into the nightclub district and suddenly come upon two gifts. I reach down, take a close look, and scan them for luck. The first is a dark red satin ankle strap; maybe the dancer caught her party shoe on the teeth of a steel grate or a car door in the middle of the night. She must have kept on moving, dancing down the street. The strap is perfectly fresh and new, its tiny brass buckle and one brass tooth still fastened to itself, and for a second the dancer appears before me in the vapours of her happiness, running along the lamp-lit alleyways to another bistro, the strapless shoe like a second skin still holding her foot. The second gift is the curled peel of an orange. Its bright spiral glows on the wet black pavement; oils still bead the leather of its own skin. This reveller was so thirsty he sucked the fruit until its miniature universe was completely gone, and so was he, on to the last bus threading the dark streets to his watchman's job in the halls of the university. Urban hiker on a trek, poet thinking a new poem in her head, I know where I am going to end up, a couple of hours from now, in the back room of my apartment, where I will sit uninterrupted. My desk waits like an unopened letter, it's there like the clean and complex room of a prose poem, a visual and musical text I will sit with, if all goes well, through the long afternoon and into the evening.

I am practising suspension, absorbing everything, distorting my peripheral vision under the influence of the sun-strands of new forsythia streaking the gray hills this early spring morning. I am walking east through the city to my desk, less than three miles from here, though it seems farther, on foot, the terrain dramatically layered with river, cliff, bridges, river. I am the unlikeliest *flâneuse* in a least likely place, neither broad metropolis nor neat town, but my own beautiful and homely and complicated small American city. The parapets and belvederes of Pittsburgh glint with silver-pink light as far as my gaze ravels into the eastern sky. While I am walking, everyone I love is, too, inside the spaces my own walk makes, and I am saving this sensation, this series of perceptions, inside the wonderful lethargy my procrastination feeds me like a delicious hangover, a little one, a parrot in my brain as I walk along the rivers.

This morning I'm momentarily winning the war between working for pleasure and working for fear, in the delicacy of knowing that on this, my day off, the desk is my only destination.

I won't be tired, I won't let anything I find on my walk go unnoticed, and then I'll give myself over to the spatial and aural gifts I receive, each time I read Baudelaire, city-poet, poet of excruciatingly inhabited place. I like thinking of the journals and the prose poems as my familiar and imaginary companions. Reading and re-reading Baudelaire, I am invited into the bifocality of his voice(s): poet/visionary, poet/philosopher, if only for an instant before I have to settle down and attempt my own poem. Baudelaire remains master of the prose poem we're still writing inside the excitement and the chaos of Post-modernism; he presides as inventor of the arc of the contemporary political poem, and perhaps most of all, he is the urban dreamer in whose care I place myself. In the moment of my own writing life inside the rich variety of communities of American poets, across regions, styles and intentions, I find my entrance through Baudelaire to spatial departures both far and intimate. My work as teacher by profession and poet by vocation finds openings in Baudelaire that I have found only rarely in film or travel. My education, formal and self-made, is infused with the laments, outrages and songs of Baudelaire. I am (his stubborn, intermittent sexist journal entries aside) oddly at home in the wisdom of the journals and the great mysteries of the prose poems, and I never tire of studying the simultaneities of his rage, indolence, wild love and beauty.

Baudelaire indeed 'found nothing to like about his time, and unlike Leconte de Lisle he was unable to deceive himself about it', Walter Benjamin wrote.[2] Baudelaire's unmediated passion gave us all the essentials for a poetry engaged, social and, hopefully, transformational. Baudelaire's terrible denunciations in 'Les Yeux des pauvres' and 'Le Joujou du pauvre', the world-weary crankiness and lovely melancholy of 'Déjà!' and the ecstatic anthems 'Un hémisphère dans une chevelure' and 'Enivrez-vous' have astonished a generation and a half of college students with whom I have worked. My students fall in love with those poems and a host of others, on first reading. They marvel and say they've never seen anything like them. My native Pittsburgh, forced by economic devastation and population drain to remake itself time and again over its three-hundred-year history, tells a very old story. Like many American cities it was imagined and designed and redesigned by stellar architects and urbanists of the last centuries, but designed for whom?

Pittsburgh was for Baudelaire distant as the ruins of Kwanstiyukwa and the caves of Chauvet. Its diminutive size and physical attitude alone – visited and duly recorded by Dickens and praised by Jane Jacobs and Lewis Mumford, city on a human scale, centre-city population 400,000 – would not have led Baudelaire to mistake it, as other visitors have, as an exercise in claustrophobia. He would have recognised the sullen rages of the sleepwalkers and the *esprit* of the fourth-generation festivals. He would have loathed – and praised – the heartbreaking perimeters of spoiled natural landscapes surely as he did his own. My Polish grandfather, my *Dziadzi*, fled the economic and physical slavery of the oilfields of 1913 Poland only to land in the coal-fields of Pittsburgh's industrial czar, Henry Clay Frick, fields reclaimed today where even in mild weather the willows snap like whips. My distressed city, once an international steel and glass empire, now a fledgling biotechnology hub, is no place for poetry. Yet poetry surely is its supreme subject. In its odd beauty, Pittsburgh might stand in for a micro-Paris, a minor Rome (visit our seven parapets overlooking the rivers), a sister-survivor city to Kobe, though our disaster was not natural, but a human-enacted economic destruction. Baudelaire's angriest prose poems are the outdoor rooms I wander. They are my centrifuge and I their eager feed. I stand protected inside their membranes of anonymity even as I am free enough to peer inside 'Les Fenêtres':

> In that dark or glowing hole life lives, dreams, suffers.
>
> . . .
>
> And I go to bed, proud that I have lived and suffered in characters other than my own. Perhaps you will say to me: 'Are you sure that that legend is the right one?' What does external reality matter, if it has helped me to live, to feel that I am, and what I am? (PP 87)
>
> [Dans ce trou noir ou lumineux vit la vie, rêve la vie, souffre la vie.
>
> . . .
>
> Et je me couche, fier d'avoir vécu et souffert dans d'autres que moi-même. Peut-être me direz-vous: «Es-tu sûr que cette légende soit la vraie?» Qu'importe ce que peut être la réalité placée hors de moi, si elle m'a aidé à vivre, à sentir que je suis et ce que je suis? (OC I 339)]

Baudelaire would recognise my students, too, though on certain evenings their strolls take them beyond the city limits to traverse the twenty-first century's hideous footprints of Wal-Mart, McMansion and the invisible cess-lakes of industrial waste in the outlying districts along thruways where there are no sidewalks. Some are the grandchildren of miners and farmers, others the sons and daughters of children who sold off their family farms in order to live. Our young writers tune into their own poetries and iPods, and they hang out at cafés called Tango, Slaughterhouse and Quiet Storm. Their intoxicants and sedatives replicate neither opium nor absinthe, but the local draft beers and, on certain nights, the brutal neo-PCP, a reconstituted angel dust from the familiar hell of no jobs/no art/no jobs.

My slipper strap and orange peel soothe me and so does a city hilltop behind me; it might be the promontory of the Janiculum, 100 stone steps above Trastevere and the green-gray River Tiber. No, it is the West End Overlook, and many of our buildings still stand face-away from the waterfronts of the rivers Ohio, Allegheny and Monongahela. Our small city built as work-bucket and money lode for the wealthy families of high industry stands within the skeleton of the outer/outsider new of the teetering US economy. Fashions from Paris and New York arrive on a six-to-twelve-month delay. A larger world of supra-consumption and innovation sounds its calls from great distances. 'New industry' is something being enacted perhaps on the other side of the world by men, women and children achingly familiar, suffering inside deadly factories. For now, for me, the morning is long and slow and I have my choice of stops, for food, drink, paintings; for magazines and international news, among the ruins of the old arcades and emporia where shoppers are buying free-range chickens, designer ales, micro-wave cakes and enough pasta and Italian sausages for the spring season's carnival of baptisms, graduations, farewells and welcomes. The wrought-iron figure eight of the Smithfield Street Bridge backdropping the ice-goth glass masterpiece of Philip Johnson is one of hundreds of cross-hatchings of our ancient on our new.

Baudelaire's city-as-outdoor museum thrives here on a micro-scale that reflects the world. The socio-economic realities of Pittsburgh are lenses on to cities as far as Manchester, Milan, Moscow. The lens of my walk functions telescopically, as, in the vista stand the ex-urban and the suburban, then the diminished pastoral: (there is no wilderness but there are plenty of wild pockets here in Northern Appalachia). Our strip-mined countryside still holds pockets of plentiful clean water, thanks to the dense woods and folds of the Laurel Mountain foothills. Far in the distance is another city. And another. In my long-vision I recognise sister-cities that stretch outward from the very Baudelaire poem in which I exist. I think of Mary Ann Caws' rites and corridors inside space-time. Like Baudelaire, like Benjamin, Caws knows all about the time-travel a poem can make, particularly when the poem composes itself inside the corridors and interiors of a living city. When writing my poem under the spell of Baudelaire, of Caws, I wander inside my city, layered and multivocal as it is with its palimpsests of histories, voices, memories. In this way, one text (city remembered and experienced fresh) crosses another (the poem I am *thinking*) crosses another (the poet/me making the poem). Baudelaire's teaching, then, infuses me with the knowledge that my aesthetic *is* the physical and literal city from which I write. I inhabit (text crossing text) Baudelaire's excruciating sense of place. I think, too, of Durer's instruction on composition and craft, as recorded in the 1901 diary of Italian painter Umberto Boccioni: '(the) vehemence of stroke, which bites, contorts, and deforms, but runs and runs toward the ideal'.[3] So moves Pittsburgh in its trajectory towards its future, even as it presents its heart on its funky sleeve. We live on top of the ancient walking grounds of the woolly mammoth, on hillsides sharp and steep as knives, and our new labs manufacture human bone mass. New archeological excavations on an Allegheny River sandbar uncover artefacts from the daily lives of people who millennia ago burned cooking fires and traded skins and beads here, on the same rivers my great-grandmother's Troy Hill house, now nearly demolished, gazes down on. In the worlds before my eyes, I give myself over to the degradations and breakthroughs the Baudelaire poem explores. The interpenetrating planes of time working their forces on the face of Pittsburgh might be read as a sequence of prose poems. The cross-hatchings of the 300 bridges and boulevards and back alleys make it so. Our elderly and new immigrants from Eastern Europe, Pan-Asia and South America – not to mention the citizens of the Pittsburgh diaspora who periodically return – walk head-on into the unpredictable weather of the world economies, the spring rain, wind, fallen blossoms and the gesture a stranger's 'Good morning' makes as we pass on the street.

Sometimes I like to read the narrative bridges of the prose poem as if they were the genius-notes of an architect or urbanist I've discovered on my own, a thinker who thinks and dreams in a language of cinematic intimacy, so I can 'see' and 'read' the poem at the same time. Alert and relaxed in the movements of Baudelaire's brilliant sentences, I take my time travelling around inside the lapidarian imagistic spheres. Then I am sucked down inside and up through the implosions the poem makes, and I lose myself. At this critical juncture the prose poem conceals, then reveals, when we least expect it, the through-the-looking-glass black hole that transports us into another dimension entirely. In Baudelaire the implosion strips and destroys the masks of kindness or irony or coyness or reverie and reveals and amplifies – for one thing, rage. In 'Le Mauvais Vitrier', the banalities of mass production (read: 'free trade') are indicted for their denial of the need for beauty.

> 'Don't tell me you have no coloured panes! No panes which are pink or red or blue, no magic panes, no panes of paradise? Well, you're an impudent wretch! You dare wander about in poor neighbourhoods and you don't even have windows that let us see life through rose-coloured glasses!' And I pushed him roughly to the stairway, into which he stumbled, muttering as he went.

I went over to the balcony and snatched up a small pot of flowers, and when the man reappeared at the doorway, I dropped my missile perpendicularly down on the hooks of his pack; and as the shock of the blow threw him down backwards, the end result was that he crushed under his back all this poor ambulatory fortune, which made the startling noise of a crystal palace pulverised by lightning.

And, intoxicated by my act of madness, I shouted furiously to him: 'Let us see life As something beautiful! As something beautiful!'

(Translation altered from PP 40)

[«Comment? Vous n'avez pas de verres de couleur? des verres roses, rouges, bleus, des vitres magiques, des vitres de paradis? Impudent que vous êtes! vous osez vous promener dans des quartiers pauvres, et vous n'avez pas même de vitres qui fassent voir la vie en beau!» Et je le poussai vivement vers l'escalier, où il trébucha en grognant.

Je m'approchai du balcon et je me saisis d'un petit pot de fleurs, et quand l'homme reparut au débouché de la porte, je lassai tomber perpendiculairement mon engin de guerre sur le rebord postérieur de ses crochets; et le choc le renversant, il acheva de riser sous son dos toute sa pauvre fortune ambulatoire qui rendit le bruit éclatant d'un palais de cristal crevé par la foudre.

Et. ivre de ma folie, je lui criai furieusement: «La vie en beau! la vie en beau!»

(OC I 287)]

What do the 'poor neighborhoods' (houses/humans) and the 'poor ambulatory fortune' (glass/humans) hold in common, the poem demands? Baudelaire's dramatic portrayal of failed imagination and mindless toil forecasts late capitalism's most insidious endgame: the more we consume the more we are consumed. Yet the person *making* the essential resources for living everyday life, like the poem, the painting, like free speech itself, is committing acts of courage. 'Le Mauvais Vitrier' both unmasks the glazier and hyperfocuses the eye on the sparkling facets of desire. Every shard of the crystal palace catches the eye of the maker in love with the making itself. Baudelaire's poems against social injustice, advertising, aesthetic and romantic degradation, and automaton complicity in class oppression were enormous foreshadowings and watchtowers and remain unsurpassed for the urban poet. Post-modernism's ever-widening canon refreshes itself in the bath of Baudelaire's multitudinous vision.

I'm heading home, but first I will buy wine and dinner and I will think about 'Projets' and pleasure: 'Why force my body to move from place to place, since my soul can travel so nimbly? And why turn plan into reality, when the plan is in itself sufficient pleasure?' (PP 65–6) ['Pourquoi contraindre mon corps à changer de place, puisque mon âme voyage si lestement?

Et à quoi bon exécuter des projets, puisque le projet est en lui-même une jouissance suffisante?' (OC I 315)].

When I get home I'll reread 'A une heure du matin' because it is, as all prose poems should be, intense and satisfying as a novel, but better, compressed, extravagantly liquid and transporting. I love it for its echoes later in Hemingway and O'Hara and poems of my own that I have tried to write in homage, but mostly because, now that I am fully awake, I want to stay up, inside the layers and surprises of Baudelaire, poet for my city.

NOTES

1. Charles Baudelaire, *Intimate Journals* (Boston: Beacon Press, 1957), p. 9.
2. Walter Benjamin, *Charles Baudelaire: A Lyric Poet in the Era of High Capitalism* (London: Verson Editions, 1983), p. 97.
3. The Durer quotation is from the diary of Umberto Boccioni, referenced in the exhibition notes on Boccioni's paintings in 'Boccioni's Materia: A Futurist Master-piece and the Avant-Garde in Milan and Paris', Solomon R. Guggenheim Museum, Spring 2004.

CLAUDE PICHOIS

Afterword

An aspect of French poetic life has changed since the middle of the nineteenth century, as it had already been altered twenty years after the death of Baudelaire by the publication of the poet's *Posthumous Works [Œuvres posthumes]*. This publication was the work of Eugène Crépet, who included an extensive biography as well as numerous documents and letters.

1953 saw the completion of the *Complete Works [Œuvres complètes]* in an edition begun by Jacques Crépet, Eugène's son, and finished by me, who am to some degree his son-in-law, his natural son being Jean Ziegler, who has been a close collaborator of mine. The nineteen volumes of this irreplaceable critical and annotated edition, which was published by Louis Conard (whose successor was Jacques Lambert), began with *The Flowers of Evil [Les Fleurs du Mal]* (1922) which, like Baudelaire's other works, the rights of which had belonged since 1867 to Michel Lévy and then to Calmann Lévy, had now entered the public domain. (Whence the more or less meticulous editions of the *Fleurs* that appeared in 1917, one of them being produced by Apollinaire.) While working on his great edition, Jacques Crépet, in collaboration with Georges Blin, gave the Librairie José Corti a far more scholarly edition of the *Fleurs* in 1942 and, in September 1949, an edition of *Intimate Journals [Journaux intimes]*, a traditional and misleading title that includes *My Heart Laid Bare [Mon cœur mis à nu]*, *Rockets [Fusées]* and the *Notebook [Carnet]* (this last, moreover, having no title).

1949 is also a date that is as important as it is ridiculous. It was on 31 May of that year that, after a lengthy procedure, the Court of Appeal annulled the verdict of 20 August 1857 that had ordered the suppression of six of the finest poems of the *Fleurs du Mal*. These poems had in any case been clandestinely reproduced several times already. Baudelaire thus became a politically correct author. The condemnation had been inept, but understandable, given the hypocritical morality of the time. It was the judges of 1857 who were condemned by this rehabilitation.

We can be thankful that it was only around the middle of the twentieth century that Baudelaire became a university author. Before that, only one doctoral thesis was devoted to him: André Ferran's *Baudelaire's Aesthetics* [*L'Esthétique de Baudelaire*], published by Hachette in 1933, accompanied by the complementary thesis, the even more useful annotated edition of the *Salon de 1845*, which was published in 1933, at Toulouse, by the Editions de l'Archer. As it happened, the period before and after the Second World War, although it saw the meetings at Pontigny,[1] was innocent of the conference malady and did not institutionalise Baudelaire's work by setting it for university examinations. This did not prevent good and great writers from interpreting Baudelaire, who was becoming a classic despite himself. One has only to think of the debt that Proust, Gide (especially in *Strait is the Gate* [*La Porte étroite*]), and later Marcel Raymond, Albert Béguin and Jean-Paul Sartre all owe to him.

It was a sign of the times that Jacques Schiffrin, when he created the 'Bibliothèque de la Pléiade',[2] which soon passed under the aegis of the Gallimard Press, should have devoted the first volume to appear (printing was completed on 10 September 1931) to the poetry of Baudelaire, edited by Yves-Gérard Le Dantec. A second volume, number seven of the collection, with the same editor, came out at the end of 1932 (printing was completed on 1 October 1932). Le Dantec was a great enthusiast of poetry, from Marceline Desbordes-Valmore to Pierre Louÿs. But he was no philologist. As a result, he included in the second volume an apocryphal text, 'The Brussels Years' ['Les Années de Bruxelles'], written by Pascal Pia, at a point when the Institut de France, to which the vicomte de Spoelberch de Lovenjoul had bequeathed his collection,[3] had not yet given permission for the notes from Baudelaire's *Poor Belgium!* [*Pauvre Belgique!*] to be published.

At the beginning of the 1950s, when book clubs flourished, the two publishing houses of Gallimard and Hachette combined to create the 'club of the best book' ['le Club du Meilleur Livre'], with the aim of rivalling the 'French Book Club' ['le Club Français du Livre']. Samuel de Sacy, who directed the collection known as the 'Golden Number' ['Nombre d'or'] entrusted to me the task of organising the publication of Baudelaire's complete works in two volumes. The new arrangement of material that I adopted was the fruit of the following reflections.

From the time when Michel Lévy had published the *Complete Works* Baudelaire's writings had been divided into categories: *The Flowers of Evil, Short Prose Poems, The Artificial Paradises, Romantic Art, Aesthetic Curiosities* [*Les Fleurs du Mal, Petits Poèmes en prose, Les Paradis artificiels, L'Art romantique, Curiosités esthétiques*]. This last title, over which Baudelaire had pondered, covers the studies on art and thus has unity and authenticity, which is not the case for *Romantic Art*, a title unknown to Baudelaire, which includes in turn pieces on art, an essay entitled *Moral of the Toy [Morale du joujou]*, the study of Richard Wagner and finally the literary criticism; it is therefore, a composite work. In his great edition of the complete works, J. Crépet had preserved these two titles, as did Le Dantec in the Pléiade, with a few modifications.

The moment had come, therefore, to abandon the previous categories and begin afresh. The texts should be arranged in the chronological order in which they were published, indeed, in which they were written. Instead of the artificial unity created by their genre, there would be the real unity of the time of their creation, all the more convincing in that Baudelaire once more threw into question the very notion of genre: one need only think of the different forms assumed by his verse poetry and the shifting frontier that separates the verse and prose poems.

The two volumes of the *Club du Meilleur Livre* came out in 1955, each with a print run of 6,500 copies. They are now extremely rare, a fact that proves how interesting this new presentation was, like S. de Sacy's idea of preceding each chronological section with an introduction that had been requested from great writers or good critics.

It was Pierre Jean Jouve who wrote the preface for the prose poems and Yves Bonnefoy who wrote the one for the *Fleurs du Mal*. Another section was entrusted to Marcel A. Ruff, whose thesis, *The Spirit of Evil and Baude-lairean Aesthetics [L'Esprit du mal et l'esthétique baudelairienne]*, the first important thesis since the Second World War, had been published by Armand Colin that same year, 1955. It was a thesis in the first meaning of the term in that it drew Baudelaire into the clan of the Jansenists.[4]

It is highly significant that Bonnefoy, whose collection of poems *On the Movement and Immobility of Douve [Du mouvement et de l'immobilité de Douve]* had appeared in 1953, should have been associated with this edition. The new French poetry thus gave its sanction to the new presentation of Baudelaire's works.

By the end of the 1950s, the Pléiade Baudelaire appeared somewhat over-taken by events, even outdated. For that reason, the Gallimard Press asked me to improve the two volumes, which had been combined into a single vol-ume. In 1961, this edition came out under the double signatures of Y.-G. Le Dantec and C. Pichois. New, corrected, print runs followed. But on the death of Le Dantec, it was time for a fresh start. This took place. Unfortunately, the chronological arrangement of the *Club du Meilleur Livre* was set aside in favour of an organisation based on genre. This was an entirely new edition, all the texts being established from the originals and the notes conceived in response to the needs of demanding readers.

The two volumes appeared in 1975 and 1976, constituting a truly serious edition, but one which was still only partly scholarly. They have frequently been reprinted, each time with improvements to details, for it is one of the virtues of this collection that the editor is allowed to make necessary corrections and a few modifications and clarifications, provided that the typographic composition is not disturbed. To give a simple example: the notes Baudelaire made about *Dangerous Liaisons* [*Les Liaisons dangereuses*][5] have remained in the place assigned to them in 1976, but, after that date, because the manuscript, which had been lost since 1903, was rediscovered, the text was made to conform to the manuscript. The annotations indicate clearly that Baudelaire did not make these notes in two stages, first in 1856–7, and then when he was in Brussels. Instead, they belong entirely to the end of his stay in Belgium. Only when a completely new composition of the second volume is undertaken will it be possible to place these fragments at the end of the section entitled 'Literary Criticism' ['Critique littéraire']. This edition is truly serious, but because the publisher wants it to remain profitable, it cannot therefore be completely scholarly. To earn that description, it would need more variants and annotations. The serious charge I would make against it, is that through the fault of a pedant, who insisted on blindly following the collection's code or policy, the title *Les Fleurs du mal* [sic] is systematically printed like that, although in the explanatory note (OC 1 797 in all the print runs) it is clearly indicated that in his letters Baudelaire most often writes *Mal* with a capital 'M' and *fleurs* with a small 'f'. *Mal* indicates clearly the metaphysical dimension of the collection: *fleurs* would have hardly any meaning (think of the etymological meaning, *anthology*) had Baudelaire not linked it to *Mal* through a powerful oxymoron. I regret the fact that numerous critics, ignoring the clarification on page 797, multiply *Les Fleurs du mal* . . .

Jacques Dupont and I noted that all previous scholarly editions had given the variants in the form of notes attached to the text of the second or rather the final edition of the *Fleurs du Mal* (1861). This presentation has a serious disadvantage: whenever there is a case offering any complexity it becomes difficult to follow the succession of changes the author has made to the text. In addition, despite the existence of concordances for all three editions of the *Fleurs du Mal*, it was difficult to get a precise idea of the collection's initial appearance, as it can be seen in the original edition of 1857, the organisation and typographical format of which had been the subject of painstaking care by Baudelaire and his publisher, Poulet-Malassis.

The new 'diplomatic' edition of the *Fleurs* aims to restore to the collection its 'historicity' since it came into being slowly over twenty years, before reaching its definitive form in 1861. No one knows what would have been the final appearance Baudelaire would have given it, had he been able to complete successfully the third edition of the *Fleurs*: the posthumous edition of 1868 has, for that reason, to be considered as being without philological value. With this new edition, the reader will henceforth be able to follow the series of the pre-original publications (those that appeared in periodicals or newspapers before their publication in the volume) preceding or following the first edition of 1857, and consult, reproduced in facsimile, the two successive editions of the *Fleurs*, as well as the poems published by Baudelaire after the 1861 edition (in reviews and even newspapers, or in the volume called *Wrecks* [*Épaves*]). I should add that for each poem, presented in the place Baudelaire finally assigned to it in the edition of 1861, there will be facsimile reproductions of all the states of the poem currently known (manuscript, pre-original publications, corrected proofs for the 1857 edition and so forth). It will be the first time that a reader will be able to see, for each poem of the *Fleurs*, what has come down to us of the stages by which Baudelaire was able to reach the definitive text. Henceforth we will have, for the first time, a dynamic, evolving presentation of the sometimes numerous and complex modifications that the poems underwent. Some of these documents, which until now have been unknown or inaccessible, have been consulted in diverse private or public collections throughout the world. They let us appreciate the beauty of Baudelaire's handwriting and his sense of how the poem should appear on the page.

These three volumes of facsimile documents are accompanied by a volume of transcribed variants and annotations. The transcriptions make it easy for the reader to trace the changes that appear, by means of a systematic and methodical comparison of the successive versions. The annotations aim to produce useful clarifications, of a philological, historical and lexicographical nature (for there is a nineteenth-century language which is sometimes, indeed frequently, different from contemporary French), and they try to shed light on the genesis of each poem, through systematic discussions of the hypotheses that Baudelairean criticism has proposed concerning dating, hypotheses that are often very diverse and even contradictory. In this genetic perspective, questions of 'sources' and 'intertextuality' and therefore of rewriting are frequently broached and a certain number of new hypotheses are put forward.

As a result, this new edition should delight poetry lovers and persuade them, in accordance with Baudelaire's wishes, that where art is concerned no attention to detail is without its usefulness.

To complete this philological, bibliographical and literary panorama, it is fitting to indicate the existence of periodicals and series that are devoted entirely to Baudelaire. The first appeared in the United States: the initial number of the *Bulletin baudelairien* is dated 31 August 1965. It was created by W. T. Bandy, James S. Patty and Raymond P. Poggenburg, at Vanderbilt University, and is the origin of the W. T. Bandy Center for Baudelaire Studies of that university. It was followed by *Etudes baudelairiennes*, created in 1969 by Marc Eigeldinger, Robert Kopp (who left the team soon afterwards) and Claude Pichois, and was published by the Editions de La Baconnière at Neuchâtel (Switzerland). These studies stopped after the publication of volume XIII (1991), *Le Soleil de la Poésie. Gautier, Baudelaire, Rimbaud*, by Marc Eigeldinger. It is particularly fitting to draw attention to one of its volumes, the critical edition produced by Michèle Stäuble-Lipman Wulf of Baudelaire's version of *Confessions of an English Opium Eater* [*Un mangeur d'opium*], in which De Quincey's text appears opposite that of Baudelaire (vols. VI–VII, 1976). *L'Année Baudelaire*, published by Klincksieck, took over from *Etudes baudelairiennes* in 1995, and after the near collapse of that press, was published by Champion; it is edited by Claude Pichois, John E. Jackson and Jean-Paul Avice, together with an editorial panel composed of Baudelaireans from around the world.

Two splendid theses have brought honour to the French universities in the last ten years, that of Jérôme Thélot, *Baudelaire. Violence et Poésie* (Paris: Gallimard, 1993) and that of Patrick Labarthe, *Baudelaire et la tradition de l'allégorie* (Genève: Droz, 1999).[6]

J. Thélot asks what can poetry do today, faced with the passions of history and the metaphysical aridity of the current age, when Western societies, losing trust in its witnesses, seem to turn away from poetry. What need is there for poetry, and what legitimises it, when Baudelaire himself finally lost the ability to speak, revealing that to lose speech is the modern experience par excellence?

Now, Baudelaire not only raises that question, but also charges each reader to answer it, to take it up again where his poems leave it, and to see, as Baudelaire did, that an answer which ends in aphasia, personal or collective, is in turn answered by another response, that of love. For there surely is violence in language, but the poem that accompanies such violence can at least know this truth, turning poetry into a study of its own conditions. And more precisely there is a murder in the heart of words, and yet the poem that grows out of that fact can also reveal it, thus making poetry, like a sacrificial drama, an act of compassion for the victim of words.

Thélot's book, in which he reads, in the following order, *Le Spleen de Paris, Pauvre Belgique!*, the poem to Sainte-Beuve, and the strange story told to Nadar, 'Clergeon in Hell' ['Clergeon en enfer'], and finally *Les Fleurs du Mal*, and which draws its inspiration from the works of Yves Bonnefoy and René Girard, is devoted to Baudelaire's passion: to his denunciation – in which ethics are stronger than aesthetics – of the violence within poetry, in order to set language free at last, beyond the poems.

Taking note both of Walter Benjamin's proposal that the perception of allegory be enhanced, and of Jean Prévost's call for a study of Baudelaire's 'deep rhetoric', Patrick Labarthe chose a historical approach. His book explores those great traditions of allegory through whose influence the poet could have trained himself, restoring the dialogues that, at different moments of his work, he carried on with the great voices of his day or of the past. Tracing the diverse allegorical traditions that have left their mark on Baudelaire, and showing the convergences and the transformations in a work in which analogy is generalised, could, however, take place only in conjunction with the various poetic systems he envisaged. This book, therefore, moves from the Christian tradition of allegory (in the writings of Chateaubriand and in the oratorical tradition of the seventeenth century for example) to the ways in which thinkers from Winckelmann to Jouffroy conceived of the symbol, and to the figures of paganism (notably in Gautier) or the tradition of the bestiary.[7] At the end of his study, Labarthe suggests we should see a kind of dialectic between Baudelaire the *critic*'s permanent image of 'correspondences' – which is what links him to an entire Romantic understanding of analogy – and Baudelaire the *poet*'s rejection of this image through a far more fragmentary representation of reality: a representation which is carried out by means of allegory, which henceforth appears as Baudelaire's fundamental mode of thought.

There are many documentary and interpretive studies one could mention, but it is the task of bibliographies to list them. But a compatriot of Baudelaire cannot but pay homage to the valuable work published in the English-speaking world, especially in the United Kingdom, many of whose authors are present in this volume.

I said at the beginning of this essay that French poetic life had changed since the middle of the nineteenth century. This is borne out by the fact that if Victor Hugo is still the most popular (in the etymological sense) of the French writers, in the eyes of the educated classes it is Baudelaire who gets the better of his elder. Hugo – so Valéry wrote to Pierre Louÿs on 28 December 1914 – 'is of an entirely different abundance from Baudelaire, and yet, it's Baudelaire who has had progeny'.[8] With Hugo we see the fading, indeed the disappearance, of poetry as rhetoric. Baudelaire has benefited from Mallarmé's image of poetry as suggestion and from Rimbaud's poetry as aggression. We can be grateful to them, and even to Hugo, who served as a springboard for Baudelaire.

(Translated by Rosemary Lloyd)

NOTES

1. These meetings, which took place in the summer at the Cistercian abbey of Pontigny, in the département de l'Yonne, were famous for their discussions of literary and philosophical topics, and were attended by such luminaries as, for instance, André Gide, Paul Desjardins, Jacques Rivière, Dorothy Bussy and Lytton Strachey. After the Second World War, these meetings were continued at Cérisy-la-Salle. (Translator's note.)
2. Created in 1931 by Azerbaijan-born Jacques Schiffrin, the collection of annotated texts known as the Bibliothèque de la Pléiade is now the standard French reference edition for works of literature. (Translator's note.)
3. Charles de Spoelberch de Lovenjoul (1836–1907) was a bibliophile and book collector who left his vast collection of books and manuscripts to the Institut de France, that 'protector of the arts, letters and sciences', that had been created in 1795. (Translator's note.)
4. A branch of Christian theology founded by the Flemish theologian Cornelius Jansen (1585–1638). It emphasised original sin, human depravity and the need for divine grace for salvation from sin. (Translator's note.)
5. Pierre Choderlos de Laclos's 1782 epistolary novel. Baudelaire made a series of suggestive notes on this book, but never completed his projected article. (Translator's note.)
6. I owe the elements of the following two analyses to these two authors.
7. François-René, vicomte de Chateaubriand (1768–1848), a pre-Romantic writer whose works paved the way for the Romantics and whose rhetorical style earned him the sobriquet of the 'Enchanter'. He is the author, among other works, of *The Genius of Christianity* [*Le Génie du christianisme*]. Johann Joachim Winckelmann (1717–68) was a German art historian and archeologist. Théophile Gautier (1811–72), in his youth an ardent supporter of Romanticism, became one of the leading proponents of the art for art's sake movement. (Translator's note.)
8. Gide, Louÿs, Valéry, *Correspondance à trois voix*, ed. P. Fawcett and P. Mercier (Paris: Gallimard, 2004), p. 1068.

Titles of individual poems and prose poems referred to in the text

Abel et Cain	Abel and Cain
Albatros (L')	The Albatross
Alchimie de la douleur	Alchemy of Suffering
Ame du vin (L')	The Soul of Wine
Amour du mensonge (L')	The Love of Illusion
Assommons les pauvres	Let's Beat up the Poor!
Aube spirituelle (L')	The Spiritual Dawn
Au lecteur	To the Reader
A une dame créole	For a Creole Lady
A une heure du matin	One O'Clock in the Morning
A une Madone	To a Madonna
A une mendiante rousse	To a Red-Haired Beggar Girl
A une passante	To a Woman Passing by
Avec ses vêtements	The Way Her Silky Garments
Balcon (Le)	The Balcony
Beau Navire (Le)	The Lovely Ship
Beauté (La)	Beauty
Belle Dorothée (La)	Beautiful Dorothea
Bénédiction	Benediction
Bijoux (Les)	The Jewels
Bohémiens en voyage	Gypsies Travelling
Bons Chiens (Les)	The Good Dogs
Brumes et pluies	Mists and Rains
Cadre (Le)	The Frame
Causerie	Conversation
Chacun sa chimère	To Each His Monster
Chambre double (La)	The Double Bedroom
Chanson d'automne	Autumn Song

Charogne (Une)	A Carcass
Chat (Le)	The Cat
Cheval de race (Un)	A Thoroughbred Horse
Chevelure (La)	Head of Hair
Chien et le Flacon (Le)	The Dog and the Flask
Ciel brouillé	Misty Sky
Cloche fêlée (La)	The Cracked Bell
Confiteor de l'artiste (Le)	The Artist's *Confiteor*
Corde (La)	The Rope
Correspondances	Correspondences
Crépuscule du soir (Le)	Dusk (FM)
Crépuscule du soir (Le)	Evening Twilight (PP)
Le Cygne	The Swan
Danse macabre	Dance macabre
Déjà!	Already!
Désespoir de la vieille (Le)	The Old Woman's Despair
Destruction (La)	Destruction
Deux Bonnes Sœurs (Les)	The Two Good Sisters
Don Juan aux enfers	Don Juan in Hell
Dons des fées (Les)	The Gifts of the fairies
Elévation	Elevation
Enivrez-vous	Never be Sober
Ennemi (L')	The Enemy
Etranger (L')	The Outsider
Examen de minuit (L')	Midnight Examination
Fantôme (Un)	A Phantom
Fausse monnaie (La)	The Counterfeit Coin
Femme sauvage et la petite maîtresse (La)	The Wild Woman and the Little Sweetheart
Femmes damnées	Condemned Women
Fenêtres (Les)	The Windows
Fin de la journée (La)	Day's End
Flacon (Le)	The Flask
Flambeau vivant (Le)	The Living Torch
Fontaine de Sang (La)	The Fountain of Blood
Fou et la Vénus (Le)	The Jester and the Goddess
Foules (Les)	The Crowds
Gâteau (Le)	The Cake
Géante (La)	The Giantess
Goût du néant (Le)	The Taste for Nothingness

Gravure fantastique (Une)	A Fantastical Engraving
Guignon (Le)	Bad Luck
Harmonie du soir	Evening Harmony
Hémisphère dans une chevelure (Un)	A Hemisphere in a Head of Hair
Hiboux (Les)	The Owls
Horloge (L')	The Clock
Horreur sympathique	Congenial Horror
Hymne à la beauté (L')	Hymn to Beauty
Idéal (L')	The Ideal
Invitation au voyage (L')	Invitation to the Voyage
Irrémediable (L')	The Irremediable
Irréparable (L')	The Irreparable
Je t'adore	I love you
Je te donne ces vers	I give to you these verses
Jeu (Le)	Gaming
Joujou du pauvre (Le)	The Poor Child's Toy
Laquelle est la vraie?	Which is the Real Benedicta?
Litanies de Satan (Les)	Litanies of Satan
Lune offensée (La)	The Insulted Moon
Mademoiselle Bistouri	Miss Scalpel
Martyre (Une)	A Martyr
Masque (Le)	The Mask
Mauvais Moine (Le)	The Wretched Monk
Mauvais Vitrier (Le)	The Bad Glazier
Miroir (Le)	The Mirror
Mort des amants (La)	The Death of Lovers
Mort des artistes (La)	The Death of Artists
Mort des pauvres (La)	The Death of the Poor
Mort héroïque (Une)	A Hero's Death
Muse malade (La)	The Sick Muse
Muse vénale (La)	The Venal Muse
Musique (La)	Music
Parfum (Le)	The Perfume
Parfum exotique	Exotic Perfume
Paysage	Landscape
Perte d'auréole	Loss of a Halo
Petites Vieilles (Les)	The Little Old Women
Phares (Les)	The Beacons
Pipe (La)	The Pipe

Plaisant (Un)	A Prankster
Poison (Le)	Poison
Port (Le)	The Port
Portraits de maîtresses	Portraits of Mistresses
Possédé (Le)	The Possessed
Projets (Les)	Plans
Remords posthume	Remorse after Death
Reniement de saint Pierre (Le)	St Peter's Denial
Rêve d'un curieux (Le)	Dream of a Curious Man
Revenant (Le)	The Ghost
Rêve parisien	Parisian Dream
Réversibilité	Reversibility
Sept Vieillards (Les)	The Seven Old Men
Sépulture	Burial
Serpent qui danse (Le)	The Dancing Serpent
Soupe et les nuages (La)	The Soup and the Clouds
Spleen: Quand le ciel lourd et bas	Spleen: When low and heavy sky
Squelette laboureur (Le)	Skeletons Digging
Sur *Le Tasse en prison*	On *Tasso in Prison*, by Eugène Delacroix
Thyrse (Le)	The Thyrsus
Tir et le cimetière (Le)	The Firing Range and the Cemetery
Tout entière	Completely One
Tu mettrais l'univers	You'd Entertain the Universe
Vampire (Le)	The Vampire
Veuves (Les)	The Widows
Vie antérieure (La)	A Former Life
Vieux Saltimbanque (Le)	The Old Mountebank
Vin de l'assassin (Le)	The Murderer's Wine
Vin des amants (Le)	The Lovers' Wine
Vin des chiffonniers (Le)	The Ragmen's Wine
Vin du solitaire (Le)	The Solitary's Wine
Voyage (Le)	Voyaging
Voyage à Cythère (Un)	A Voyage to Cythera
Yeux des pauvres (Les)	The Eyes of the Poor

GUIDE TO FURTHER READING

Charles Baudelaire: reference texts used throughout this volume

Œuvres complètes, 2 vols., ed. Claude Pichois and Jean Ziegler (Paris: Gallimard, 1975–6)
Correspondance, 2 vols., ed. Claude Pichois (Paris: Gallimard, 1972–3)

Charles Baudelaire: other works cited in this volume

Un Mangeur d'opium, ed. Michèle Stauble-Lipman Wulf, Etudes baudelairiennes VI–VII (Neuchâtel: A la Baconnière, 1976)
Intimate Journals, trs. Christopher Isherwood (Boston: Beacon Press, 1957)

Translations

Brown, Andrew, On Wine and Hashish (London: Hesperus, 2002)
Cameron, Norman, Intimate Journals (New York: Syrens, 1995)
Clark, Carol and Robert Sykes, eds., Baudelaire in English (Harmondsworth: Penguin, 1997)
Kaplan, Edward, The Parisian Prowler (Athens: University of Georgia Press, 1997), second edition with new preface
Lloyd, Rosemary, The Conquest of Solitude: Selected Letters of Charles Baudelaire (Chicago: Chicago University Press, 1986)
The Prose Poems and 'La Fanfarlo' (Oxford: Oxford University Press, 1991)
Martin, Walter, Charles Baudelaire: Complete Poems (Manchester: Carcanet, 1997)
Mayne, Jonathan, Art in Paris 1845–1862 (London: Phaidon, 1965)
The Painter of Modern Life (London: Phaidon, 1964)
McGowan, James, The Flowers of Evil. Oxford: Oxford University Press, 1993.
Shapiro, Norman R., Charles Baudelaire: Selected Poems from Les Fleurs du Mal (Chicago: University of Chicago Press, 1998)

Biographical and other

Pichois, Claude, Baudelaire, trs. Graham Robb (London: Hamish Hamilton, 1987)
Pichois, Claude and Vincenette, eds., Lettres à Baudelaire (Geneva: A la Baconnière, 1973)

Critical and general

Benjamin, Walter, *Charles Baudelaire: A Lyric Poet in the Era of High Capitalism*, trs. H. Zohn (London: NLB, 1973)

Bersani, Leo, *Baudelaire and Freud* (Berkeley: University of California Press, 1977)

Burton, Richard, *Baudelaire and the Second Republic: Writing and Revolution* (Oxford: Clarendon Press, 1991)

   Baudelaire in 1859: A Study in the Sources of Poetic Creativity (Cambridge: Cambridge University Press, 1988)

Caws, Mary Ann and Hermine Riffaterre, eds., *The Prose Poem in France: Theory and Practice* (New York: Columbia University Press, 1983)

Chambers, Ross, 'Baudelaire's Street Poetry', *Nineteenth Century French Studies*, 13, 4 (Summer 1985), pp. 244–59

   Loiterature (Lincoln: University of Nebraska Press, 1999)

   Mélancolie et opposition. Les débuts du modernisme en France (Paris: Corti, 1987)

Chesters, Graham, *Baudelaire and the Poetics of Craft* (Cambridge: Cambridge University Press, 1988)

Clark, T. J., *The Absolute Bourgeois. Artists and Politics in France 1848–1851* (London: Thames and Hudson, 1973)

Clements, Patricia, *Baudelaire and the English Tradition* (Princeton: Princeton University Press, 1985)

Evans, Margery, *Baudelaire and Intertextuality: Poetry at the Crossroads* (Cambridge: Cambridge University Press, 1993)

Fairlie, Alison, *Baudelaire: 'Les Fleurs du Mal'* (London: Edward Arnold, 1960)

Hannoosh, Michele, *Baudelaire and Caricature: From the Comic to an Art of Modernity* (University Park: Pennsylvania State University Press, 1992)

Hiddelston, J. A., *Baudelaire and 'Le Spleen de Paris'* (Oxford: Clarendon Press, 1987)

   Baudelaire and the Art of Memory (Oxford: Clarendon Press, 1999)

Jackson, John E., *Baudelaire* (Paris: Livre de Poche, 2001)

   La Mort Baudelaire (Neuchâtel: A la Baconnière, 1982)

Johnson, Barbara, *The Critical Difference: Essays in the Contemporary Rhetoric of Reading* (Baltimore, MD: Johns Hopkins University Press, 1980)

Kaplan, Edward K., *Baudelaire's Prose Poems: The Esthetic, the Ethical, and the Religious in 'The Parisian Prowler'* (Athens and London: University of Georgia Press, 1990)

Killick, Rachel, 'The Sonnet in *Les Fleurs du Mal*', *Dalhousie French Studies*, 2 (1980), pp. 21–39

Lawler, James R., *Poetry and Moral Dialectic: Baudelaire's 'Secret Architecture'* (Madison, NJ: Fairleigh Dickenson University Press, 1997)

Leakey, Felix, *Baudelaire and Nature* (Manchester: Manchester University Press, 1969)

Lloyd, Rosemary, *Baudelaire's Literary Criticism* (Cambridge: Cambridge University Press, 1981)

   Baudelaire's World (Ithaca, NY: Cornell University Press, 2002)

Maclean, Marie, *Narrative as Performance: The Baudelairean Experiment* (London: Routledge, 1988)

Miner, Margaret, *Resonant Gaps: Between Baudelaire & Wagner* (Athens: University of Georgia Press, 1995)

Mossop, D., *Baudelaire's Tragic Hero* (Oxford: Oxford University Press, 1961)

Murphy, Steve, *Logiques du dernier Baudelaire. Lectures du* Spleen de Paris (Paris: Champion, 2003)

Prendergast, Christopher, *Paris and the Nineteenth Century* (Oxford: Blackwell, 1992)

Raser, Timothy, *A Poetics of Art Criticism: The Case of Baudelaire* (Chapel Hill: University of North Carolina Press, 1989)

Salines, Emily, *Alchemy and Amalgam: Translation in the Works of Baudelaire* (Amsterdam: Rodopi, 2004)

Sartre, Jean-Paul, *Baudelaire*, trs. M. Turnell (London: Hamish Hamilton, 1964)

Scott, Clive, *Translating Baudelaire* (Exeter: University of Exeter Press, 2000)

Stephens, Sonya, *Baudelaire's Prose Poems: The Practice and Politics of Irony* (Oxford: Oxford University Press, 1999)

Tester, Keith, ed., *The Flâneur* (London: Routledge, 1994)

Wing, Nathaniel, *Limits of Narrative: Essays on Baudelaire, Flaubert, Rimbaud and Mallarmé* (Cambridge: Cambridge University Press, 1986)

Wright, Barbara and David Scott, *'La Fanfarlo' and 'Le Spleen de Paris'* (London: Grant and Cutler, 1984)

Bibliographical

Robert T. Cargo, *Baudelaire Criticism 1950–1967* (Tuscaloosa: University of Alabama Press, 1968)

The *Bulletin baudelairien* keeps an up–to–date list of Baudelaire criticism

Online and electronic resources

http://baudelairelitteratura.com Site maintained by David Smadj

INDEX

Amiel, Henri Frédéric 38, 39–40
Ancelle, Narcisse-Désiré 3, 10
Apollinaire, Guillaume 176, 179
Artaud, Antonin 179
Asselineau, Charles 11
Auden, Wystan Hugh 197
Aupick, Jacques 2–3, 9, 24
Avice, Jean-Paul 218

Balzac, Honoré de 16, 33, 118, 139, 142,
    169, 171, 172, 177
Bandy, W. T. 218
Banville, Théodore de 51, 60, 66, 172
Barbey d'Aurevilly, Jules 9, 31
Barthes, Roland 43, 48, 146, 157, 196
Bataille, Georges 180
Baudelaire, Caroline Archenbaut
    Defayis 1–2, 3, 8, 9
Baudelaire, François 1
Beckett, Samuel 49, 177, 179
Béguin, Albert 214
Belgium, Baudelaire's experiences in 11
Benjamin, Walter xiv, 24, 43, 44, 45, 106,
    207, 219
Bersani, Leo 161
Bertrand, Aloysius xiii, 70, 71
Betjeman, John 197
Blanqui, Louis-Auguste 28, 29
Blin, Georges 4, 213
Boccioni, Umberto 210
Bonnefoy, Yves 94, 200, 215, 218
Boudin, Eugène 141–2
Brecht, Bertold 179
Brooks, Peter 157
Brunel, Pierre 195
Buber, Martin 189
Buchanan, Robert 202
Burton, Richard D. E. 157

Butor, Michel 123
Byron, George Gordon Lord 171

Camp, Maxime Du 50
Campbell, Roy 200
Carson, Ciaran xiv
Castle, Terry 149, 152
Caws, Mary Ann 209
Cézanne, Paul 179, 184
Chambers, Ross 152, 153
Champfleury (Jules Husson-Fleury) 170–1
Chassériau, Théodore 47
Chateaubrand, François René de 133, 219
Chenevard, Paul 118
Chennevières, Philippe de (Jean de
    Falaise) 169
Chevreul, Michel Eugène 138
Christophe, Ernest 34
Cladel, Léon 168
Clark, Carol 200
Clements, Patricia 194
Collins, Wilkie 118
Coleridge, Samuel Taylor 118
conseil judiciaire 3–4, 11
Crépet, Eugène 165, 213
Crépet, Jacques 213, 215
Cruikshank, George 141

Daix, Pierre 135
Dante xiv, 18, 37
Daubrun, Marie 38, 159
    poems inspired by 35, 38–9
Daumier, Honoré 11, 16, 22, 25, 118, 141,
    183
Delacroix, Eugène xiv, 11, 19, 34, 118, 131,
    132–9, 142, 143, 183, 184
Deleuze, Gilles 105, 110
Demeny, Paul (Rimbaud's letter to) 51

Derrida, Jacques xiv, 26
Desbordes-Valmore, Marceline 164, 173
Dickens, Charles 208
Dulac, Germaine 179
Dupont, Jacques 216
Dupont, Pierre 27, 28, 164
Duras, Marguerite 176
Durer, Albrecht 210
Duval, Jeanne 3, 5–6, 8, 37, 186
   poems inspired by 35–7, 38, 39, 40–1

Eigeldinger, Marc 218
Eliot, Thomas Stearns xiv, 91, 130

Ferran, André 214
Feydeau, Georges 194
Fitzgerald, Robert xiv
Flaubert, Gustave 11, 12, 15, 32, 50, 132,
   164, 170, 172, 175
   L'Education sentimentale 18
   Madame Bovary 32, 165, 170, 172
Fleurs du Mal (Les), trial of 4, 9, 10–11
Fontaine, Jean de la 194
Foucault, Michel 43
Fourier, Charles 16, 18, 22
Fraisse, Armand 58
Frick, Henry Clay 208

Gauguin, Paul xiv
Gautier, Théophile 11, 15, 42, 50, 51, 60, 66,
   118, 164, 166, 168, 172, 177, 219
   Emaux et camées 54
Gavarni, Paul 141
Genet, Jean 179
Genette, Gérard 196
Gide, André 39, 41, 179, 214
Girard, René 218
Goya, Francisco de 22, 36, 131, 141
Gray, Gustave Le 43
Guattari, Félix 105, 110
Guys, Constantin 11, 142–4, 178, 183

H. D. (Hilda Doolittle) 197
Heaney, Seamus xiv
Heine, Heinrich 16
Hemmingway, Ernest 212
Hoffmann, E. T. A. 33, 177
Hogarth, William 22, 141
Houssaye, Arsène 69, 70–1, 73, 79, 83, 84,
   85, 110, 182
Howard, Richard xiv
Hugo, Victor 15, 24, 42, 44, 83, 87, 89, 164,
   173, 180, 219

Baudelaire's dedications of poems to 50,
   92, 180
   Les Contemplations 173
   La Légende des siècles 165
   Les Misérables 25

Ingres, Jean-Auguste-Dominique 138, 142

Jackson, John E. 218
Jacobs, Jane 208
Johnson, Barbara xiii, 94, 187, 188–9
Jouve, Pierre-Jean 215
Jouffroy, Théodore Simon 219
Joyce, James 172, 176
Juvenal (Decimus Iunius Iuvenalis) 36

Kaplan, Edward K. 188–9, 191
Karr, Alphonse 118
Kierkegaard, Søren 98
Kock, Paul de 172
Kopp, Robert 218

Labarthe, Patrick 218, 219
Lacan, Jacques xiv
Laclos, Pierre-Ambroise-François Choderlos
   de 132, 216
Laforgue, Jules 130, 131
Lamartine, Alphonse de 33, 38, 39
Lautréamont, Isidore Ducasse, comte de
   179
Leakey, F. W. 200
Leconte de Lisle, Charles-Marie 207
Le Dantec, Yves-Gérard 214, 215
Lerner, Laurence 197, 200
Levinas, Emmanuel 25
Liddy, James 200
Liszt, Franz 77
Lloyd, Rosemary 153, 162
Louÿs, Pierre 219
Lowell, Robert 194, 200, 201
Lukacs, Georg xiv, 44
Lyu, Claire 149, 150

Machiavelli, Niccolo 20
Maistre, Joseph de 10, 29, 49
Mallarmé, Stéphane xiv, 66, 109, 176, 179,
   184, 192, 219
Man, Paul de 188–9
Manet, Edouard 11, 34, 139, 179, 183,
   184
   Déjeuner sur l'herbe 34
   Maîtresse de Baudelaire 37
Manet, Mme 12

Marx, Karl 20, 102, 106
Martin, Walter 199
Matisse, Henri xiv
   Luxe, calme et volupté 39, 41
Maturin, Charles Robert 132
McGann, Jerome 203
Meisonnier, Jean 118, 136
Ménard, Louis 170
Mercier, Louis-Sébastien 42
Meryon, Charles 11, 183
Menard, Louis 27
Meurice, Mme Paul (Eléonore-Palmyre
   Granger) 12
Michelangelo (di Lodovico Buonarroti
   Simoni) xiv, 131
Milton, John 47
Molènes, Paul de 146, 155
Montaigne, Michel de xiv
Moore, Nicholas 197
Moreau, Hégésippe 167
Moreau de Tours, Joseph 118
Morisot, Berthe 184
Mumford, Lewis 208
Musset, Alfred de 19, 33, 180

Nadar (Félix Tournachon) 11, 48, 50, 160,
   218
Nerval, Gérard de Labrunie 33, 46, 47, 118,
   167
Nodier, Charles 118
Nolan, Sidney xiv

O'Connor, Ulick 197
O'Hara, Frank 212
Ovid (Publius Ovidius Naso) xiv, 39, 41,
   180

Paley, Elizabeth 158
Patty, James S. 218
Petrarch, Francesco 37
Pia, Pascal 214
Picasso, Pablo xiv
Pichois, Claude 157, 215, 218
Plato 122
Poe, Edgar Allan xiii, 11, 29, 88, 101, 132,
   165, 167, 173, 184, 186, 193
Poggenburg, Raymond P. 218
Poulet, Georges xiv
Poulet-Malassis, Auguste 11, 29
Pradier, Jean-Jacques 118
Prarond, Ernest 145, 155
Prévost, Jean 219
Proudhon, Pierre-Joseph 29

Proust, Marcel 42, 45, 176, 177–8, 179, 214
   A la recherche du temps perdu 177
Puget, Pierre 131

Quincey, Thomas de xiii, 118, 120–1, 126,
   148, 149, 150, 165, 184, 187, 218

Rabelais, François xiv
Raphaël (Raffaello Sanzio) 137
Raymond, Marcel 214
Rembrandt, Harmenszoon van Rijn xiv, 131,
   137
Rethel, Alfred 183
Richard, Jean-Pierre xiv
Ricœur, Paul 93
Rilke, Rainer Maria 179
Rimbaud, Arthur xiv, 51, 66, 176, 179, 219
   Le Bateau ivre 44
Robb, Graham 34
Robertson, James 203
Rossetti, Dante Gabriel 202
Rousseau, Jean-Jacques 6
Rouvière, Philibert 145, 167
Rubens, Peter Paul 131, 137
Ruff, Marcel 215
Ryle, Anthony 200

Sabatier, Aglaé-Apollonie 186
   poems inspired by 35, 37–8
Sacy, Sameul de 214, 215
Sade, Donatien Alphonse François de xiv
Sainte-Beuve, Charles-Augustin xiv, 11, 34,
   59, 167, 171
   *Tableau historique et critique de la poésie
   française* 58
Sarraute, Nathalie 176
Sartre, Jean-Paul xiv, 1, 12, 19, 214
Senancourt, Guy de 118
Senneville, Louis de 61
Scheffer, Ary 133, 136
Schiffrin, Jacques 214
Schultz, Gretchen 162
Séraphin, Joseph 149, 152
Shakespeare, William 77
   Hamlet 177
Shanks, Lewis Piaget 200
Shapiro, Norman xiv, 194, 199
Socrates 89, 96
Spoelberch de Lovenjoul, Charles, vicomte
   de 214
Staël, Germaine de 137
Stevens, Wallace 197
Swedenborg, Emanuel 33, 177

Swinburne, Algernon 193, 194–5, 202, 203
  Ave atque vale 195
  Dolores 195
Swift, Jonathan 17
Sykes, Robert 200
Symons, Arthur 193, 194

Tate, Allen 201–2
Thélot, Jérôme 48, 218–19
Thoré, Théophile 193
Tisserant, Hippolyte 145, 156
Todorov, Tzvetan 72
Treadwell, James 146, 147
Truffaut, François 179–80

Valéry, Paul 184, 219
Van Gogh, Vincent 184
Varda, Agnès 180
  Jacquot de Nantes 180
Vauvenargues, Luc de Clapiers, marquis
  de xiv
Verlaine, Paul 11, 19, 65
Vernet, Horace 18, 136
Vigny, Alfred de 31, 47, 180
Vinci, Leonardo da xiv, 34, 131

Virgil (Publius Virgilius Maro) xiv, 43, 180
Voltaire, François-Marie Arouet 132

Wagner, Richard xiii, 11, 33, 146–63
  Fliegende Holländer (Der) 154, 162
  Lettre sur la musique 152, 153
  Lohengrin 33, 152, 154, 157, 158
  The Revolution 28
  Tannhäuser xiii, 152
  Tristan und Isolde 152
Watkins, Vernon 201
Watteau, Antoine 46, 131
Weber, Carl Maria von
  Invitation to the Waltz 39, 41
Weil, Simone 93
Whitman, Walt 101
Wilbur, Richard xiv
Winckelmann, Johan Joachim 219
Woolf, Virginia 176
Wulf, Michèle Stäuble-Lipman 218
Wratislaw, Theodore 195

Yeats, William Butler 33

Ziegler, Jean 213

INDEX TO BAUDELAIRE'S WORKS

Abel et Caïn 27–8
Albatros (L') 6, 19, 33, 43
Alchimie de la douleur 61
Ame du vin (L') 26, 46
Amour du mensonge (L') 56
Assommons les pauvres 10, 17, 28, 29, 80, 84, 95, 96
Aube spirituelle (L') 59
Au lecteur 19–22, 23, 32–3, 53–4, 58, 90–1, 176
A une dame créole 59
A une heure du matin 81, 84, 212
A une Madone 4, 39, 41, 186, 195
A une mendiante rousse 44
A une passante 19, 28–9, 45, 102, 105, 114, 184
Avec ses vêtements 36, 59, 195

Balcon (Le) 37, 38, 64
Beau Navire (Le) 38, 40
Beauté (La) 34, 59, 91
Belle Dorothée (La) 95, 186
Bénédiction 19, 22–3, 32, 33, 178
Bijoux (Les) 186
Bohémiens en voyage 60, 131
Bons Chiens (Les) 98–9
Brumes et pluies 60, 63

Causerie 59
Chacun sa chimère 131
Chambre double (La) 19, 72, 74–7, 79, 81, 118, 121, 153, 186
Chanson d'automne 39, 41
Charogne (Une) 36–7, 38, 179
Chat (Le) (34) 59
Chat (Le) (51) 54, 56–7
Cheval de race (Un) 97

Chevelure (La) 35–6, 37, 77, 141, 186
Chien et le Flacon (Le) 27, 72, 73
Ciel brouillé 38, 39, 42, 49
Cloche fêlée (La) 39, 40, 59
Comment on paie ses dettes 169
Confession 38
Confiteor de l'artiste (Le) 75–6, 77, 79, 168
Conseils aux jeunes écrivains 165
Corde (La) 95, 190
Correspondances 33, 39, 41, 61, 122, 177, 201–2
Coucher du soleil 172
Crépuscule du matin (Le) 12
Crépuscule du soir (Le) 72
Cygne (Le) xiii, 12, 19, 43–4, 58, 92, 107–9, 115, 180–1

Danse macabre 28
Déjà! 131, 207
De l'essence du rire 139–41, 154–5
Désespoir de la vieille (Le) 95
Destruction (La) 46
Deux Bonnes Sœurs (Les) 46
Don Juan aux enfers 131
Dons des fées (Les) 81
Drames et les romans honnêtes 87, 145
Duellum 36, 131
Du vin et du haschisch 88, 119

Ecole païenne 88, 136, 166
Edgar Poe: sa vie et ses ouvrages 87
Elévation 33
Enivrez-vous 125, 131, 207
Ennemi (L') 34, 59
Epaves, Les 11
Etranger (L') 23, 72–3, 74, 95
Exposition universelle (1855) 134

Fantôme (Un) 54
Fausse monnaie (La) 25–6, 81, 166
Femme sauvage et la petite maîtresse
    (La) 72, 81
Femmes damnées 46, 93
Fenêtres (Les) 75–6, 78–9, 80, 81, 83, 85,
    95, 96–7, 190–1, 208
Fin de Don Juan (La) 145, 156
Fin de la journée (La) 48, 58
Flacon (Le) 38, 55
Flambeau vivant (Le) 37, 59
Fleurs du mal (section) 32, 46–7, 92
Fontaine de Sang (La) 46
Fou et la Vénus (Le) 72
Foules (Les) 79–80, 95
Fusées 51

Gâteau (Le) 28, 80, 84, 85, 95, 96
Géante (La) 34, 60, 195
Goût du néant (Le) 64–5
Gravure fantastique (Une) 131
Guignon (Le) 34, 59

Harmonie du soir 38, 63, 141
Hémisphère dans une chevelure (Un) 77, 207
Héautontimoroumenos 39, 41, 55
Hiboux (Les) 54
Horloge (L') 41
Horreur sympathique 39, 41, 61
Hymne à la beauté (L') 91, 197–9, 202

Idéal (L') 34, 59
Idéolus 155
Invitation au voyage (L') 39, 40, 63, 186,
    188
Irrémédiable (L') 41, 54
Irréparable (L') 39, 41, 64, 158–9, 160
Ivrogne, L' 145, 156–8

J'aime le souvenir 23, 195
Je t'adore 36
Je te donne ces vers 37
Jeu (Le) 131
Joujou du pauvre (Le) 80, 84, 95–6, 186,
    207
Journaux intimes 88–9

Laquelle est la vraie? 72, 79, 97, 131, 186
Lesbiennes (as title for Les Fleurs du mal) 46
Liaisons dangereuses, Baudelaire's notes
    on 216
Litanies de Satan (Les) 10, 27–8, 47
Lune offensée (La) 22

Mademoiselle Bistouri 81, 95, 97–8, 102,
    104, 121, 187
Mangeur d'Opium (Un) (Baudelaire's
    translation of De Quincey's Confessions of
    an English Opium-Eater) xiii, 120, 148–9,
    158
Marquis du 1er housards 10, 155
Martyre (Une) 92, 134
Masque (Le) 34, 91, 131
Mauvais Moine (Le) 34, 59
Mauvais Vitrier (Le) 28, 83–4, 85, 95,
    210–11
Miroir (Le) 81, 82–3
Moesta et errabunda 64
Mon cœur mis à nu 51, 88, 153, 160, 162
Morale du joujou 152
Mort (La) (section) 32, 48–50, 94
Mort des amants (La) 48, 54
Mort des artistes (La) 48
Mort des pauvres (La) 48, 60
Mort héroïque (Une) 85, 134, 140, 154–5
Muse malade (La) 34, 59
Muse vénale (La) 34, 59
Musique (La) 38, 40, 59–60, 161–3

Obsession 39, 41, 61

Paradis artificiels 46, 88, 117–28
Parfum (Le) 37
Parfum exotique 35–6, 37, 62, 109, 196, 197
Paysage 42, 49
Peintre de la vie moderne (Le) 79, 80, 94
Perte d'auréole 19, 131
Petits Poèmes en prose (Les) (Spleen de
    Paris) 6, 19, 94
Petites Vieilles (Les) 6–7, 44, 45, 58, 92,
    179, 197
Phares (Les) 34, 41, 131
Pipe (La) 54
Plaisant (Un) 81, 131
Poème du haschich 46, 120, 149–50
Poison (Le) 56
Port (Le) 72
Portraits de maîtresses 81
Possédé (Le) 59
Prefaces to Les Fleurs du mal 51
Projets (Les) 79, 80, 81, 83, 87, 211

Que diras-tu ce soir 37

Remords posthume 59, 197
Reniement de saint Pierre (Le) 28, 47
Rêve d'un curieux (Le) 48, 158, 159–60, 162

Revenant (Le) 59
Rêve parisien 19, 54, 118
Réversibilité 38, 64
Révolte (section) 26, 32, 47, 93
Richard Wagner et *Tannhäuser* à Paris 145, 147–63

Salon de 1845 138, 142
Salon de 1846 15–18, 19, 20, 90, 131, 135, 138, 142
Salon de 1859 19, 43, 137, 141
Sed non satiata 36, 59, 62
Semper eadem 59
Sept Vieillards (Les) 28, 44–5, 57, 92, 105
Sépulture 59
Serpent qui danse (Le) 36, 186
Servante au grand cœur (La) 8
Sisina 59
Soupe et les nuages (La) 72, 73, 187
Spleen et Idéal (section) 32, 91
Spleen (group of poems with this title) 38, 39–41
Spleen (1) 60, 200
Spleen (3) 134, 197
Spleen (4) 56

Squelette laboureur (Le) 54
Sur *Le Tasse en prison* 131

Tableaux parisiens (section) 19, 26, 32, 41, 91, 101, 142, 143
Thyrse (Le) 77–8
Tir et le cimetière (Le) 72
Tout entière 54
Tu mettrais l'univers 36

Vampire (Le) 55
Veuves (Les) 80, 84, 95, 186
Vie antérieure (La) 62
Vieux Saltimbanque (Le) 81, 84, 95
Vin (Le) (section) 32, 45–6, 92
Vin de l'assassin (Le) 26, 46, 145, 156
Vin des amants (Le) 46
Vin des chiffonniers (Le) 26, 45–6, 184
Vin du solitaire (Le) 46
Voyage (Le) 28, 32, 48–50, 94, 195, 196
Voyage à Cythère (Un) 46–7, 55, 93

Yeux des pauvres (Les) 25, 26, 80, 82, 83, 95, 111–14, 189–90, 207

CAMBRIDGE COMPANIONS TO LITERATURE

*The Cambridge Companion to Greek
Tragedy*
edited by P. E. Easterling

The Cambridge Companion to Roman Satire
edited by Kirk Freudenburg

*The Cambridge Companion to Old English
Literature*
edited by Malcolm Godden and Michael
Lapidge

*The Cambridge Companion to Medieval
Women's Writing*
edited by Carolyn Dinshaw and David
Wallace

*The Cambridge Companion to Medieval
Romance*
edited by Roberta L. Krueger

*The Cambridge Companion to Medieval
English Theatre*
edited by Richard Beadle

*The Cambridge Companion to English
Renaissance Drama, second edition*
edited by A. R. Braunmuller and Michael
Hattaway

*The Cambridge Companion to Renaissance
Humanism*
edited by Jill Kraye

*The Cambridge Companion to English
Poetry, Donne to Marvell*
edited by Thomas N. Corns

*The Cambridge Companion to English
Literature, 1500–1600*
edited by Arthur F. Kinney

*The Cambridge Companion to English
Literature, 1650–1740*
edited by Steven N. Zwicker

*The Cambridge Companion to English
Literature, 1740–1830*
edited by Thomas Keymer
and Jon Mee

*The Cambridge Companion to Writing of the
English Revolution*
edited by N. H. Keeble

*The Cambridge Companion to English
Restoration Theatre*
edited by Deborah C. Payne Fisk

*The Cambridge Companion to British
Romanticism*
edited by Stuart Curran

*The Cambridge Companion to
Eighteenth-Century Poetry*
edited by John Sitter

*The Cambridge Companion to the
Eighteenth-Century Novel*
edited by John Richetti

*The Cambridge Companion to Gothic
Fiction*
edited by Jerrold E. Hogle

*The Cambridge Companion to Victorian
Poetry*
edited by Joseph Bristow

*The Cambridge Companion to the
Victorian Novel*
edited by Deirdre David

*The Cambridge Companion to Crime
Fiction*
edited by Martin Priestman

*The Cambridge Companion to Science
Fiction*
edited by Edward James and
Farah Mendlesohn

*The Cambridge Companion to Travel
Writing*
edited by Peter Hulme and Tim Youngs

*The Cambridge Companion to American
Realism and Naturalism*
edited by Donald Pizer

*The Cambridge Companion to
Nineteenth-Century American Women's
Writing*
edited by Dale M. Bauer and Philip Gould

*The Cambridge Companion to Victorian and
Edwardian Theatre*
edited by Kerry Powell

*The Cambridge Companion to the Literature
of the First World War*
edited by Vincent Sherry

*The Cambridge Companion to the Classic
Russian Novel*
edited by Malcolm V. Jones and
Robin Feuer Miller

The Cambridge Companion to the French Novel: from 1800 to the Present
edited by Timothy Unwin

The Cambridge Companion to the Spanish Novel: from 1600 to the Present
edited by Harriet Turner and Adelaida López de Martínez

The Cambridge Companion to the Italian Novel
edited by Peter Bondanella and Andrea Ciccarelli

The Cambridge Companion to the Modern German Novel
edited by Graham Bartram

The Cambridge Companion to the Latin American Novel
edited by Efraín Kristal

The Cambridge Companion to Jewish American Literature
edited by Hana Wirth-Nesher and Michael P. Kramer

The Cambridge Companion to the African American Novel
edited by Maryemma Graham

The Cambridge Companion to Canadian Literature
edited by Eva-Marie Kröller

The Cambridge Companion to Contemporary Irish Poetry
edited by Matthew Campbell

The Cambridge Companion to Modernism
edited by Michael Levenson

The Cambridge Companion to American Modernism
edited by Walter Kalaidjian

The Cambridge Companion to Postmodernism
edited by Steven Connor

The Cambridge Companion to Postcolonial Literary Studies
edited by Neil Lazarus

The Cambridge Companion to Australian Literature
edited by Elizabeth Webby

The Cambridge Companion to American Women Playwrights
edited by Brenda Murphy

The Cambridge Companion to Modern British Women Playwrights
edited by Elaine Aston and Janelle Reinelt

The Cambridge Companion to Twentieth-Century Irish Drama
edited by Shaun Richards

The Cambridge Companion to Homer
edited by Robert Fowler

The Cambridge Companion to Virgil
edited by Charles Martindale

The Cambridge Companion to Ovid
edited by Philip Hardie

The Cambridge Companion to Dante
edited by Rachel Jacoff

The Cambridge Companion to Cervantes
edited by Anthony J. Cascardi

The Cambridge Companion to Goethe
edited by Lesley Sharpe

The Cambridge Companion to Dostoevskii
edited by W. J. Leatherbarrow

The Cambridge Companion to Tolstoy
edited by Donna Tussing Orwin

The Cambridge Companion to Chekhov
edited by Vera Gottlieb and Paul Allain

The Cambridge Companion to Ibsen
edited by James McFarlane

The Cambridge Companion to Flaubert
edited by Timothy Unwin

The Cambridge Companion to Proust
edited by Richard Bales

The Cambridge Companion to Baudelaire
edited by Rosemary Lloyd

The Cambridge Companion to Thomas Mann
edited by Ritchie Robertson

The Cambridge Companion to Kafka
edited by Julian Preece

The Cambridge Companion to Brecht
edited by Peter Thomson and Glendyr Sacks

The Cambridge Companion to Walter Benjamin
edited by David S. Ferris

The Cambridge Companion to Lacan
edited by Jean-Michel Rabaté

The Cambridge Companion to Nabokov
edited by Julian W. Connolly

The Cambridge Companion to Chaucer,
second edition
edited by Piero Boitani and Jill Mann

The Cambridge Companion to
Shakespeare
edited by Margareta de Grazia and
Stanley Wells

The Cambridge Companion to Shakespeare
on Film
edited by Russell Jackson

The Cambridge Companion to
Shakespearean Comedy
edited by Alexander Leggatt

The Cambridge Companion to Shakespeare
on Stage
edited by Stanley Wells and Sarah Stanton

The Cambridge Comanion to Shakespeare's
History Plays
edited by Michael Hattaway

The Cambridge Companion to
Shakespearean Tragedy
edited by Claire McEachern

The Cambridge Companion to Christoher
Marlowe
edited by Patrick Cheney

The Cambridge Companion to Ben Jonson
edited by Richard Harp and
Stanley Stewart

The Cambridge Companion to Spenser
edited by Andrew Hadfield

The Cambridge Companion to Milton,
second edition
edited by Dennis Danielson

The Cambridge Companion to John Dryden
edited by Steven N. Zwicker

The Cambridge Companion to
Aphra Behn
edited by Derek Hughes and Janet Todd

The Cambridge Companion to
Samuel Johnson
edited by Greg Clingham

The Cambridge Companion to
Jonathan Swift
edited by Christopher Fox

The Cambridge Companion to Mary
Wollstonecraft
edited by Claudia L. Johnson

The Cambridge Companion to
William Blake
edited by Morris Eaves

The Cambridge Companion to
Wordsworth
edited by Stephen Gill

The Cambridge Companion to Coleridge
edited by Lucy Newlyn

The Cambridge Companion to Byron
edited by Drummond Bone

The Cambridge Companion to Keats
edited by Susan J. Wolfson

The Cambridge Companion to
Mary Shelley
edited by Esther Schor

The Cambridge Companion to Jane Austen
edited by Edward Copeland and Juliet
McMaster

The Cambridge Companion to the Brontës
edited by Heather Glen

The Cambridge Companion to Charles
Dickens
edited by John O. Jordan

The Cambridge Companion to
George Eliot
edited by George Levine

The Cambridge Companion to Thomas
Hardy
edited by Dale Kramer

The Cambridge Companion to Oscar Wilde
edited by Peter Raby

The Cambridge Companion to George
Bernard Shaw
edited by Christopher Innes

The Cambridge Companion to Joseph
Conrad
edited by J. H. Stape

The Cambridge Companion to
D. H. Lawrence
edited by Anne Fernihough

The Cambridge Companion to
Virginia Woolf
edited by Sue Roe and Susan Sellers

The Cambridge Companion to James Joyce,
second edition
edited by Derek Attridge

The Cambridge Companion to
T. S. Eliot
edited by A. David Moody

The Cambridge Companion to
Ezra Pound
edited by Ira B. Nadel

*The Cambridge Companion to
W. H. Auden*
edited by Stan Smith

The Cambridge Companion to Beckett
edited by John Pilling

*The Cambridge Companion to Harold
Pinter*
edited by Peter Raby

*The Cambridge Companion to
Tom Stoppard*
edited by Katherine E. Kelly

*The Cambridge Companion to
Herman Melville*
edited by Robert S. Levine

*The Cambridge Companion to Nathaniel
Hawthorne*
edited by Richard Millington

*The Cambridge Companion to Harriet
Beecher Stowe*
edited by Cindy Weinstein

*The Cambridge Companion to Theodore
Dreiser*
edited by Leonard Cassuto and Claire
Virginia Eby

*The Cambridge Companion to
Willa Cather*
edited by Marilee Lindermann

*The Cambridge Companion to Edith
Wharton*
edited by Millicent Bell

*The Cambridge Companion to
Henry James*
edited by Jonathan Freedman

*The Cambridge Companion to
Walt Whitman*
edited by Ezra Greenspan

*The Cambridge Companion to
Ralph Waldo Emerson*
edited by Joel Porte and Saundra Morris

*The Cambridge Companion to
Henry David Thoreau*
edited by Joel Myerson

*The Cambridge Companion to
Mark Twain*
edited by Forrest G. Robinson

*The Cambridge Companion to
Edgar Allan Poe*
edited by Kevin J. Hayes

*The Cambridge Companion to Emily
Dickinson*
edited by Wendy Martin

*The Cambridge Companion to
William Faulkner*
edited by Philip M. Weinstein

*The Cambridge Companion to Ernest
Hemingway*
edited by Scott Donaldson

*The Cambridge Companion to F. Scott
Fitzgerald*
edited by Ruth Prigozy

*The Cambridge Companion to
Robert Frost*
edited by Robert Faggen

*The Cambridge Companion to
Ralph Ellison*
edited by Ross Posnock

*The Cambridge Companion to
Eugene O'Neill*
edited by Michael Manheim

*The Cambridge Companion to
Tennessee Williams*
edited by Matthew C. Roudané

*The Cambridge Companion to
Arthur Miller*
edited by Christopher Bigsby

*The Cambridge Companion to
David Mamet*
edited by Christopher Bigsby

*The Cambridge Companion to
Sam Shepard*
edited by Matthew C. Roudané

*The Cambridge Companion to
Edward Albee*
edited by Stephen J. Bottoms

CAMBRIDGE COMPANIONS TO CULTURE

*The Cambridge Companion to Modern
German Culture*
edited by Eva Kolinsky and
Wilfried van der Will

*The Cambridge Companion to Modern
Russian Culture*
edited by Nicholas Rzhevsky

*The Cambridge Companion to Modern
Spanish Culture*
edited by David T. Gies

*The Cambridge Companion to Modern
Italian Culture*
edited by Zygmunt G. Barański
and Rebecca J. West

*The Cambridge Companion to Modern
French Culture*
edited by Nicholas Hewitt

*The Cambridge Companion to Modern
Latin American Culture*
edited by John King

*The Cambridge Companion to
Modern Irish Culture*
edited by Joe Cleary and
Claire Connolly